"From the moment I met Anna, [illegible] integrity in her relationships. She and her husband live and parent their children intentionally, and it is remarkable how committed they are to being globally-aware. It is inspirational to our family, and I hope we can continue to learn more from her on how to nurture a Christian, global mindset ourselves."
-Amy Bassett

"Anna Goodworth is living what she teaches. She is finding ways to teach her kids to think globally, compassionately, and with Christ at the center. In LESS, she combines humor, honesty and keen insights as she encourages us to be missionally-minded ourselves.
-Mary Gleason

"This book is for everyone! Anna's words will inspire you and your family to open your eyes to the world and real issues going on outside your yard: in your town, state and world. Raising mission minded, compassionate, caring children takes time and effort. The practical ideas and stories in this book with help your family on this journey!"
- Summer Bergantino

"Anna is the most passionate person about missions I know... Her desire and commitment to helping others is evident in her life, her family & her decisions and interactions with others. Anna weaves startling facts, statistics, personal stories and scripture together with humor and a mother's heart. She not only informs you about the issues and makes you want to take action, she also provides hope and examples of how our families can have an impact."
-Laurie Swanson

"To take up our cross and follow Him: that is the life of unconditional surrender that Jesus call us to. Is that the life we are living and modeling for our children? L.E.S.S is a challenge to raise our level of discipleship as we parent our children. Everything Anna writes about, she actually lives out with her family. The concrete strategies to put our faith in action and love the poor and vulnerable make it easy to join in the adventure. The choice is ours."
-Jenny Estabrook

"Anna has lived her life for the sake of people who need to know the love of Christ. Through the many years I have had the privilege of knowing Anna, Micah 6:8 consistently describes her conviction:

> *He has shown all you people what is good. And what does the LORD require of you? To act justly and to love mercy and to walk humbly with your God.*

As a mother, Anna, along with her husband, have taken seriously the obligation of teaching their children to live out Micah 6:8. For all parents who have the desire to raise children to love God, be globally aware and missionally minded, Anna's book is worth reading."
- Donnis Pallaoro

"Anna is able to foster awareness of this world's difficult places in a way that is empowering for kids to feel they can do something to improve it. She has melded her experiences gleaned from missions around the world, addressing some of our most perplexing problems with vignettes of her kids and how she has nurtured a desire in them to serve as He calls us to do."
-Craig and Natalie Prins

"This is the book every parent needs to help raise more informed, compassionate kids to live out their God given purposes. With a conversational style, Anna educates you and guides you through numerous ways our kids can be engaged with the world and follow where God leads them. There is something for every parent and kid in this book,"
-Carri Grimditch

"Anna has been walking this journey into a missional life with her family for years now. In what she has learned, she hopes to humbly (and sometimes hilariously) invite us to take our children further into the call of Christ to be lights into the world both far and close. We can choose to be comfortable with our families in our suburban Christian lives or we can reach beyond, only to find ourselves even more blessed by a life passionate about the world. Anna gives us some ideas".
-Megan Meyers

L.E.S.S.

Raising Youth for a Missional Life

By Anna Goodworth, M.Div.

Editor: Matthew Brennan

Table of Contents

Chapters		Page
Introduction		5
1	My Journey So Far	12
2	"Why?" For the Bible Tells Me So	39
3	"Why?" Saying the "S" Word at Church	53
4	"Why?" Finding God in a Cardboard Box	63
5	"Why?" The Spoiled Little Thrill Seeker	72
6	"Why?" Safe and Lukewarm	87
7	"Why?" Not just Why? But Why Now?	100
8	Introduction to L.E.S.S.	117
9	Live It! Introduction	124
10	Live It! Brave the Darkness	132
11	Live It! Get Your Hands Dirty	143
12	Live It! Raise Your Voice	158
13	Live It! Looking at the Camel in the Mirror	170
14	Exposure and Education—Introduction	191
15	Exposure—Scared of the Dark	206
16	Exposure—Love Hurts	213
17	Exposure—Raised Fists	227
18	Exposure—A Cure for the Disease of Apathy	234
19	Serve With Them—Introduction	241
20	Serve With Them—Build Them Up	250
21	Serve With Them—The Power of the Narrator	263
22	Send Them Out—Introduction	281
23	Send Them Out—Little Birds	289
24	Send Them Out—Releasing the Arrow	299
25	Do Something Big!	310
26	The Joy of Isaiah 58 and Living with LESS	324
27	Resources for Further Enrichment	333

Introduction

My husband, Adam, loves to liven up family devotional time. One evening, when my daughter was three and my son was five, Adam wasn't just reading to them the story of Jesus healing the blind man, but having them act it out instead. I walked into the room close to the beginning of the grand performance and saw that, apparently, my son, Lukas, was playing the part of Jesus.

If you knew my son even at the age of five, you would know that this role could only lead to a sketchy debut from a little boy whose sarcasm was both scary and yet, brilliant. In his divine role, Lukas stood very tall, strong, and ready to heal (not unlike a televised preacher ready to unleash his incredible power on whomever he chose to have mercy).

Though only three, my daughter did her best to also play her part of the award-winning production as the blind man. When it was Adelaine's turn to come to Jesus, seeking healing for her eyesight, she dramatically blundered around the room with her eyes closed, running into furniture, yelling (I swear, in a southern accent), "Heal me, Jesus! I'm blonde! I'm blonde! Heal me, Jesus!"

Throughout the journey of writing this book, I found myself feeling both very blind and very blonde (in the worst sense of the word). I feel very young and like I have so much more of my life to experience, so much more of motherhood to perfect, so much more of my own faith to build up, and so much more of this world of global issues to digest, dive into, and change. Yet in spite of my insecurities, I could not deny that God was giving me ideas, thoughts, experiences, and reflections on this topic quicker than my hands could type. I very much still question if I should write a book while I do not yet have all my kids successfully graduated into adulthood living purposeful lives for Christ, instead of being still in the thick of backseat sibling battles and stepping on Lego pieces in the middle of the night. I wish I could prove that each one of my children has successfully grown up either as a missionary, to work for non-profits, or just giving 90 percent of their huge Wall Street salaries to charity to validate how I could write such a book.

Not fully trusting my own perspective, I tried to research and gain knowledge from parents, writers, and church leaders whom I see are raising a younger generation to engage the world around them, empowering them to love with their hearts and hands for Christ for the rest of their lives. The key is that I want to do that now, while they are young and not wait until my kids are more grown up. The pages of this book hold many conclusions from witnessing the lives of those I want to emulate, engaging scripture, and making some notes of youth development in our culture.

The only other things that may perhaps make any of my words valid are the experiences and passions that God has graciously given me as well. I was heavily involved in youth ministry for seven years, serving full-time in Northern Ireland for one year before my passions for Youth, Missions, and God's Word collided when I got my Masters of Divinity at Denver Theological Seminary, specializing in Youth and Family Ministry. I still work with youth in many capacities …especially elementary and teens. Two years working in foster care, volunteer efforts for World Vision, and my own youth mission curriculum development further pushed me toward writing this book. Though God had been doing work in me for some time toward missions, it was actually after I became a mom that God completely broke my heart for the broken both locally and globally. As I learned about so many sorrows in this world, I was forever ruined for this happy, Christian, suburban life.

Even while very young my kids would catch me in a moment broken by the reality of AIDS or sex trafficking or the injustice of the poverty of just one precious child. They looked at my tears and asked me, "Why are you crying, Mama?"

So I told them.

I told them it was because someone hurt a little girl and it breaks God's heart … or I told them an earthquake killed thousands of people and left little kids without their mamas and daddies … or I told them that there are kids in countries far away who are sick and have nothing and yet we have everything.

Sometimes it wasn't tears of sorrow I cried, but instead it was tears of extraordinary joy when I learned of God redeeming and restoring lives through the work of community development, child sponsorship, missionary work, and the ordinary work of serving others in word or deed. I told that to them as well.

Sometimes when I told them of these things, my children just kissed me and waddled away unfazed (having become used to the scene of their mama broken). But sometimes … oh, the precious sometimes, they would ask more.

So I told them.

They asked how to pray for the people … so I told them.

They asked what they could do to help these people …

so I told them.

And so began my journey to seek more and more new ways to educate them on God's heart for the world. I found many great resources (many of which I note in this book), but nothing quite like what I was looking for … not one source that proposed a possible backbone structure for how to instill empathy, information, vision, and actual ability into my children to love and serve God's mission for the rest of their lives, whether they go overseas, live in suburbia, or somewhere in between. I wanted to educate them in ways that empower them, ways that won't leave them hopeless, and ways for them to know without a doubt that they are part of the solution for the rest of their lives. I feel very much in the middle of this dialogue, but something tells me that I may only still be at the beginning of it.

I know another thing: I find that I have social remorse for foolish things I said or did after about 90 percent of my interactions. After parties or social interactions, my husband and I sometimes engage in "post-game analysis" where we casually critique ourselves for all of the inevitable social flaws we committed that evening. I have no doubt that my flaws will become evident through my writing as well. I apologize in advance if I make incorrect assumptions or mock something about Christian subculture that a reader actually holds near and dear. My intention is not to offend. My intention is to empower us (possibly myself most of all) to live what we say, to walk what we believe, and to be all Christ desires of us, young and old. I hope this for us, but also for those younger ones who mimic us, look to us, and ask us, "Mama, why are you crying?"

This book is broken up into five parts. The first big chunk is dedicated to the why. Why would we drastically incorporate global issues into our parenting? I say "drastically" because a real effort in this area often requires drastic measures for us to step outside of our normal routine, circles of life, and even our faith to engage these topics and change our lives so that we can truly incorporate them intentionally. Don't put the book down yet, fearing I am asking too much of us all in our busy lives! I think we all want a change, don't we? We want to make decisions based on a bigger calling to decide what we say "yes" and "no" to in our schedules and budget. When we are convinced that the change is right, anything remotely drastic feels right, refreshing, and clear! You can still read this whole book and decide you don't buy into any of it. However, I give a lot of WHYs. I approach scripture and youth psychology not just to address why we would raise kids who know the world, but why we would engage them now, while they are young-even very young. The why takes up a big portion, and as you read, you may just realize that there are more reasons to engage with this idea than you ever thought.

The last four parts of the book are focused on the how: HOW do we engage and raise children up in these global issues coupled with the Great Commission so that they are not only exposed to them, but also empowered, enabled, and mobilized to do something about them for the rest of their lives. I use the structure of the word LESS (L.E.S.S.) as an acronym: Living—Exposure—Serving—Sending, not just for a memory cue of the steps we make in teaching our children, but as a reminder that we can use a lot less stuff and distraction in our lives to focus on this mission. We must be less, in order for Christ to be more. However, to reiterate, we don't want to just talk to them about what they can do when they get older, as if they have to wait or receive a special call. It is not just for the future, but for right now, too. Though we can teach about Christ's heart, embody the Great Commission call, instill their identity, and give them skills for the future, certainly, it is now also when God can use even little children to serve Him, empowering them for even more in the future. Now is when they are shaping their identities, either as onlookers of God's purpose or as the ambassadors of it, in a living relationship with and following Christ. I know that these are lofty goals. Chances are that each topic I approach could require a book of its own, but I will attempt to at least get the conversation going in all of our hearts. L.E.S.S. will form the structure of the last four sections of the book. And finally, the last chapter includes loads of specific resources (books, movies, websites, etc). Though there is an intended structure to the book with a thick understanding of WHY laid down before completely embracing HOW, you are welcome to jump to the HOW chapters if you are already convinced of WHY.

It is crazy to think that our little rascals or sarcastic teenagers are part of God's plan to redeem the broken places and hearts of this world. It is hard to believe, but totally true … all because God is just sweet enough to include us as we reveal the true Redeemer.

I hope that L.E.S.S. may be a guide for when the youth in your life see you in sorrow or passion over this lost, broken world and ask, "Why are you crying?"

Chapter 1
My Journey So Far

Livin' the Dream

I was walking toward baggage claim in Portland International Airport trying to get to the meeting spot to pick up my best friend, Carrie, who was visiting from Colorado. I had the hand of my sticky, distracted 2-year-old son tightly grasped in one of mine. My other hand awkwardly pushed a stroller, which cradled my new, 3-month-old little girl.

Rumor had it … in these young mothering days, I was living the dream.

Realizing that I was late for the rendezvous, I started to push the stroller faster, wondering how a stroller could possibly be so heavy with only one small child in it. Granted, I was only pushing with one arm and part of my hip because I was trying to, at the same time, pull my son along with the other arm, who for no apparent reason began to sit down in the middle of the airport floor at random.

Push. Pull. Push. Pull. Push. Pull.

Needless to say for any new moms, I was sporting my pregnancy pants with the fabulous elastic band because none of my pre-pregnancy pants fit yet–much to my disgust and late night tears. However, these pregnancy pants didn't fit, either. They were too big. This is the unspoken wardrobe sorrow of new moms (besides those instantly skinny moms that we all secretly despise). Therefore, every few steps the saggy-bottom pants fell a little too far off my hip, revealing the stretch marks that served like a dog whistle call to liposuction clinics, who sent me flyers in bulk. So about every third step, I had to stop and hike up my pants to cover the pure paleness and indecency of my backside.

Push. Pull. Hike. Push. Pull. Hike. Push. Pull. Hike.

Time seemed to go on forever, and yet somehow I had still not reached my friend at baggage claim. Then apparently my sporadic jerking around of the stroller during my wiggle-jiggle walk woke up my daughter because she started to cry. I knew this not just because I heard her cries with my ears … but because I felt it. Yeah, I said, "I felt it." I felt it just under my bra … and then I felt it through my bra … and then I felt it through my shirt.

So there I was in the middle of Portland International Airport unable to simply get to baggage claim because I couldn't do the Push-Pull-Hike, and then add on some sort of rapper, cross-armed move, hiding the huge wet, leaky-milk headlights now staining my shirt. (I'm sorry if you opened this book and didn't know it would be this … well … awkward. It gets better soon … I hope). It was only my sheer desire to see my friend and have her laugh with me about the entire situation that prohibited me from sitting on the floor and bawling my eyes out. I was at the lowest of my young mom flustered days–I didn't feel like a human being. I felt like a cross between a cow and a zombie. And yet it was here, during this diaper-filled time in my life, that God was breaking my heart. He was literally causing me to be ill as I learned the atrocities of sex trafficking, the sorrows of AIDS, and the plight of orphans. It was in my most humble (dare I say humiliating?) days that God did some of His greatest work to inspire me to raise children who were both broken and empowered. I didn't know how some freaky, leaky, tiger-striped lady who had at least 30 pounds and a whole lot of insecurities to lose could help the global situation, but I knew I had to be a part of the conversation or my heart might literally break inside me.

Mission Trip Frequent Flyer Miles

God's story for me didn't start in the Portland Airport. I can see His hand all through my life, though my family did not attend church regularly when I was growing up. I see the thread of how God kept me in the random avenues of churches during times of significant childhood traumas, giving me glimpses of truth, hope, and love. In high school, I asked Jesus into my heart about 500 times (you know, just to be sure), but I didn't understand that asking Jesus into my heart meant giving Him all of my life. So while His grace was apparent on me in many ways, my life was scattered and uncertain throughout adolescence. Of all places, it was during my freshman year of college at University of Colorado at Boulder (the land of granola and dreadlocks), that I gave my whole life to God–not just in faith, but also in missions.

I quickly found myself on a plane to Haiti.

I remember feeling like I was going to meet my maker before we even landed in Haiti. We were flying in a mini commuter plane, not unlike the metal shell the monkeys build in the animated film, *Madagascar 2*. At the time, I was sure the pilots were making bets on which passenger was going to toss their over-salted pretzels first in the barf-bags. However, I now realize that most of those tin vomit-comets feel like a terminal roller-coaster ride. As we approached the ground, I couldn't quite comprehend where we were going to land because I saw no landing strip, no sign of an airport, and just mini-huts made out of straw or tin and fields of laundry laid out like a giant quilt. Finally, a mini-airstrip came into view (though I swear it was just a bike path). Goats ran for their skinny lives and we landed in one piece. We all recovered with anthems of praise, and doors opened on the plane, revealing heat and humidity that almost knocked us over.

After bribing security to let us actually take our own luggage and supplies with us, we found ourselves piling into the back of a truck. (No, no, no—I don't mean piling in the back seat of a truck, but climbing up and piling in to stand in the bed of a huge pick-up truck.) Forget safety regulations! The next exciting task was merely to hold on for dear life as the truck darted in and out of traffic, with no respect to proper sides of the road or how many kamikaze animals were left dead behind. There was just loud honking to the car (or semi) we were currently playing chicken with to warn them that we were about to collide. I knew this mere image of me would be absolute horror to my parents, so as a freshman in college who hadn't rebelled much in high school beyond becoming a "fundamental" Christian, I was *loving it*!

This trip to the poorest parts of Haiti, as well as the next year when I co-led the trip, was a place of deep absorption of all the sights and sounds of poverty. I remember one distinct moment when the truck was stopped on the road and I glanced down to see a sweet little boy, probably four years old, with distended belly and dirty clothes, sitting down amidst trash, eating a rat. Another time we were arriving at a village with some food supplies of rice, beans, and dried milk. When the car abruptly stopped, some of the milk spilled in the bed of the truck. We just hopped out ready to clean it up, but several Haitians ran up to collect it. They then held the dirty dried milk in their hands as a precious commodity and licked it up out of sheer hunger.

On another adventure, we drove a long way to a far-off village. It was 1997 and they had rarely seen white skin, so we were definitely a strange, blinding sight for them. It was the first time I had truly digested the scene of starving kids taking care of other kids. A malnourished 4-year old carried a baby dressed in rags. Other children were running around without the protection and dignity of any clothing at all. In this mountain village, we were working on building a church and school, but no sides were built yet, so we were literally surrounded 24/7 by curious eyes. I still don't know what to do with the confusing shame of watching them watching us eat our meals. We hadn't brought food for the whole village, so there we were, obviously already well-fed individuals, eating our meals. They didn't ask us for any. They just watched. Some even brought some of their precious food to offer us as gifts. We finally got a clue and skipped a couple meals so we could provide at least a small amount of food for the village.

Between the rat, the dried milk, and the hungry village, I was given probably one of the most humbling realizations: in my sheltered, privileged life, I had to do *nothing* to be able to have food every day.

It isn't like I deserved it and they didn't.

It isn't like I worked hard and they didn't.

It isn't like by some nature of who I was, I should have something they didn't.

The stark reality that I did *nothing* to be born into a family that had love and opportunities felt blinding in a valley dark with little hope or education. Now I was in college and *got* to travel--never having the fear of not having enough food. They, on the other hand, just happened to be born in Haiti, in a society without much education or resources – historically abducted from Africa during the slave trade and later struggling under corrupt leaders, poverty, and natural disasters. Yet the mothers of Haiti wanted to provide for and protect their children just as my mother and father did—just as I want to provide for my children now.

But their hands were empty and mine were overflowing.

This realization of my undeserved blessings now slammed home when I saw actual faces of people before me. It was a realization that completely changed my life. It has taken most (though I fear not all) of the entitlement out of me. Living in a country filled with an entitlement mentality in children, I can't help but believe that God wishes to bless our children with similar realizations as well. With L.E.S.S. is more.

My deepest "less is more" is realizing that I don't deserve anything. What I deserve is death because I am a sinner.

What I have been given is forgiveness and *life* through Christ, and with it, a chance to use what opportunities I have been blessed with to restore the lives of others. I thank God that He did not allow me to be blind to this, but pray He reminds me again every single day and helps me to instill it in my children. For in the realization that I don't deserve any blessing more than the enslaved girl in Cambodia has brought with it the freedom to pursue joy, meaning, and passion in the things that do not fail.

God led me to many mission trips after my first to Haiti. Each trip left me conflicted as to how my life was supposed to go on. Knowing that I wanted to be a part of this work for the poor, oppressed, and lost, I kept doing what I knew … which was to go on more mission trips. I spent a summer in Thailand and Laos teaching English, ministering to persecuted Christians, and caring for babies with AIDS. I went to a Mexican orphanage and assisted on a trip to Vancouver, Canada, where we cared for prostitutes, drug-addicts, and the homeless. I also spent a year in Northern Ireland as a youth worker. But I admit that besides a valuable period of culture shock in varying degrees after each trip (where I was sickened by all my possessions), most of my life seemed to go on as before. It wasn't until the end of seminary that my actual theology (my understanding of God—who He is and what He cares about) collided with these seemingly peripheral missionary passions.

Seminary Revival

Denver Seminary was an incredible experience for me. I had amazing professors and found some really extraordinary friends and acquaintances, who—I am extremely proud—are now leading churches across the country. However, there were unexpected struggles for me at the beginning. At seminary, you really take apart the Bible and your faith, piece by piece, to evaluate it and build it up in truth. I confess, though, at times it felt as if I was in a biology lab experiment, where the frog had to be dead before we could dissect and learn about it. Similarly, it felt like my faith was being ripped apart bit by bit to look at in detail. Despite the school offering many spiritually rich opportunities (worship, discipleship, mentorship, authentic teachers), halfway through the program, I struggled *not* to read my Bible as merely a textbook and *not* to listen to a sermon just in order to critique it. I had become too much of a scientist in the process and had missed so much of God in the process. I wasn't far from Jesus, but not thriving either. Luckily, our God is a living God.

God made sure He got through to me just before I finished my degree. I went on a required "Immersion Experience." I had gotten married eight months before, and was now seven months pregnant (oops … honeymoon baby) at the time of the immersion. For the immersion, our class had to spend over a week living in a hostel in downtown Denver. We went to homeless shelters, refugee schools, juvenile detention centers, soup kitchens, and inner-city churches to understand how our seminary education was to actually apply missionally—not just far away, but near and everywhere. We were instructed to take the theology of redemption and witness God in it . . . tangibly. Words can't describe my gratitude for this experience. Otherwise, I would have never had the chance to march in the Martin Luther King's Day Parade with all nations and tribes … and have contractions the whole way. What a memory! But seriously, I had lived 25 years of my life in the suburbs just west of this city and never knew *any* of that suffering or poverty, as well as the life and hope, existed in these parts of Denver. I was embarrassed by my ignorance and enlightened by the rest. This immersion experience impacted me (and my husband) more than Denver Seminary will ever know.

It was in the uniting of my theology with seeing God's work in the poor that my seminary experience was "resurrected," if you will. I had lost my connection, to some degree, with God. I knew the Bible. I could write one heck of an IBS (Inductive Bible Study—though I think there is a reason it has the same acronym as Irritable Bowel Syndrome). I could even write a decent sermon. But my heart was truly starting to find God with the poor and oppressed.

I shouldn't have been surprised.

That is where He told us He would be all along.

Becoming Whole Never Hurt So Much

Just after seminary and having our little boy, our family moved to Portland, Oregon, for my husband's graduate program. I had no idea what God had in store for me these next few years. Having just been exposed to a deeper world of missions in my own backyard of homelessness, poverty, drugs, and refugees, I was excited to get involved wherever and whenever I could as a new mom in inner-city work or maybe in overseas missions.

I happened upon a group called Women of Vision. They are a volunteer organization of women who support World Vision's global community and spiritual development work, particularly for oppressed women and children. As I began to digest the additional information I was receiving about the atrocities around the world, I felt almost drug-addicted. I couldn't get enough information. The more I learned, the more I needed to learn. I felt like I needed to catch up. I began checking out every documentary I could on any related subject. Kay Warren (wife of Rick Warren) describes a similar experience as she became passionate about the AIDS epidemic: "Suddenly I was consumed with a desire to learn about HIV/AIDS. I devoured every book, article, and video I could get my hands on. I searched the Internet for websites that would teach me about this global crisis … I was disturbed—almost frantic—in my hurry to make up for lost time."[1]

In the midst of all the insane tragedies that I might take a lifetime to investigate, advocate for, and seek to change, four topics in particular destroyed me: the AIDS epidemic, child soldiers, genocide, and human trafficking. Fun topics? Not a chance. *Don't put the book down.* The next section is a snapshot of some horrible realities in the world. Read through the realities—feel free to cry or clench your fist in rage. God is honored by our tears and anger against the things that so disgust Him. He is sad and angry, too. Brokenness is not bad. With LESS control over what makes us feel good, we can gain MORE of His heart. Here we go.

AIDS

During the last few days of my summer-long mission trip in Thailand, we were in Chang Mai and helped at an orphanage. We held several babies who had tested positive with HIV and several that had progressed to full-blown AIDS. My friend, Tara, held the most precious little girl named Nuk, and I held this fat munchkin named Woot. Both had AIDS. They nestled into our necks and rested there. It was so far beyond my comprehension to think that these babies would be dead before long. This was in 1999, and this orphanage didn't have a great deal of resources. They certainly did not have the money for antiretroviral drugs (which were barely accessed by developing countries at the time) for two orphaned babies who already had AIDS.

HIV lives in prostitutes and drug users, but is also just as easily given to the faithful wife from an unfaithful husband, and passed on to her unknowing children through birth and breastfeeding. It often passes on to the next generation, painfully and shamefully living out its fate at a younger and younger age. It leaves children without parents and burdened with responsibilities they are too young to have … leaving them vulnerable to more tragedies. Isn't that just how we picture evil—robbing the vulnerable? That is why the lights of education, advocacy, compassion, and Scripture are its worst enemies and our best weapons.

But I ask, "Why are we numb to the conversation of AIDS?" Perhaps it is because the sheer numbers are overwhelming or perhaps because statistics aren't personal. Hold a baby who did nothing to be born with a *preventable* disease. If he is in a third world country and has no access to medication, his life will be short and filled with illness. That isn't a statistic. That is personal. It is a life that could have been different if his or her community had better health and spiritual education. It is a life that could have been different if the mom had medication before she got pregnant or while she was pregnant. Did you know that if a mom is receiving treatment during pregnancy, there is a 95-98 percent chance that she will not pass HIV on to her child.[2] Surprised? I was, too.

It is inexcusable that babies born with AIDS don't have a better chance at life when we have answers. Children with HIV that receive antiretroviral drugs can grow up to be adults (a conservative life span estimate is 65 years).[3] Although still needing to be wise and careful, people with HIV on medication can have spouses and children without passing the disease on to them because the virus is so low in their system that it is considered undetectable.[4] Somehow, I think this information changes things! We must respond in truth (and not fear), and the above statistics are, in fact, true. If we understand HIV better, we will act differently about adoption of HIV kids, about those with HIV in our community (and there are more than you think), about how seriously we give toward HIV prevention globally, and about how we educate our own children. This knowledge has changed our family.

Child Soldiers

Visiting a good friend of ours in Uganda a couple times recently, my husband, Adam, saw where he had hidden in the bushes every night to keep the Lord's Resistance Army from abducting him. Adam also met a girl who had been held as a slave by the LRA. She'd hidden in an active ant hill to escape the torture of the soldiers, but is still struggling to escape the torment that remains in her memory. Seeing that hideout and meeting that girl was surreal for Adam but definitely made "child soldiers" more tangible. It no longer could remain as a story in a book or newspaper headline that is read, questioned, and forgotten. I'm grateful for movies like *Invisible Children* that reveal the horrible atrocities done by the LRA, led by Joseph Kony, in Uganda, Southern Sudan, and The Democratic Republic of the Congo, taking young boys and girls while massacring their families. I'm grateful that even Hollywood hits like *Blood Diamond* are revealing the realities of some of the industries that propagate child soldiers—how they are abducted into being a soldier, forced into doing horrific things to their own family (killing and raping), and often brainwashed by ideology, drugs, and war movies, as well as the lies that their own families do not want them anymore. "LRA commanders often force children to kill their own siblings, just to ensure that the children's loyalty will be to the movement, not to the family. The leaders require every abducted child to kill another child within a week of being captured. This helps to create alienation against society in the mind of the child."[5]

I confess that this feels SO appalling I cannot quite grasp that it is true. It's absolute horror makes it seem impossible, not just in Africa, but all over the world. Yet I must grasp its reality or I will not act in order to help stop it.

Books (like *Running for My Life* and *A Long Walk to Water*) or movies (like *War Dance*) that show rescued child soldiers, are helpful because they make the impossibility of this kind of evil more approachable in the story of one child—particularly one that is on the road to recovery. Yet not all are on this road to recovery…

In my own life, my passion for wanting to fight injustice was heightened when I became personally responsible for a younger generation. When I see a movie with boys being forced to use guns, I see my own son. Who is to say it couldn't be him? Do we really think the hearts of some dark Americans in a confused political time couldn't pull something like that off even in our own land? I am responsible not only to those "invisible" children, but to those "voiceless" mothers who are longing for their sons and daughters to come home. Their call and cry may seem powerless to them, but at the very least, I can raise my voice in prayer and in politics on their behalf. I must.

Genocide

I honestly didn't know much about more recent genocides than the Holocaust until I saw *Hotel Rwanda* in the theaters. I walked out in shock. I just kept thinking, "What? This can't be real. How did that happen? How did it happen *again*? How did *no one* stop that?"

Why? How could we let that happen even after we swore that it would never happen again after the Holocaust? There is an exceptional clip in *Beyond the Gates* where a reporter from the BBC admits how differently she is affected by the killings she witnessed while reporting in Europe versus reporting in Africa. She says, "When I was in Bosnia, I cried every day. I looked at the white faces of women dead in the gutter and thought, 'That could be my mother.' In Rwanda, I look at the bodies and I think, 'It's just dead Africans'."[6] Pretty raw, huh? Makes your stomach sick? Mine, too. Yet—I know it is true. It isn't true that the slaughter of one group of people is more tragic than another. Yet it is true that somehow we can't as easily identify or sympathize with (and thus act on behalf of) those who are different from us in appearance, language, and culture. The less alike they are with us, the less likely we are to help. It is a pretty gross reality.

The movie *Tears of the Sun*, set in Nigeria, expresses a similar mentality of a bunch of American soldiers (led in a surprisingly moving role by Bruce Willis' character). They initially feel indifferent toward the Nigerian people, yet as they slowly gain relationships, their hard, separated hearts change—demanding a compassionate response that costs many of them their lives. So we see that there may be hope for our calloused hearts.

First of all, hope arrives in our own efforts to step into the lives and hearts of those who are different from us—God's call empowering us to make heart to heart connections and see His image in others. Relationships and connections break down impossible walls.

Secondly, only God has the ability to make beauty from ashes … and He does it! In Oregon, my husband and I met an amazing man and his family who lost almost everything in the Rwandan Genocide. Emmanuel Sitakis lost 35 of his closest family members in the genocide and has somehow had the grace from God to forgive, even having some interactions with those who literally chopped up his family. He has started ERM Rwanda—an extraordinary ministry that trains and pairs up orphans and widows to care for each other in Rwanda. And thousands have come to know Jesus through this ministry!

In recent decades, there have been other genocides, but I will just mention one more: Cambodia. Again, this was after the WWII Holocaust. During the 70's, the Khmer Rouge led a genocide that resulted in approximately two million deaths. Again, other countries left and let it happen. If one goes to Cambodia to visit some of the sites of torture prisons and execution sites, there are visuals from the genocide that are almost too much to handle. Murals tell stories of mass graves of people buried alive, burned alive, and starved, as well as other torturous deaths. "One scene was of a mother lying on the ground, straining to grab her baby away from a gleeful soldier. He was swinging the infant toward a tree trunk in the same way a batter swings at a baseball."[7]

I feel sick. I can't take much more … yet there's more.

This genocide left the door open for another tragedy that runs rampant all over the world. In places like Cambodia particularly, where the infrastructure doesn't exist to fully prosecute the sickest of men, the grossest of evils thrives: human trafficking.

Human Trafficking

The numbers truly are insane. "More than 30 million slaves live in our world today. Girls and boys, women and men of all ages are forced to toil in the rug-loom sheds of Nepal, sell their bodies in the brothels of Rome, break rocks in the quarries of Pakistan, fight wars in the jungles of Africa, and sew clothes in the garment factories of California. Go behind the façade in any major town or city in the world today, and you are likely to find a thriving commerce in human beings. You may even find slavery in your own backyard."[8]

We shouldn't only be teaching the slave trade to our kids as a past American sin on African Americans. The Trans-Atlantic African slave trade was horrible and our country still bears the scars of it. It is something to mourn deeply, especially because it was seen as "acceptable" for so long. However, unfortunately, it can also serve as a teaching point for the illegal (though overlooked) atrocities that are occurring still. The scary thing is that if we aren't part of actually changing this tragedy, we aren't doing anything more than being a bystander or a propagator of the tragedy, just like those who allowed slavery before the Civil War.

In Cambodia (and other countries like India and Thailand…and the United States), a man can go on a sex vacation, filling his days and nights with the raping of little girls for profit, almost as easily as planning a bus tour. Witnessing a brothel in Cambodia, Kay Warren describes, "My skin crawled with horror to know that on the other side of those padlocked doors were little girls—some of them as young as five or six—who would be offered as sexual partners to men sitting in the cafes as soon as it was dusk. We were told that the younger the child, the more money she was worth—virgins are highly prized in the world of sexual perversion. For a mere $300, a man could 'buy' one of these little ones, take her to a hotel for up to a week, use her in any way he chose, and then return her to the brothel where he had found her."[9] These girls are raped 10 to 40 times a day. Reread that sentence. No—I'll do it for you. *These girls are raped 10 to 40 times a day*. Imagine a life like that. Day after day. Week after week. Is that not an actual Hell in which we are allowing little girls to remain?

Gary Haugen, president of International Justice Mission, in his book, *Terrify No More,* tells about real girls his organization met and worked to rescue. In the midst of the undercover rescue operation, the stories of young girls came to life. One girl, like many, was tricked into thinking that there was a great opportunity of a "restaurant job" in hopes of sending money to her family. She then found herself trapped in a room with a sick middle-aged man who had bought her virginity. This particular girl recounts the experience of her first rape as she is screaming initially out of fear and then screaming out of physical pain. The screaming apparently bothered the pedophile, so he complained to the brothel owner. The brothel owner, wanting to keep the customer happy, taped the girl's mouth shut so the man could finish the job.[10]

Don't know what to say? I don't either. If I'm honest, I feel so angry and sad that the only things I feel like saying are the biggest cuss words I could ever think of and they don't even do it justice. I'm not just being lazy with my tongue or feel like a rebellious Christian with my urge to cuss. These atrocities are from Hell and they are damned! They are worse than every cuss word out there; there are no words even bad enough to come close to describing it! How pathetic that we can't even describe those acts with our stupid, little cuss words. No words would even do justice to God, for how He feels about this evil. It is unfathomable and yet it is happening at this moment to a little girl … a little girl as precious as one you know … maybe your little girl. I say "your little girl" because maybe some of us are called to adopt or called to sponsor these children or these raids. (You can do that, you know. You can "buy" a brothel raid at www.IJM.org for a gift—how cool is that? I know what I want for Christmas next year!) I also say, "your little girl" because they *are* "our" little girls. They are our little girls because they are God's little girls and we must identify them as just like our own.

On my daughter's 5th birthday, she had two sweet girls over to dance, do crafts, play with dolls, and have cake. They did exactly what sweet little girls should do—coloring, playing with dolls, making bracelets, and twirling about in safety and joy. Yet they could be kidnapped in another country or…in America. I've now heard of too many horrific stories of moms in our own country who have lost children to nasty men, never to hear from their daughters again.

I can't even picture my daughter getting taken—raped by a nasty old guy. Yet I believe that in order to help bridge the gap of "that girl" and "my girl," I have to visualize it, at least for a moment, because those little girls in other countries are just as precious as she is. They are just as confused and traumatized as she would be if she were taken into a strange room with a bunch of people she didn't know and a man took off his pants. Their brains and bodies are shutting down because they can't handle all the pain and fear from what is happening to them. Why shouldn't I (in my own mind) put my own daughter in their shoes? Because they aren't blonde-haired and blue-eyed? I know that some people may think it is inappropriate for me to go so far as to imagine my own child in this situation, but I can guarantee you that it makes me more uncomfortable than it makes you! It sends me into absolute convulsive tears! I can barely type. It feels as if putting it in writing actually tempts it to happen or that writing about it happening is in itself victimization. I get it. But if it gets me emotionally to a place where I can "get" that these little girls are *just like mine* and feel ill the way I am *supposed* to feel for each little child—then I believe it serves its purpose. I believe that we are *supposed* to feel that ill. It makes me intensely sick, and though I don't think it is something that I think I can or should dwell on for too long, I need to somehow get this:

This *is* happening to millions of Jesus's little girls and I am supposed to be in puddles of convulsive tears about them, too. Do we get that? If I knew that my baby girl was in a brothel being raped, it would take death to stop me from getting her out. Can you imagine if all of us felt that kind of fire and said, "One of my kids is in there"? We wouldn't need organizations. We'd all get on planes in mass floods and bust down every brothel door in every part of the world as enraged and scared moms and dads and aunts and uncles and brothers and sisters. Perhaps that isn't the best method of justice (which is why I'm grateful for the wisdom and expertise of groups like IJM), but the point is, we wouldn't just be crying about it—or too sad to really dive into the topic—or changing the channel. *Nothing* would stop us if it were our little girl.

If only we thought they were ours … if only we dared to remember that they are *His*.

A Little Balance

First of all—congratulations!

You made it through reading about those atrocities, though I doubt unscathed.

When I first learned about the above topics (and others such as hunger, dirty water, homelessness, and orphans), I literally became ill … for a few months. I think my body couldn't take all of the information my mind and heart were receiving. I would read and cry, then watch a documentary and cry and all the while get physically sicker. Though there may have been better ways to go about it all, I personally don't regret this time, for it felt like I had purged myself of ignorance as I dealt with an intense amount of anger and sadness.

I was even angry at the church (not any church in particular, just my experience of church). Why had the church not told me about these issues? *Why had I not known until now*? I would have made different decisions in my life. I would have spent LESS time, thoughts, and money on stupid and insignificant things and could have done more. I may have made MORE impactful and empowered decisions early in my life. These are some of the *Whys* of educating our children on God's broken heart for the world.

As you can imagine, it was during this time of global education that my social life peaked, since I was the life of the party (or not). If asked about how I was, I often just changed the subject (because I didn't want to watch the person in front of me pop an entire bottle of Zoloft before my eyes) or because I didn't want to watch another person's eyes glaze over. When I did tell someone about all the global issues I was learning and struggling with, you could almost hear the record player scratch and the Satuday Night Live skit Debbie Downer play out right before my eyes.

I don't think most people will be called to dive into these issues with such intensity over such a short amount of time. To focus entirely on these issues can obscure other beautiful truths in the world. However, I suspect that for most American Christians, the evil realities across the globe are avoided (or simply unknown) to a much greater extent than God intends. There are great blessings for those who identify with the suffering (remember the Sermon on the Mount), and not least of all is the joy of seeing God redeem broken situations.

Hope for the Suffering

Indeed, God doesn't break our hearts if not to reshape them for His purposes, and that is what He did for me. Particularly through my World Vision/Women of Vision chapter, I learned a great deal about community development. Their education through Bible Studies, books, and speakers included a deeper understanding of God's heart for the broken, which added another incredible layer to what God did in me at Denver Seminary and through mission trips. I saw that all of my passions could exist in one world for me. At seminary, my immersion experience had been a huge step in an amazing direction to work often with the urban poor and refugees, but it was through World Vision (and other wonderful organizations and resources since) that I truly grasped that I don't have to be limited by only doing things locally or hop on a mission trip internationally.

I have seen the power of a church banded together with a heart to serve. We watched lives, communities, and villages transform in other countries because of money we were able to raise, allowing both clean and living water to reach them. I saw the lives of everyday folk change in America who were empowered by what their lives could mean for others across the globe and for all of eternity.

We *can* do things globally without actually traveling there. I learned the power of my voice in advocacy. I learned the power of what any group of people can get done with one common purpose. Luckily, World Vision's motto is two-fold: "Our vision for every child, life in all its fullness. Our prayer for every heart, the will to make it so." Therefore, we also educated those around us, so they too could be part of these amazing life-changing stories … and they did.

In 2009, I was blessed to go to Mozambique with World Vision to visit one of our chapter's projects. Though we were mainly visiting an AIDS education initiative, we got to see the whole scope of community development—villages at every stage of the process. We saw those just beginning the process—identifying kids to sponsor. We saw those who were years and years into the process—healing and thriving communities that were self-sustaining, alive in Christ, and taking care of their communities' orphans. And I could not believe the youth! World Vision is training youth to be leaders of change of the future as they put their faith in Christ. Indeed they are already changing the present. I have never seen leadership development and youth ministry so powerful—ever! It was extraordinary.

It was also in Mozambique that I saw firsthand how incredible sponsorship is: how it is the backbone of most good community development work. It was there that I met Matete, an incredible girl whose father was made blind by acid during Mozambique's Civil War and whose mother was chronically ill. We are blessed to now be Matete's sponsor (a whole other amazing story). I could not feel any better about giving away any of the money God blesses us with than with the different sponsorship checks we write. I've never seen money used so efficiently, so transparently, and so wisely.

Hope for my Family

If you hated a lot of what you read earlier—the evils that exist and the horrible things that are happening at this very moment to little kids—then I wonder, what is your response? I personally get angry and sad for a while, but then I get all fired up and demand to see God and the church act … *right now.*

I ask, "What's the plan, God?"

Well, guess what?

It turns out we are part of the plan. "'You are the light of the world'. According to Jesus, we are it. You are it"[11]

My family is part of the plan … *now*. So, we are taking that seriously … *now*. In a process of change, we are trying to do things differently—with our time, our efforts, and our money. (I said "process," so if I've overwhelmed you so far, please take a deep breath—it is, indeed, a slow process!) But, we aren't waiting until our kids are older. It is actually now that I am certain that I must infuse this call into their DNA even as I am hearing the call myself. This "global education" has drastically changed the kind of parents we are and want to be. With this missions-based faith, I have seen a depth in my marriage, my relationship with Christ, and in the hearts of my children that I don't think is just an added bonus. I believe it is what was supposed to be there all along because this redemption plan has always been what God intended (from the call of Abraham through the vision of the tribes in Revelation).

As I recall the earlier days of motherhood (like *push, pull, hike, leak* in the airport), I think about how far God has brought me in so many ways. I am okay that I don't know exactly each next step to take, so long as I know that one of my end goals in life is to be a restorer of the broken and lost alongside Christ. My children are learners with me. But now I am seeing this mess in the mirror and around me differently than I saw it on that embarrassing airport day:

I *am*, in fact, living the dream.

It is just a different dream … and honestly, it is *so much better* than I could have ever imagined for myself or my family.

Chapter 2
"Why?" For the Bible Tells Me So

"Christians don't tell lies; they just go to church and sing them."
–A. Z. Tozer

My son is a bit of a prankster. He has been as long as I can remember. The first significant prank I can remember was when he was two.

We had just transitioned him to a toddler bed and were trying to train him to stay in his bed. He had knocked on our door many times previously that night and we had just laid down the law that there had "better not be *one more knock on the door or else*" and he was to "*stay in bed.*" But, sure enough, about five minutes later came a sound that made my blood boil: *knock, knock, knock*. I said (in the most "Mary Poppins," patient voice ever, of course), "Bummer, buddy, this is so sad." Then I opened the door not to a two-year old in trouble, but to find only a multicolored clown wig left on the floor outside the door, hearing a faint giggle from his room. Two years old! He was only two!

We quickly saw his pranks progress into tormenting his sister, who is younger by two years. As a four-year old, I overheard him calmly beckoning her as if to play. "Addy, come find your princess dolls." I looked over to find that he had turned the laundry basket upside down, trapping the princesses inside. Sitting on top of the basket was a nice, full cup of water waiting … just waiting to be spilled all over an unsuspecting two-year-old sister. The list truly has grown longer and longer, and with it he has grown more confident of his pranking skills.

One night, just before he turned five, the phone rang and I answered. On the other end, I hear, "This is 911 emergency. We received a call from your residence. Is everything okay?"

Oh dear. It looked like someone wasn't sleeping upstairs like I thought he was. I quickly told the 911 dispatcher that I believed my son had prank-called, sent my husband upstairs to make sure everything was fine, and asked what my son had said on the phone. The dispatcher said (in a blunt and annoyed tone), "Your son asked if we wanted to come to a booger party."

Well, of course he did.

He couldn't just do the average giggle prank call, could he? Have to go the extra mile, doesn't he? So we went upstairs, and Lukas was instantly in balls of tears without us even saying a word. Adam had to leave the room during the discussion because he was about to laugh too hard about the whole situation and ruin the "learning opportunity."

But then came a *knock, knock, knock* on the front door that wasn't a joke! It was the cops. The police came first to make sure that everything was fine, and second to make sure that my son peed his pants in fear so he would never call 911 again unless it was an emergency (and rightly so). The look on that kid's face was utter disbelief and embarrassment to see two police officers telling him that 911 is nothing to play around with, that it is for people who need help, and that a prank call takes the help away from the people who really need help. WOW. Not much more needed to be said.

Well, I can tell you two things for sure were learned that night:

1. Though Lukas still loves a good prank (He'll randomly answer the phone, "Papa's pizza—can I take your order?"), he has not even hinted at messing around with 911 again. He figured out pretty quickly that it was to be taken seriously.
2. The 911 dispatchers and police officers do not actually want to go to a booger party. They apparently don't even like being invited to one. Don't bother asking.

Hard Verses to Swallow

God's Word, too, is quite clear about what things we are to take seriously and what things we are not to mess around with! In the last few years, my heart has been absolutely shocked by the things God says in Scripture about His standards for how we are to treat others … to the point that He says He will bless us if we obey it and will not if we don't. Ouch!

The call to compassion and action doesn't give extra credit points for those who are *really* committed to Him. It is a requirement of all following Christ. But how didn't I know? In the next chapters, we will look at the great verses about God's heart for the poor, how He dwells with the struggling, oppressed, and fatherless, and how church is supposed to be about more than just our individual relationships with God. Yes, our relationship with God is vital to everything. We can do NOTHING without Him. Our love of Christ and identity in Him is the source of everything we do and truly above all, but we were never meant to settle for learning about how God feels about us or about just dealing with our own sin issues (which certainly need to be dealt with). But our call to follow Christ was a call *to* something … to be fishers of men, next door and to the ends of the earth. We are restored as we help restore others. We were called to redemption—of us, those around us, and the whole earth, whether we live in America or go overseas.

In this chapter, we see some of the even harder verses to swallow. You'll read the ones that make us squirm in our seats and say, "Did He really just say that?" or "Is that really what it means?" If we are honest with ourselves, we sometimes ask those questions about Scripture when it make us uncomfortable, not just because they are statements that sound extreme in our tempered, "balanced" culture. Sometimes, we want an excuse not to change anything about our cushioned lives. But God is kind to us, wanting to urge us on to be and do more. He gives us motivation with both promises and warnings in Scripture—not completely unlike me giving my kids motivational rewards and consequences for important behaviors they really need to change. "Not only does God warn us of certain loss if we are unfaithful to our responsibilities, He seeks to motivate by assuring us of the great reward that awaits those who are faithful to the missionary mandate."[1]

If you have read any of my favorite books to motivate adults (that I quote often in this book) like *The Hole in Our Gospel, Just Courage, Dangerous Surrender, Radical,* or *Interrupted,* then you are somewhat familiar with these verses. I share them again for a few reasons:

1. Many aren't familiar with these verses. The reality is that our days don't give us God's Word as often as Hollywood gossip and we possibly don't seek it out as often either.
2. If you are like me and suffer from undiagnosed short-term memory loss, then you have heard these verses, but forgot them, either out of convenience or because you never saw them in action.
3. I have read the above books and many like them and I am *still* impacted by these Scriptures. Each time I rest on them they find their way deeper inside me. Each time, it is like a little crack in my heart (or my bank account) opens up a little bit and fresh

water comes in. It is super cold at first and totally shocks and stings my system so that I cringe and want to run away … but then the truth is refreshing and life-giving, something my body and soul have been waiting for all this time. God's Word is like that. So whether it is the first time or the hundredth time looking at just some of these verses, please gander again.

First—Blessings

> *He who is kind to the poor lends to the LORD, and He will reward him for what he has done.* (Proverbs 19:17)

I've always heard that Proverbs is considered a book a principles and not necessarily promises, but even as a principle, we will be rewarded for lending to the poor. It isn't that we should serve at a homeless shelter and "happen" to mention it in our Christmas letter and get a self-designated praise that way. We *will* get rewards, either on earth or in Heaven.

Peter also calls to us:

> *Live such good lives among the pagans that, though they accuse you of doing wrong, they may see your good deeds and glorify God on the day he visits us.* (1 Peter 2:9–10)

Are you living this? Not just living a holy, separate life, but living a good life *among* the lost and broken. This isn't just living among them, trying to give some glimpse of what holiness looks like (because who are we kidding about our own sin issues?), but it is genuine living, loving, and following Christ and also doing *good deeds* . . . deeds that stand out. Are you doing this? Is your church? Is your community? If you are, then spread it— like wildfire! I *beg* you. I have been seeing more glimpses of it lately, as God is moving! But if you don't have this already, read this:

> *They devoted themselves to the apostles' teaching and to the fellowship, to the breaking of bread and to prayer. Everyone was filled with awe, and many wonders and miraculous signs were done by the apostles. All the believers were together and had everything in common. Selling their possessions and goods, they gave to anyone as he had need. Every day they continued to meet together in the temple courts. They broke bread in their homes and ate together with glad and sincere hearts, praising God and enjoying the favor of all the people. And the Lord added to their number daily those who were being saved.* (Acts 2:42–47)

Did you catch that? "Selling their possessions and goods, they gave to anyone as he had need." You knew I was going there, didn't you? I'm going here next: "And the Lord added to their number daily those who were being saved."

Something makes me nervous, yet excited, that He is calling me and my family into something deeper still, something costly like this. Honestly, it scares me, but I think history tells us time and time again that it is this kind of radical selfless living that changes lives, churches, and cities. But are we really willing to get rid of our stuff? Really willing to live with LESS?

Fine, fine—it isn't just "stuff." It is nice items, efficient appliances, and vacations we worked hard for. It is mass extracurricular activities that will "surely" get our kids scholarships or make them "well-rounded," while they eat all the best organic food and literally get "well-rounded." It is all the "developmental" toys that our kids "should" have because it will supposedly increase their IQ and all the other kids have them. It is the newest phone or even last season's phone or iPad, iPod, or iPoo (that last one is the latest technology device for toddlers to track their potty training success if you didn't know … okay, maybe not, but I am about to iPuke about all the devices we all have). And don't forget that iBankrupt is almost on the market, so put in a preorder for that baby! Meanwhile, please forgive the slight puns, but kids in other countries, as well as our own, are saying: iHungry, iAbused, iAlone, iDying, and iLost.

It is crazy. It is wrong.

I am desperate to avoid putting this consumer culture on my children later in life for them to figure out on their own. I don't want to spring this information on my kids after they have created all their cultured habits and misconceptions about the world. I want them to get it now … to hear God's commands, promises, warnings, and heart *now* and try to live it out. It is definitely a high responsibility and not easy, but man, I personally regret the years I didn't live my life responding to the call of the broken, missing out on a fuller faith. Gary Haugen, President of International Justice Mission, suggests that "certainly the work of justice brings out marvelous rescue and joy to the *victims* of injustice, but God wants his people to know that the work of justice benefits *the people who do it* as well."[2] How gracious of God! I will say again: We are restored as we help restore others.

Alright— if *those* were the blessings and they kind of killed me, well shoot, what are the warnings going to be like? Let's breathe deep and take a look. It isn't going to be pretty.

The Warnings

> *For I know how many are your offenses and how great your sins. You oppress the righteous and take bribes and you deprive the poor of justice in the courts. Away with the noise of your songs! I will not listen to the music of your harps. But let justice roll on like a river, Righteousness like a never-failing stream!* (Amos 5:12, 23–24)
>
> *For I desire mercy, not sacrifice, and acknowledgment of God rather than burnt offerings.* (Hosea 6:6)

First, let's look at the Amos passage. God counts "depriving the poor of justice" as a sin. We don't usually talk about that in church during our confession time, do we? It isn't up there with our lust, pride, or anger list, is it? But God is saying here that it isn't just what people do *to* the poor that is a sin, it is not stepping in and giving them justice for whatever was done to them by others, as well.

Whoa. God is talking about the bystander. Being a bystander is a sin.

If God is talking to His children like that and I see His heart, that means God is talking about *me,* too.

That is a blow to my stomach. It is a blow to my very soul. What is the consequence? Well, He tells us. God says He will not listen to the music they offer. Basically, He is saying He won't receive their praise. It isn't pleasing to Him and He doesn't want it. In the Hosea verse, it is similar. God is saying that He wants mercy, not burnt offerings, as the real praise and acknowledgement that a person knows God. He wants justice to roll on like a river. I don't know about you, but this seems a little strong. Maybe this is just one passage for a particular group of people. What else is there?

> *O house of David, this is what the LORD says: "Administer justice every morning; rescue from the hand of his oppressor the one who has been robbed, or my wrath will break out and burn like fire because of the evil you have done—burn with no one to quench it."* (Jeremiah 21:12)

Uh oh! This one is obviously a little stronger . . . okay, a LOT stronger. It isn't just God saying He won't receive the praise of the one that doesn't administer justice and rescue the oppressed or poor. He is saying that He will unleash His wrath on those who don't because it is considered *evil* to not do it.

I confess, it seems a bit harsh. Doesn't seem quite like God, at first. But when I think about the person standing by while a little girl gets raped, or the person who intentionally does *not* intervene while a child starves to death, I long for God's wrath. I ache for it and I praise Him for it. There is a part of us, in our heart of hearts, that knows that the sin of the bystander is just about as sick as the sin of the perpetrator, don't we? It makes us uncomfortable to acknowledge it, mostly because it talks about us, but our souls know it. We know that God's wrath is right and just. We want to be different. At least I do.

> *The LORD looked and was displeased*
> *that there was no justice.*
> *He saw that there was no one,*
> *He was appalled that there was no one to intervene.*
> (Isaiah 59:15b–16a)

I find this interesting. God is appalled. Why? Is He appalled that the poor are suffering and that the sick are dying? Is He appalled that evil people are doing unspeakable things to innocent children? Is He appalled that millions are dying without Jesus? Yeah, in other passages we see His anger against these things, but not in this passage.

Here, God is appalled that no one is *intervening*. He is appalled at us: the church as a whole, and again, I believe He is appalled at my lack of intervening.

We only like to talk about God's love and mercy in our lives. God's love is truly amazing and *yes*, we are covered by Jesus's blood if we have accepted His work on the cross and repented with our lives. There are indeed seasons where we need to focus primarily upon God's love for us, but in the process we must not cheapen God's heart and call to the church. I believe God can be (and often is) angry at the church for not hearing Him (or for hearing Him and not obeying). We have gotten a lot of things right in the church, but I think we have royally missed some of this. We have missed (or just shot the arrow too low) in responding to most of the Bible's heart for the oppressed. However, we have missed even more. We have missed clues about where God resides (with those who are suffering) and we have missed a deeper kind of living and faith that God has for us. It truly says something about our hearts. "Why does the church of Jesus Christ live so complacently in a world where each year nearly eight million children die before the age of five, or where nearly one million children are sold into sex-trafficking? Why, if God is all-good and all-powerful, is the church so unchanged, so untransformed? . . . The heart is hard to change. The heart is the heart of the matter."[3]

A Sheep or a Goat?

> *When the Son of Man comes in his glory, and all the angels with him, he will sit on his glorious throne. All the nations will be gathered before him, and he will separate the people one from another as a shepherd separates the sheep from the goats. He will put the sheep on his right and the goats on his left.*
>
> *Then the King will say to those on his right, 'Come, you who are blessed by my Father; take your inheritance, the kingdom prepared for you since the creation of the world. For I was hungry and you gave me something to eat, I was thirsty and you gave me something to drink, I was a stranger and you invited me in, I needed clothes and you clothed me, I was sick and you looked after me, I was in prison and you came to visit me.'*
>
> *Then the righteous will answer him, 'Lord, when did we see you hungry and feed you, or thirsty and give you something to drink? When did we see you a stranger and*

invite you in, or needing clothes and clothe you? When did we see you sick or in prison and go to visit you?'

The King will reply, 'Truly I tell you, whatever you did for one of the least of these brothers and sisters of mine, you did for me.'

Then he will say to those on his left, 'Depart from me, you who are cursed, into the eternal fire prepared for the devil and his angels. For I was hungry and you gave me nothing to eat, I was thirsty and you gave me nothing to drink, I was a stranger and you did not invite me in, I needed clothes and you did not clothe me, I was sick and in prison and you did not look after me.'

They also will answer, 'Lord, when did we see you hungry or thirsty or a stranger or needing clothes or sick or in prison, and did not help you?'

He will reply, 'Truly I tell you, whatever you did not do for one of the least of these, you did not do for me.'

Then they will go away to eternal punishment, but the righteous to eternal life. (Matthew 25:31–46)

This is just too much! It has me shaking in my boots, and, honestly, it is *supposed* to. Jesus meant for people to have little puddles running down their legs in fear. (New vision of a biblical story, eh? You can tell I have a fourth grade boy, can't you?) Seriously, He wanted to scare them straight. The narrow road is the harder road. Jen Hatmaker expresses: "It won't suffice to claim good intentions. Saying 'I meant well' is not going to cut it. Not with God screaming, begging, pleading, urging us to love mercy and justice, to feed the poor and orphaned, to care for the last and least in nearly every book of the Bible. It will not be enough one day to stand before Jesus and say, 'Oh? Were you serious about that?'"[4]

Service to the poor and oppressed (or rather, if I fail to serve and become a passive, or merely sympathetic, bystander to the poor and oppressed) is not just a mirror of my service to God, but perhaps *actually* serving Christ in flesh. I have to dare to ask myself, “Have I passed Him by? How many times have I passed my sweet Lord by? How many times was I too busy or distracted or nervous to get involved?”

Tony Campolo writes, “A friend of mine was taking a tour of an inner-city church with a huge social ministry that included a soup kitchen. He was there just before the noon hour. The kitchen crew had gathered in a huddle to pray before they opened the door and let in the hungry street people. Among the prayers lifted up was one by an African-American woman who simply said, ‘Lord, we know You’ll be comin’ through the line today, so help us treat You well.’”[5]

I don’t want to fail this test. I want God to hear my worship. I want the songs I sing to reflect how I live my life, not to be lies about my adoration of Him only to live a lesser devotion the rest of the week. I hear again, or perhaps for the first time, what God’s Word tells me about what He desires from me as I live my life for Him.

Chapter 3

"Why?" Saying the "S" Word at Church

I don't preach a social gospel; I preach the Gospel, period. The gospel of our Lord Jesus Christ is concerned for the whole person. When people were hungry, Jesus didn't say, 'Now is that political or social?' He said, 'I feed you.' Because the good news to a hungry person is bread.

–Desmond Tutu

We were driving home from church during Lent one season, and I heard my son (almost six at the time) start to laugh. Knowing my son, I knew that a certain kind of laugh meant that he was either up to something (which usually meant my daughter would soon be screaming in response) or that he had found something randomly amusing. My husband was driving, so I looked into the back seat fully expecting fists to be flailing. (Isn't this what your car rides are like . . . especially on the way to or from church? Oh, they aren't? Just me?) Instead of a fight, I found my son holding up a Sunday School picture of the angel and the stone rolled away at Jesus's resurrection. I barely glanced at it (a picture of a tan, blonde angel casually sitting on top of the empty tomb), didn't think much of it, and still wondered why he was laughing. But then Lukas looked at me, handed me the picture, and said in his father's monotone, "Looks like Ken and Barbie found a new home." Man, that kid kills me.

The Real Thing

We all know when something isn't quite real. My son understood that the resurrection scene isn't supposed to look like a new Mattel merchandise display or an Abercrombie model turned angelic. Something didn't match. Similarly, but no laughing matter, I can guarantee that our kids and the *whole world* know when the actions of those who say they are Christians didn't match who they claim to be. I know what the world thinks about hypocritical Christians, and I find it a tragedy. But I truly shudder when I think of what our children will say if we don't live out our faith. Whether we call it an active, compassionate faith or whether we coin it "Social Justice" (the "S" word dreaded in some conservative corners), it must exist no matter what the phrase. Our actions must coincide with our faith. An amazing young woman, Katie Davis, wrote *Kisses from Katie,* an extraordinary book about her journey to Uganda to start Amazima ministries and adopt 13 kids. She writes about some of her early journey in Uganda:

> *As I thought about the discrepancies between the culture I came from and the one I now lived in, I could not stop thinking about my life and the lives of many of my friends in the States—and being appalled by our luxuries when people on our same planet were living in such poverty and need. I began to realize huge flaws and gaps in my faith, a wide chasm between what I proclaimed to believe and how I was actually living. I had to do something.*
>
> *I thought about these things as I lay in bed at night exhausted, devastated, and angry that people were living (and dying) like this while I had lived such an extravagant life for the past eighteen years. As abject poverty confronted me every day, I felt deeply convicted about one thing: God did not make too many people and not enough resources to go around. Because we were living in His world, there had to be a solution.*[1]

Luckily, Katie had the ability to take what she saw as hypocritical in her faith and make it real, aligned with scripture and the God she loved. So here's the thing … just in case we all missed it: The Good News isn't just about spiritual salvation. God has bigger plans than that.

Jesus's Mission

I'm a missionary girl at heart. As I shared in the first chapter, I was on mission trips pretty much from day one of my faith. I'm passionate about God being glorified when nations come to know Him. My heart breaks for those who are trapped in the darkness of sin . . . forever. This *is* the Great Commission, and God's desire for all tribes and tongues to come to know Him. However, just saving someone from eternal Hell is not all Christ came to do. It is not all He showed us and it's not all we should be showing our kids. We have missed key elements of His mission and our mission if we are only using our mouths to tell people about Jesus. My pastor reminded me of the verse in Luke, where Jesus quotes the book of Isaiah to refer to Himself:

> *The Spirit of the Lord is on me, because he has anointed me to proclaim good news to the poor. He has sent me to proclaim freedom for the prisoners and recovery of sight for the blind, to set the oppressed free, to proclaim the year of the Lord's favor.* (Luke 4:18–19)

Stop here! Where did Jesus just come from when He refers to this passage in Isaiah? If you look into this passage in Luke, you see that He has just returned from the desert after being tested for 40 days. He is introducing Himself to the world now. This is a big moment. He could have chosen a lot of things to express, a lot of different Hebrew passages to recite. His mission is to bring good news to the poor, proclaim freedom for prisoners, give sight to the blind, and set the oppressed free. These all have *both* physical and spiritual purposes. Those are bold, amazing statements and so much bigger than us. They must go together.

Rich Stearns, president of World Vision, reflects in *The Hole in Our Gospel*, "Proclaiming the whole gospel then means much more than evangelism in hopes that people will hear and respond to the good news of salvation by faith in Christ. It also encompasses tangible compassion for the sick and the poor, as well as biblical justice, efforts to right the wrongs that are so prevalent in our world."[2] We saw many scriptures that spoke of this in the last chapter, but honestly, when you really start to look through the Bible, you see what looks like that "S" word ("Social Justice") basically everywhere: "'He defended the cause of the poor and needy, and so all went well. Is that not what it means to know me?'" (Jeremiah 22:16). And:

> *What good is it, my brothers, if a man claims to have faith but has no deeds? Can such faith save him? Suppose a brother or sister is without clothes and daily food. If one of you says to him, "Go, I wish you well; keep warm and well fed," but does nothing about his physical needs, what good is it? In the same way, faith by itself, if it is not accompanied by action, is dead. But someone will say, "You have faith; I have deeds." Show me your faith without deeds, and I will show you my faith by what I do. You believe that there is one God. Good! Even the demons believe that—and shudder. You foolish man, do you want evidence that faith without deeds is useless.* (James 2:14–20)

Don't get me wrong, this kind of faith in word and deed is being lived out by some for sure! Big organizations like World Vision, Compassion International, World Relief, IJM, Salvation Army, Mercy Ships, and countless other organizations, churches, and nameless missionaries and lay people are making absolute life, community, and country-transforming efforts and giving their lives for it. This work is rocking eternity with the people that are also following the call to know and serve Jesus.

But, for some strange reason, in many churches and youth groups, there is a separation of evangelism and activist faith . . . going too far with one or the other and missing the link. "Social Justice" is often categorized as a liberal word, for some reason. "*Justice* seems to trigger one of two images: radical druggie hippies from the 1960s or 'liberal' believers who talk more about freedom and rights than Jesus or salvation."[3] Missions is thus sometimes characterized as evangelism overseas, but not always with feeding the homeless. However, even work without initial words does lead people to Christ. Even in Muslim countries, where Christian groups aren't allowed to openly share the gospel, the people ask, "Why are you doing this … why are you helping me?" opening the door for conversations about Jesus, which is then legal and often results in a saving faith.

> *But in your hearts acknowledge Christ as the holy Lord. Always be prepared to give an answer to everyone who asks you to give the reason for the hope that you have.* (1 Peter 3:15)

In researching this division of the "liberal-social gospel churches" and "conservative-evangelical churches," I found that, for the most part, this division is nationwide and not just in the Northeast, where we currently reside. Though there are some exceptions, Jim Wallis states: "Churches today are tragically split between those who stress conversion but have forgotten its goal, and those who emphasize Christian social action but have forgotten the necessity for conversion."[4] Each group seems to focus on one, but not on both. They focus on evangelism or on social action, but seem to struggle at keeping the two together (and many focus on neither). If we want to bring the two sides together, we need a theology which deals with both evangelism and compassion, both theologically sound and tangibly lived out.

Why would this ever surprise us? Why would these two sides ever come apart? So often it seems that in the work of mercy and justice we too are healed. An Isaiah 58 passage (that I engage a little more fully at the end of the book) reveals God's promises for those who do His work, and honestly, it is all over the Bible. It has always been there. If we focus simply on obedience of His Word, we will automatically have both evangelism and social justice tied together in our hearts and lives. It is in the Old Testament, in Jesus's ministry, and in how He called us to minister, live, and worship in Acts and the epistles. And yet, in it, it must *all* be about Him … our obedience for His glory, our acts of mercy and call for the redemption of His people … *all* of it. It is here that we show our children where they fit into God's great redemption story and what true faith looks like…when LESS is so much more.

The Whole Gospel

So, in the last chapter I used a nightly news tactic of fear to get your attention with God's blessings and curses. In this chapter, let's take a real, hard look at just a few more scriptures of the whole gospel. The term "Whole Gospel" has been used before by others, but has been used today most prominently by World Vision's president Rich Stearns in his book *The Hole in Our Gospel* to explain how we have preached a gospel with a hole in it. The gospel itself doesn't have a hole … many American churches just do as it is often a gospel of words with a huge hole where action should be. A "whole" gospel comes together with both word and action. Similarly, Compassion International declares practically that anyone "wanting to proclaim the glory of Christ to the ends of the earth must consider not only how to declare the gospel verbally but also how to demonstrate the gospel visibly in a world where so many are urgently hungry."[5]

When it comes to just looking at Scripture, even Rick Warren confesses: "I found those 2,000 verses on the poor. I went to Bible college, two seminaries, and I got a doctorate? How did I miss God's compassion for the poor? I was not seeing all the purpose of God. The church is the body of Christ. The hands and feet have been amputated and we're just a big mouth, known more for what we're against."[6]

We don't need to jump on a new bandwagon, we just need to read the Bible. So, just to make sure we are all reading the same Bible—without the holes, I'll state a few of these verses. Though they are convicting, if I sit in them and think about God's heart, I am humbled beyond belief by the love of my Lord and what He is working out for His church and the world. Don't skim them! (If you are like me, you might justify skimming, thinking that you surely already know them all.) Actually read them:

> *Command them to do good, to be rich in good deeds, and to be generous and willing to share. In this way they will lay up treasure for themselves as a firm foundation for the coming age, so that they may take hold of the life that is truly life.* (1 Timothy 6:18–19)

Heal the sick, raise the dead, cleanse those who have leprosy, drive out demons. Freely you have received, freely give. (Matthew 10:8)

John answered, "The man with two tunics should share with him who has none, and the one who has food should do the same." (Luke 3:11)

This is how we know what love is: Jesus Christ laid down his life for us. And we ought to lay down our lives for our brothers. If anyone has material possessions and sees his brother in need but has no pity on him, how can the love of God be in him? Dear children, let us not love with words or tongue but with actions and in truth. (1 John 3:16–18)

But when you give a banquet, invite the poor, the crippled, the lame, the blind, and you will be blessed. Although they cannot repay you, you will be repaid at the resurrection of the righteous. (Luke 14:13)

And if anyone gives even a cup of cold water to one of these little ones who is my disciple, truly I tell you, that person will certainly not lose their reward. (Matthew 10:42)

Defend the weak and the fatherless; uphold the cause of the poor and the oppressed. Rescue the weak and the needy; deliver them from the hand of the wicked. (Psalm 82:3-4)

It is easy to skip over one or two verses, but once the verses compile one on top of the other, my soul begins to break and I feel the weight of God's Word on my heart. For there are other words that I don't wish to hear, like:

Why do you call me, 'Lord, Lord,' and do not do what I say? (Luke 6:46)

And there are words I long to hear like:

> *His master replied, "Well done, good and faithful servant! You have been faithful with a few things; I will put you in charge of many things. Come and share your master's happiness!"* (Matthew 25:21)

The choice of which words I hear, in the end, are mine and mine alone. However, as a parent, the words my children hear are somewhat on my shoulders until they leave my home. That is a heavy weight. If the church has been missing this priority, it follows that our parenting is also likely missing this priority.

It isn't meant to scare us, but to wake us up and make us pay attention . . . now. So, it is a weight that I wish to share with you, as fellow parents and teachers, so that we can carry it together in hopes of passing on an incredible calling from God that is deep in His Word.

We are to live His Word. Christ came as the Word in flesh to the sinful, sick, dying, abused, hurting, and lonely. He went to all these places . . . not just to find these "other" people, but to find us.

We, with our children, will also find Him, our Lord, there in these hard places. That is where we always start. Where is the heart of God?

We will find Him with the poor.

Chapter 4
"Why?" Finding God in a Cardboard Box

God is in the slums, in the cardboard boxes where the poor play house. God is in the silence of a mother who has infected her child with a virus that will end both their lives. God is in the cries heard under the rubble of war. God is in the debris of wasted opportunity and lives, and God is with us if we are with them.
–Mother Teresa

I am beyond grateful when I see evidence of God's work in my children's lives and hearts. However, beyond scripture memory, spiritual disciplines, and a real relationship with God, my kids exhibited some normal for us (strange for others) behavior one morning:

1. Rather than stuff a pillow in her shirt to play a mommy pregnant, my daughter would have dolls of many different races that she adopted her play children.

2. My son tracks where his toys are made, knowing some work conditions in countries like China.

3. My son finished another of too many drawings of Sonic the Hedgehog to send to his sponsored child/friend

4. My daughter's pet dogs get referred to as her "foster dogs" So, I may need to explain that one: I worked in foster care, my in-laws were foster parents for 25+ years, and other dearly loved family members are adopted from the foster system

Granted, these little exchanges are a mixture of wonder and just downright weirdness. As a mom, I am constantly fighting self-centeredness in my kids and trying so hard to engage their hearts and faiths in these global and local issues. These glimpses are beautiful for me.

Where in the World is . . . God?

So, where is God? He is everywhere, and as believers, He even resides within us. However, we also see glimpses in Scripture and in the world as to where His Spirit resides. One powerful example was evidenced in the movie *Beyond the Gates* that I mentioned earlier about the Rwandan genocide. It is one of the best movies I have ever seen. It is depressing (obviously), but also inspirational. In the movie (based on a true story of a Catholic school), a priest refuses to leave with all the other Americans, French, and British, who have taken their passes out of the country during the massacre. All those leaving know that once they are gone, the Hutus will burst through the gates and slaughter the Tutsis. The main character, a friend of the priest, is ashamed for leaving, but still feels shocked to see at the last minute that the priest is staying. He begins to beg the priest to come, knowing that if the priest stays, he will surely die a brutal death. Father Christopher replies:

> *You asked me, Joe, where is God in everything that is happening here ... in all this suffering? I know exactly where He is. He is right here. With these people. Suffering. His love is here, more intense and profound than I've ever felt. And my heart is here, too. My soul. If I leave, I think, I may not find it again.*[1]

Wow. I don't even know what to do with those words. They are so intense, and if you watch the movie, your heart breaks both for the story unfolding as well as in longing to know God's presence that intensely. But, I ask myself: Do I dare to even come close to any pain like this in order to experience God?

Over and over, we learn that here, with the least of these, is where our Lord loves to be found. He is with the poor and the broken. He is with the oppressed and the lost. In many ways, with the LESS, He is MORE.

Why is this a surprise? Why do we want to argue and say "Well now, He is also in our nice churches." Well, yes, He is. Absolutely! But, I ask, what were we when He first came for us and why did He first come? We too were chained, broken, and lost, weren't we? In many ways, we still are chained to old patterns of thinking and living as we are being sanctified, and in many ways the world keeps breaking us. This brokenness is where our Lord is. This is where He comes to heal us. He came to a dark, dirty place as a baby in Bethlehem and continues to find extraordinary ways into those physically and spiritually dark places. We don't want it any other way or we are lost indeed. So if we want to know Him, His heart, His fullness of living, then we too must be found there in our own honest messes before Him and in the messes of the world.

Then our children must go, too, if we want them to see our Lord in the fullness of His love. That makes us uncomfortable. Heck, it can sometimes make my skin crawl. Yet, when I see my son feeling completely defeated by his own weaknesses (he is only nine, but he has one intense soul), I long to reveal to him a Lord that is holding the drunken, homeless man and the street orphan just as much as the rich, godly woman in church. He will find both his own healing and purpose in the reality of this kind of love that God has for him and for the whole world.

Katie Davis in Uganda, witnessing disease, poverty, orphans, and sorrows upon sorrows, echoes the vision of God in this dirty form:

> *Through all the challenges and contradictions and through the gracious people all around me, God was opening my eyes to a whole new world of living and most important to a whole new way of living out the Gospel. Every day I spent in Uganda has been beautifully overwhelming; everywhere I have looked, raw, filthy, human need and brokenness have been on display, begging for someone to meet them, fix them. And even though I realize I cannot always mend or meet, I can enter in. I can enter into someone's pain and sit with them and*

> *know. This is Jesus. Not that He apologizes for the hard and the hurt, but that He enters in, He comes with us to the hard places. And so I continue to enter.*[2]

It is because we know Jesus that we follow Him in these dark places. It is because we know that He is both good and powerful that we can courageously engage the dark alley or dusty village.

The Heart of God

The founder of World Vision and Samaritan's Purse, Bob Pierce, prayed: *"Let my heart be broken by the things that break the heart of God."* God answered that prayer, and the hearts of Bob and his family nearly broke into pieces, but out of their brokenness and willingness to serve, World Vision now serves in almost 100 countries, currently facilitating community development and sponsorship for millions of children.

What does God's heart sound like? Here are some verses that give us a glimpse beyond the ones we have read in the other chapters and beyond what we already know about God's character:

> *A father to the fatherless, a defender of widows,*
> *God sets the lonely in families,*
> *He leads forth the prisoners with singing;*
> *but the rebellious live in a sun-scorched land.* (Psalm 68:5–6)

> *He defends the cause of the fatherless and the widow, and loves the alien, giving him food and clothing.* (Deuteronomy 10:18)

Why does God's heart break so? Let's look at a few million reasons why:

"In developing countries, approximately 130 million children and teens—age 17 or under—have lost one or both parents.

More than nine million children under age five die each year. Two-thirds of these deaths—more than six million every year — are preventable.

Malaria kills approximately one million children per year, many of them under age five and most of them in sub-Saharan Africa...

Roughly 12 percent of the world's population, or 884 million people, do not have access to safe water...

Approximately 1.8 million children die each year as a result of diseases caused by unclean water and poor sanitation. This is around 5,000 deaths a day...

To date about 65 million people have been infected with HIV, and AIDS has killed more than 25 million people since it was first recognized in 1981...

Already 923 million people worldwide are undernourished, and there are more than nine million deaths related to hunger each year...

An estimated 1.2 million children—both boys and girls—are trafficked each year into exploitative work, including mining, factories, armed conflict or commercial sex work."[3]

In his book about sex trafficking, *Terrify No More*, Gary Haugen asks the question that we all are dying to ask God when we face evil:

For many of us the ugliness of abuse and oppression in our world leads us, quite understandably, to ask: Where is God in the midst of such suffering? Even if we have drifted to a place in life where we rarely address God, there is something about the rank cruelty of exploitation and the naked brutality of human violence that seems to lift our objection almost involuntarily to something larger and beyond ourselves. This was the cry that most resonated within my own heart while I struggled with the smell and mess and waste of genocide amid the mass graves of Rwanda. It was an appeal I heard echoing in an ancient cry of the psalmist:

'Why, O Lord, do you stand far off? Why do you hide yourself in times of trouble? In his arrogance the wicked man hunts down the weak, who are caught in the schemes he devises...He says to himself, 'God has forgotten; he covers his face and never sees.'

But over time, having seen the suffering of the innocent and the crushing of the weak all around the world, my plea has changed. More and more I find myself asking not, 'Where is God?' But 'Where are God's people?' . . . The little girls of Svay Pak were not suffering because of vague and inexplicable forces of nature. They were suffering because men and women with names and faces chose to beat them, rape them, and terrorize them. They suffered because other men and women with names and faces chose to provide shelter and protection for the abusers. And at the end of the day, they suffered because the rest of us let it happen.[4]

That is where I suppose I have landed as well. God has told me where He is. He has told me that He is with the poor, the broken, and the oppressed … those whom He has called me to help. I know I want Him and I want my children to know Him and rest in His merciful, powerful heart. Now, with my increasing knowledge about the world, I know more what the needs are. I know how big the gap is between me and them. I know I have done nothing to deserve this life I have been given. I know a lot of the problems are fixable if people like you and I choose to fix them (and thus choose *not* to do other things with our time, money, and image). Max Lucado reflects:

> *Ours is the wealthiest generation of Christians ever. We are bright, educated, and experienced. We can travel around the world in twenty-four hours or send a message in a millisecond. We have the most sophisticated research and medicines at the tips of our fingers. We have ample resources. A mere two percent of the world's grain harvest would be enough, if shared, to erase the problems of hunger and malnutrition around the world. There is enough food on the planet to offer every person twenty-five hundred calories of sustenance a day. We have enough food to feed the hungry. And we have enough bedrooms to house the orphans. Here's the math. There are 145 million orphans worldwide. Nearly 236 million people in the United States call themselves Christians. From purely a statistical standpoint, American Christians by themselves have the wherewithal to house every orphan in the world...God has given this generation, our generation, everything we need to alter the course of human suffering.*[5]

I know I want my children to be part of something that matters. I want them to be part of something that restores and transforms others, but also that transforms them and, most of all, glorifies God. I see no better chance to help my kids find God's heart and find their true hope than in this work amidst the broken, lost, and vulnerable. I'm not worried I'll forget to give them good theology … for all of this will require me to daily give them good theology about how God originally made the world originally, what went wrong, what He intends for it, as well as who He is, what He is doing in us, what He can do through us, and so on. I just see it as an *awesome* foundation for living out that theology. I don't want to give them a life of ten percent church, 35 percent school, ten percent family, ten percent extracurricular, and fill in the remaining 35 percent with meeting the standards placed by the culture around them by media and friends. That is what naturally happens unless we intentionally (sometimes drastically) intervene.

Those who are broken need us to engage in this work, but we need it, too, don't we? Tim Dearborn of World Vision shares the words of a local worker: "'Our job is to connect those who are rich in commodities with those who are rich in community.' Isn't that beautiful? Who's poor? Who's rich? We all are. What we have, they need. Sometimes desperately. What they have, we need. Just as desperately."[6] Again, we are restored when we help restore others.

I want to take my children to places where they can best see God in touchable, livable flesh so they can see and know that He is real, good, and just. I want them to see the bare bones of life and faith in more clarity--perhaps more color. I want them to see that He has mapped out an amazing mission and purpose for their lives and that no other God or plan could ever compare.

Chapter 5
"Why?" The Spoiled Little Thrill Seeker

It is better to lose your life than to waste it.

–John Piper

A Cheap Substitute for Purpose and Gratitude

I recently got the stomach bug REALLY BAD. I will spare you the details, but it was a painful, messy ordeal. In the past I would have been dramatic and have prayed to die amidst what feels like utter torture. However, due to my ever-increasing knowledge and connection with those in other dire circumstances, I viewed my illness quite differently. Even during a vomit session, I found my thoughts went toward another mom in another country--a village perhaps, where she'd have to walk for water. After I was sick, I took a shower to clean all the disgust off me. However, someone in a hut, without easy access to water, couldn't do that. Similarly, when I was sick, my husband took over all duties and tended to me. However, a child stuck in slavery would have no comfort or rest in spite of their illness. These thoughts gave me perspective, compassion, and a desire to act in a new way. I am humbled and grateful for these reflections and felt they were straight from the heart of God.

We all have a tendency to get stuck in our own world without intervention. I believe that ignorance and choice are the two reasons for selfish living and lack of purpose. Ignorance is something we can help ourselves and others with, and then the choice is up to them and us. Our children, our schools, and our churches' youth are desperate for purpose. Without perspective and purpose, they are headed straight for hearts and lives that reek of entitlement and either flounder without purpose or seek purpose in the wrong things.

The last couple chapters described God's heart for the poor and His call to us all to enter uncomfortable situations to love in word and deed. There are blessings for all ages in that. This chapter, however, focuses on a few blessings that are particularly important for youth to receive--in contrast to what the world offers them.

The contrast is drastic. Ungrateful teens waffling between lack of purpose or seeking thrills contrast with grateful youths engaged and fulfilled in God's global redemption story. Though it may not be easy, we can give them a bigger purpose—a global, Biblical one. Offering the Biblical one, however, requires our intentional intervention … and buying the line ourselves, which is why I'm going so much into the *whys* of all of this. Let's look at the effect of culture on our youth first and then engage an alternative.

OPTION 1 for Teens: Led by Culture Without Intervention

"Because I want it"—Generations of the Entitled

Jeanne Twenge, author of the book *Generation Me* believes that self-focused youth are a product of their families and cultures teaching them that life is about making themselves happy.[1] Though there are so many things that I want to give (and often do give) to my children (in terms of things and experiences), I am realizing that some of this is selfish parenting in the long run. I'd get their happiness now, but not necessarily in the future. I know that if my children don't learn most of the time to earn money for a toy they want, pay for a broken item, or work to buy a gift for someone else, then they aren't going to be ready for the real world. They often just see the world as a big ATM. They are growing up in economies that, sadly, will most likely be even harder to succeed in than when we grew up, and they will be unprepared.

I don't know about you, but I know some grownups who were unprepared to be self-sufficient, assuming someone else will take care of them and will fix their mess, having been sheltered from hard work, consequences, and serving others. They make lousy friends, uncommitted employees, and undesired spouses. Tim Kimmel reports in his book *Raising Kids for True Greatness*, "There are always exceptions, but for the most part, kids who don't serve will grow up self-absorbed and hard to satisfy, and they will become quite unattractive and costly to the people around them."[2]

I would never want an entitled life for my child. Then, why do we feel like we can't do much about it? Why do we assume that all teenagers are going to be lazy and self-centered? They don't have to be! Not only is allowing our children to fail, teaching them to work hard, and honestly dealing with sin a huge part of intentionally fighting selfishness, but giving our children a global vision of God's plan in a world of suffering with opportunities to serve are part of that battle as well. It is part of the same strategy for the purposelessness disintegrating the hearts of youth across our country.

Most of us fear the teenage years, hoping that our kids won't rebel too much when it comes to sex, drugs, and drinking. We aren't sure how we will stop it beyond maybe increasing our prayer life and restrictions, as well as hoping some foundational teaching has stuck somewhere in there. This fear is legitimate because teenage rebellion can have long-term or even terminal effects. If, by God's grace, we are able to barely breeze by those big casualties, there's a load of other landmines to walk through where our children could get stuck. Though they seem less scary at large, they erode the hearts of our youth. Julie Ferwerda reflects: "To fill their need-for-speed, many of our kids bury themselves in gaming, social networking, and amusement, often at the expense of meaningful family relationships or selfless contributions in the lives of others. Our little ones grow up having almost everything their hearts desire, yet for so many, their hearts are still beyond empty."[3]

Drugs

Sadly, alcohol use remains the norm among teenagers today. Nearly 75 percent have significantly consumed alcohol by the end of high school and more than 30 percent by eighth grade. Marijuana is also prevalent, seen as the gateway to other drugs, and it is being used at earlier and earlier ages.[4] On average, marijuana is now ahead of cigarette smoking. Street marijuana today isn't like what it used to be, either. For example, in 1978, Marijuana's THC (potency) was 1.37 percent. In 2008, it was 8.49 percent.[5] Today, it's also occasionally laced with cocaine, making it even more addictive. It is now commonplace in schools and part of the whole party scene. I know way too many families losing children to marijuana addictions alone, and it breaks my heart and burdens my prayers.

After marijuana, prescription and over-the-counter drugs are the most used drugs by high school seniors.[6] Reading that statistic, if we feel relieved that they aren't younger kids that are so high in this statistic, we should stop ourselves and think again. These high school seniors are about to leave home and go into college, jobs, and apartments with this drug use. This is tragic, not only for what the drugs might do to their lives, but because of what it says about how they feel about the purposefulness of what they are about to embrace in adulthood. We have failed if we haven't shown them a world full of need and purpose. There is plenty of purpose. Again, the choice is theirs, but our job as parents, pastors, and teachers is to show them the need in the world and God's heart to redeem it … and them.

Risk-taking

As parents, we are all naturally scared of risk-taking. We get a little nauseous when our children climb too high on playscapes or when they try a new, crazy skateboard move. Not many parents celebrate the day their children want to bungee jump or cliff dive, though internally they know that there is something really good about living with some risk. In an article about how teenagers are expected to be risk-takers because of the development of their brains, Dr. McArnarney says, "Novelty seeking, sensation seeking, and risk taking is the basis for considerable growth during adolescence, as well as for the seemingly reckless behavior of some adolescents."[7] Bottom line: teenagers will take risks! We can expect it.

So, if we know that risk-taking is coming and a part of development (that God made), then we are foolish not to tap into it! Todd Ahrend suggests, "This is a generation of risk takers. If we can attach some purpose and meaning to those risks, it's almost irresistible."[8] That gives me goose bumps—the idea of turning something we fear (like risk-taking) into a tool for God's glory. I love it—youth that risk for *God*! Amen!

Purposelessness

Though there are a billion opportunities to find thrills outside of God's identity and plan, the other temptation that Satan is luring youth with is purposelessness. When a person doesn't find fulfillment in the risks or thrills, they lose purpose and desire. "The enemy wishes nothing more than to coax our kids, if not into rebellion, then into pursuing passionless, insignificant, and potentially empty lives. As long as he can hamstring them with apathy, he need not worry about them doing damage to his kingdom."[9]

As Christians, we have the best plan in our grasp: God's plan of redemption! We have a dangerous and exciting plan. We have an adventure written out for us, one marked with more people that need saving than any action game could pull off. It is a story with good guys and the worst enemy imaginable to fight. We can travel, learn new skills and change lives. We have an awesome story to hand to our children, one of great risk and eternal reward! Our story, however, is real, and once the video game turns off, it is still going on, needing heroes! How have we not made it a more approachable revolution for the youth? It is kind of insane if you think about it.

Boredom

Schools are doing a lot to keep kids engaged…finding it hard to compete with virtual reality video gaming that is readily available to most kids. An article investigating other reasons contributing to boredom in school found a huge correlation with the perception by many students that school learning is meaningless, or not connected with their goals and interests, and not valuable in their lives.[10]

We may be fooled into thinking that this boredom is only occurring at high school before higher education, but educators are now seeing a serious problem of perceived meaninglessness in young people in higher education. They are reporting on a lack of purpose even from the most high-achieving kids at Ivy League schools.[11]

We cannot afford to allow church to be the same type of boring experience. It is here (and hopefully not only here) that they hear the words of eternal life. However, if we fail to connect God's Word practically with the gifts He has given our children for the world, church will become just as boring and meaningless as school. This has to happen before they leave for college so it becomes their lifeline to truth and purpose. Otherwise, our adult sons will spend their Sundays like most of America: only in Home Depot (or "Holy Depot" as my son used to accidentally call it), instead of church.

Depressed

In *Generation Me*, the author, Jeanne Twenge, recalls, "In past generations, suicide and depression were considered afflictions of middle age, as it was unusual for a young person to be depressed, but for Generation Me, these problems are a rite of passage through adolescence and young adulthood."[12] Sadly, the statistics on depression in teens is something at which we need to take a serious look. About 20 percent of teens will experience depression before adulthood, and about 5 percent will suffer a major depression. Depression itself is sad and scary, but the actions that it can lead to are also horrifying. Teenagers with depression are less likely to engage in social activities and future career goals. They often engage in risky sexual activity, and untreated depression is the number one cause of suicide, which is the third leading cause of death among teenagers.[13]

I will not for a second say that, for some, depression is not a real, chemical disease. I believe clinical depression is real. I am not a doctor. But I also think that some are depressed due to a lack of purpose. Tony Compolo recounts a story he heard from M. Scott Peck, a famous psychologist and author. Dr. Peck was treating a woman suffering from extreme depression. Before her appointment, her car broke down. Dr. Peck offered to pick her up for her appointment, but explained that he had to make a hospital call before he got to the office. The woman agreed to come along. "At the hospital, he gave her the names of two of his patients who were convalescing there, and told her that each of them would enjoy a visit from her. When they met again, an hour and a half later, the woman was on an emotional high. She told Dr. Peck that making the visits and trying to cheer up those patients had lifted her spirits, and she was feeling absolutely wonderful."[14]

So … let's give youth (and everyone in our churches) a purpose! Where is it? It is throughout the Bible. We see it in the calling of Abraham to be a blessing to the nations and all the way in Revelations when all the nations will be praising God. We see the end game already. Youth need to hear that although they may feel chained to depression, there are those literally chained across the world who need their help. They need to know that although they are hungry for thrills, there are those so hungry that they are dying for food. It certainly doesn't fix all the struggles of a teen, but perspective is *so much* and knowing that *their* life and action could change the life of someone else gives amazing, life-transforming purpose. Or, better said: "Rather than just badgering kids with the message 'Don't Do Drugs,' wouldn't it be more effective to teach them how else to really enjoy their free time?"[15]

We are not required to (nor could we) pay Jesus back for what He did for us with good works, but there is something about someone sacrificing for us that allows us to know deeply that our life is supposed to count for something more. God told us what we were to run toward for a worthy race and how to know if we were running a good race. So, let's take a look at the flip side of the equation. What does it look like if we *do* give youth a purpose and introduce them to the kinds of thrills God intends for them to have?

> *However, I consider my life worth nothing to me; my only aim is to finish the race and complete the task the Lord Jesus has given me—the task of testifying to the good news of God's grace.* (Acts 20:24)

OPTION 2: Engaged in Culture with Intentional Perspective

Purpose

God has given us a purpose … and it goes beyond our Christian bubble. Claude Hickman writes, "Why does God even have Christians on planet earth right now? Why are you here? There is more to the Christian life than just going to Heaven when you die. Otherwise your pastor might as well just baptize people, hold them under, and send them to Heaven right then! It would save time and parking. Instead God has left us here with a purpose beyond our salvation."[16] (I love this quote … sarcastic, but it definitely has a point.)

It reminds me of The Parable of the Ten Talents (Matthew 25:14-30), in which two farmers had invested their talents, but one had hidden his, giving back to the landowner the talents given to him and never using them to make something more. How tragic to end our lives not using all of the gifts (giftedness, possessions, money, and time) we were given, and just handing them back to God? But, I confess, in my time in youth ministry, I wasted a lot of time and energy playing ridiculous games with *absolutely no point*. I'm not saying that there isn't a time and place for games … even strange games. However, many weird youth games feel a little like handing talents back to God … or more like keeping the talents and just handing pretend money back to God … really weird play money with pictures of clowns and vomiting children on the dollars instead of presidents.

In his book *58: Fast Living*, Dr. Scott Todd acknowledges the very tough job of youth workers. However, he makes a pretty good jab at silly games that seem never-ending in youth ministry, like chubby bunny contests:

> *If we intend to raise up an army of Christ-followers who will pursue justice for the oppressed and who will fight the adversary in a world afflicted by poverty, then we must begin training our youth for that fight. They are our greatest asset. They are young and full of energy. They are uncompromising idealists and they actually believe that God is all-powerful. To end extreme poverty for good requires nurturing the strength and future of the Church—our youth. They are sick of all the weak substitutes ... We should listen to them, challenge them, live our own lives in ways to demonstrate world-changing intentions, and save the marshmallows for a camping trip or a mug of hot chocolate.*[17]

Once again, for any defensive folk reading this who just can't get enough of your egg tosses, I will acknowledge many love the fun youth games for an icebreaker or team builder. There can be a time and a place for them. However, if they are engaging in adult activities like sex and drinking, then maybe we can step above the kiddy games and give them more meat and purpose than that? I'm just wondering.

Grateful instead of Entitled

So, what is the flip side of entitled/selfish kids? What would it look like to have children that didn't think they were somehow owed the right to own the same phone their friends have?

I grew up believing that I should have what others had. I didn't whine or behave overtly spoiled, but I confess, I knew that I could basically work the system at my house. I'm not proud of that, but it's true. Before I knew God, I was pretty darn selfish. After God changed my life, I grew a conscience, but I still listened to all the mottos of "you deserve this" and "you have to have that." I believed them and still fight not to listen to the lies. It wasn't until I was in Haiti during my freshman year of college that I literally woke up from the delusion and so began a deep change in my heart that has only grown more every day.

Katie Davis, author of *Kisses from Katie,* writes similarly, "But as I think through my life, I see how blessed and loved I have been. I think it is only normal that God would ask, even require, me to share this love with others who may not know it."[18] Sharing, giving, serving, and being grateful are the natural outpourings of this realization that we are blessed. It is extraordinary. It happens easily when it is real. Julie Ferwerda also reflects on what led her into her missional work:

> *But in the back of my mind, a nagging question began to surface: why did God pick me to live this life and not a desperate, poverty-stricken one? When I looked around at all the intense suffering and lost dreams in this world, where my brothers and sisters in Christ were born into circumstances beyond their control, I thought, why isn't that me? And why doesn't somebody do something? And then one day I realized ... I am somebody.*[19]

I can honestly say that my children have become more grateful, less-entitled kids because of their global education. They can honestly answer the question with a heart/knowledge of the lives of others around the world, "Do you think God loves you more than those kids who are hungry or are hurting?"

Of course I want to avoid bratty, entitled children, but on the more proactive side, I want to offer them the gift of thankfulness. True gratefulness is something that I feel I didn't fully embrace until after my global education. One would think that I would be depressed all the time with all I know about the world—the little girls raped for profit, the genocides, babies dying of AIDS. Honestly, I *am* actually deeply depressed at times, out of my skin outraged about these things. My heart is extremely heavy and I often feel as if it could absolutely shatter with sorrow, yet somehow, I have never lived more thankfully for my life than today in the midst of this knowledge. Let me explain:

Should something horrible happen to one of my children or husband (i.e., we have an accident and I lose one or both of them), though I may certainly lose my heart to sorrow, I do not think I will ever be one of those people that regrets the past and says, "I didn't know how good I had it. I wish I wouldn't have taken it for granted." Why? Because *I do know how good I have it*. I check on my children every night before I go to sleep. I know their safety is not to be taken for granted. I know their health is not to be taken for granted. It is my gratitude about my children, my husband, my little home, and my purpose that literally makes me cry at least once a week.

Somehow, all of that happened not just because God gave me really overwhelming gifts (which I confess in my husband and children and blessings, He has), but because He also has allowed me to see the other side of the world, the other side of other people's stories … and guess what? He lets me be even a small part of changing that horrible stuff. I am so grateful for it. I have messes in my own life and heart that I am certainly still trying to work out like everyone. (Seriously—do you have a few days for me to tell you about the mess I am?) My marriage isn't perfect, and my kids can absolutely drive me up a wall. I am forever trying to lose weight and manage time better, but I can say with all my heart that I have lived a full and good life (and I am only 35). It is all just a bonus from here on out. When God gave me a global perspective, He painfully ripped entitlement and wandering from my life and sewed gratitude and purpose in its place. I have the scars to prove it: they are on my knees. Those scars are fresh each time I fall on my knees in humility and surrender when I remember the answer to what I asked my children: *"Do you think God loves you more than those kids who are hungry or are hurting?"*

Chapter 6
"Why?" Safe and Lukewarm

If you read history you will find that the Christians who did most for the present world were precisely those who thought most of the next.

–C.S. Lewis

Let me start this chapter by saying that my husband, Adam, is an amazing father. We are usually on the same team when parenting. I am beyond blessed by him. I am, however, going to tease him a little, or perhaps myself and my controlling nature, with this story.

When my son was two, my husband took him on a trip to Arizona to visit my husband's brother. I knew they would have a good time, but the trip proved to me an experience of loosening my grip on my first-born child. First of all, it took a lot of convincing to get my husband to take a diaper bag on the airplane. He swore that his cargo pants, with all the pockets, could do the trick of any diaper bag. He just planned to put a diaper in one pocket, Sippy cup in another, snacks in another, and so on. Thus the "diaper cargo pants" were born! I should have clued in at this point that the trip and parenting weren't going to go "my way" on the trip.

After the first full day, I got a recount of all the things they did on their trip. As my husband told me about the day, I found out that they went on a fun, long walk through the woods and my son's shoes got very muddy. Knowing that I would be anxious about cleanliness, my husband quickly assured me that he had hosed off the shoes and they were now drying. However, as my husband was talking, I also knew my son was now again playing in the woods. I knew that he didn't have any other pair of shoes because my husband didn't want to bring "excess stuff" on the trip. So … what was he wearing while running around in the forest? All of my internal mother alerts were going off about my first-born and I not-so-calmly asked Adam about Lukas's feet (picturing his feet getting punctured and bloody from sticks or envisioning parasites going into his feet—all very dramatic and ridiculous). Adam answered calmly (as if his answer was totally within the realm of normal), "Oh Anna, don't worry. I just put duct tape on his socks to make shoes. He's wearing those."

This became legendary among our friends as the new shoe trend. Duct tape is good for just about anything, I suppose. This was only one of many strange parenting strategies that occurred that weekend, including Lukas's "bath" (i.e., getting hosed off while sitting in a swimsuit in the jogging stroller). Though my son was fine and having a ball, as a mom, who had bought into all the "correct" ways of doing everything to the utmost for the safety of my first-born, it was a major hit to my control issues. (He could have gotten a rash or something with that stroller bath right? Anyone? Anyone? Bueller? Throw me a bone here!)

Safety Town

We all crave a degree of safety, don't we? I think it's a longing inside of us for the world God originally created us for … a residue in our souls from the Garden of Eden. However, I think it can also get twisted as something we want to control in a world, life, and God that we can't predict. We take it ever more seriously when it comes to parenting. Our need for safety is born inside us the moment our child is conceived, to protect them from all harm. Every parenting magazine, email forward, or safety recall adds another injection to our addiction to safety. Safety and wisdom are good traits from God. We are to care well for our children. However, I believe we can take it too far and at times actually end up trying to protect our children from God. We can harbor our children from the lives they were meant to live.

Leaving "Safety Town"

We are called not to live so "safely" with our children. (I know your back just stiffened. If someone else said that to me, I would get tense, too.) Helen Lee says it well:

> *This does not mean we willfully endanger or unwisely put our children or ourselves at risk. But it means that we don't shelter our families from experiencing and witnessing the challenging parts of the world we live in. When we spend all our days in well-manicured communities that do not display a hint of the pain and suffering of this world, raising our children in neighborhoods where the most striking things they ever see are the growing sizes of McMansions on the street, we are not raising them in a world that fully reflects reality.*[1]

First of all, we aren't safe in our cul-de-sacs. Kids get killed by cars and kidnapped, and they get cancer in cul-de-sacs and good neighborhoods, too. The best drugs are in rich neighborhoods. I know some in super nice neighborhoods who have all of the above. We are not relying on God but instead are relying on circumstance and surroundings if we believe that these safeguards truly make us safe. I say "we" because I do it, too. I LOVE (and have been known to triple-check) the locks on my doors and the gates on my backyard. I love our vitamins and general safety rules. I think they are wise and I will continue to do the best I can, but they cannot take the place of teaching my children safety, and they can never, ever take the place of #1—prayers of protection over my children, and #2—following the safest thing of all: God's call leading my family.

We need to take our kids out of this "safety illusion" to make sure they are safe in God's will and truly engaging God's mission. The central way out of this illusion is faith that living out God's mission is in fact the safest place in town. But, mind you, it's a different kind of safe. It's the kind of "safe" (obeying and trusting God as our guide and protector, while still using our wisdom) we were all made for and it's the kind of "safe" that many of our neighbors simply don't get.

We must dive into some of these hard topics if we want to raise our children up in a strong faith. Tim Kimmel, author of *The Danger of Raising Nice Kids,* writes, "Parents whose goal is to raise a spiritually safe kid usually get a spiritually safe kid in the process. But they also often get a spiritually *weak* kid. The child is weak when it comes to standing up against the harsh pressures of a lost world. Once they are exposed to the full gale, down they go. On the other hand, parents who want to raise strong children realize that it cannot happen without the children having to work their spiritual muscles."[2]

Gary Haugen, too, shares honestly about sheltered youth:

> *I think something in them dies. They either go away and perish in safety, or they go away looking for adventure in the wrong places. Jesus, on the other hand, affirms their sense of adventure and their yearning for larger glory. In fact, he is encouraging us to affirm this calling in our children and raise them up to be brave, to be loving, to be significant. But honestly, sometimes I just want my kids to be safe. And I think they can smell my fear, and it builds little prisons that can last a lifetime.*[3]

Itsy Bitsy Tick

A month after we moved to the Northeast, we found our first tick. It was on my son, who was five at the time. He found it in the morning. It was in an unfortunate location. Poor kid. He was briefly traumatized (as was I), particularly in the charade of pulling it off, but then he miraculously recovered and went to kindergarten, only to sing a new rendition of "Itsy Bitsy Spider" that I'm not sure his teacher fully appreciated.

For about a week, I didn't want my kids to go outside to play. I swore I felt ticks all over my body. I itched all the time and insisted that they were crawling over me all night long. Even though I did find one in my sheets once, I eventually sent my children out to play again, obviously realizing that keeping them inside was paranoia and could never be an abundant life at all. My paranoia kept them from experiencing the gift of our backyard and the beauty of the outdoors. We have had more ticks in our days, and I'm sure I will be haunted again and again by those blood-sucking insects, but they will not stop us from living (unless we get Lyme disease, of course … for those of you who are playing the pessimist right now—thank you very much). We do, however, check our bodies every night for ticks. I give the kids rules on where to go in the yard and where not to go. I can be wise with them and still let them live. We can do this in every area of parenting. We can do this in our life of following God.

We have a call to be proactive, but how the heck do we do this? I would propose we stop defining ourselves and our children by what we *don't do* (though this is needed sometimes) and what we are scared of, and instead define what we *are* and what we are *fighting* for. "What if they were defined by their actions of justice and mercy, forgiveness and love, strength and courage, generosity and humility, and faithfulness? What if they were a generation who lived in the world and still proclaimed these things by their very lives?"[4] I am the first to acknowledge that this can look different for every family.

Lukewarm

Okay, let me bring it back around. Safety: the feeling that nothing can hurt our kids. I love the safe, warm feeling when I see them tucked in at night and our house is all locked up. I sleep well when I feel safe and often struggle with giving my kids to God when I am uncertain of my illusion of safety. I get it. I want that warm feeling, too. We seek safety in more than just our physical safety. We want to have cushion in our bank account, a change of clothes in the car, and a granola bar in the purse. The "just in case" always ready to go. Some people are truly gifted at it and can bless others with it. These things are awesome. They are good planning and often good signs of a steward, but if being safe in any way keeps us from giving or serving, then that idea of safety has made us lukewarm. In that situation, safe living isn't what we want.

> *I know your deeds, that you are neither cold nor hot. I wish you were either one or the other! So, because you are lukewarm—neither hot nor cold—I am about to spit you out of my mouth. You say, 'I am rich; I have acquired wealth and do not need a thing.' But you do not realize that you are wretched, pitiful, poor, blind and naked.* (Revelation 3:15–17)

Francis Chan shares his reflection on this in our contemporary society in a way that cuts to the heart. I wouldn't consider myself a lukewarm Christian, but when I read this list, I see myself in its reflection more than I'd like to admit:

> *Lukewarm people give money to charity and to the church ... as long as it doesn't impinge on their standard of living ... Lukewarm people gauge their morality or 'goodness' by comparing themselves to the secular world ... Lukewarm people will serve God and others, but there are limits to how far they will go or how much time, money, energy they are willing to give ... Lukewarm people are thankful for their luxuries and comforts, and rarely consider trying to give as much as possible to the poor ... Lukewarm people do whatever is necessary to keep themselves from feeling too guilty ... Lukewarm people are continually concerned with playing it safe ... Lukewarm people do not live by faith; their lives are structured so they never have to. They don't have to trust God if something unexpected happens—they have their savings account*[5]

Apathy is Unsafe

I don't want us to fear every corner, but I wanted to expose the lies, such as: the Northeast has experienced more natural disasters in recent years than for decades before, but each time the storm leaves, we feel safe again. The swine flu came and sent everyone into hysteria a few years ago, but shoot me up with a vaccine and I feel like Superwoman. We can't sleep when there is an uncaught kidnapper in the area, but we rest easy once he is arrested. However, there is always another storm, another virus, another kidnapper. While I totally have my emergency kits ready to go and my kids know their stranger danger stuff to the core, I *hate* that I cannot guarantee their safety. We are scared to go anywhere with a higher mortality rate or to a war-torn country—and of course, I get that. I'm not raising my hand to send my kids there either, but when I am realistic, I remember something. We are indeed at war. It is just a different war that I'm supposed to care about. I want to be part of that fight, but my safe living can't give me what I want. We must ask, "What have millions of Christians done? We have stopped believing that we are in a war. No urgency, no watching, no vigilance. No strategic planning."[6]

Shattering Our Safe Feeling

On December 14th, 2012, in Newtown, Connecticut, about an hour away from me, Adam Lanza entered Sandy Hook Elementary and killed 26 people, 20 of them children, ages six and seven. This shocked the country, bringing mobs to their knees as prayer vigils were held nationwide. The devastated families will never have the peace of understanding why this happened, for the reason lies only in the fall of mankind and in evil still leaving us breathless in a world that has hope, but is not yet redeemed.

I've stayed awake so many nights crying for the families of those little children, begging for God's peace and mercy as they deal with all of this. Many homeschool moms I know expressed a newfound reason why they homeschool, but unfortunately, I know in my soul that this could happen anywhere—the mall, a baseball game, the airport. I can't handle these realities most of the time.

All I suggest is surrender. I don't mean giving up wisdom and safety precautions, but I mean releasing them back to Him. Sometimes we release them easily because we feel secure and joyful that He has the best things planned for them, but sometimes we have to release them finger by grasping finger as we realize that we truly have no other choice or we'll go insane. I've recently had a couple panic attacks which I believe stem from my desire to protect my children. I can't let fear run my life, in any way. All those children that were victims of those crimes I believe are safely with our Lord, redeemed and whole, but it is our horrible ache on this side of eternity that cries on.

In Light of Eternity

I'd like to offer something even bigger, even harder, perhaps, for us (perhaps me most of all) to grasp with little kids. We are built with such protective natures of our children (which were God given) that it doesn't feel natural to look at our children in light of eternity. We don't want to think about the death of our children someday. Yet I believe that we must because Jesus does and because it offers so much freedom. David Platt shares:

> *The key is realizing—and believing—that this world is not your home ... Though you and I find ourselves surrounded by the lure of temporary pleasure, we must fasten our affections on the one who promises eternal treasure that will never spoil or fade. If your life is going to count on earth, we must start by concentrating on heaven*[9]

Alright, alright—chill out people. I don't go and drop my seven-year-old in the middle of drug-abuse alley in inner-city Hartford with a Bible in his hands and say, "Do some convert'n! Pick you up at seven or see you in Heaven … whichever comes first. Have a good time!" Get real. All I know is that there is great wisdom in thinking about our lives in context of our death and eternity. My husband claims that he makes his wisest decisions when he considers his death and eternity.

What if we could actually believe in Heaven? I mean seriously. What if we could live like Heaven is real? Those I know who study Heaven live differently. Consider this scripture:

> *So do not be afraid of them, for there is nothing concealed that will not be disclosed, or hidden that will not be made known. What I tell you in the dark, speak in the daylight; what is whispered in your ear, proclaim from the roofs. Do not be afraid of those who kill the body but cannot kill the soul. Rather, be afraid of the One who can destroy both soul and body in hell. Are not two sparrows sold for a penny? Yet not one of them will fall to the ground outside your Father's care. And even the very hairs of your head are all numbered. So don't be afraid; you are worth more than many sparrows.* (Matthew10:26–31)

We are safe, but just in a different home. This world feels right in all the beautiful and lovely ways and so very wrong in all the evil and sad things. We must work to give children an identity with their home in Heaven:

> *But our citizenship is in heaven. And we eagerly await a Savior from there, the Lord Jesus Christ, who, by the power that enables him to bring everything under his*

> *control, will transform our lowly bodies so that they will be like his glorious body.* (Philippians 3:20–21)

Once they have submitted to Jesus, our children are citizens of Heaven. We can give that to them in the language we use about who they are, in how we describe their struggles, in how much we teach them about Heaven, in how we view death, and most of all, in how we actually treat them. They'll know we are faking it if we cannot let them step out the door for God's purposes in light of eternity. They have to see that *we* believe in Heaven, that *we* believe that they were created for eternity, for greater things, and that death is a reward. If we shelter our kids too much from the battle on this earth, are we not indirectly giving them the message that earthly life is all that exists?

How do we hand off this idea to our kids? How do we give them a vision for a selfless life, a passion for God's heart, a desire to help others, and the ability to actually do it? It is completely against what they receive every day in their schools, in the media, in their own little self-consumed minds, as well as sometimes in our churches. If I truly believe that my children are safest and fullest in Christ's will and hand, then I will choose to parent with an open hand. "Hannah in Scripture "we must realize that our child is actually God's child—entrusted to us for only a short time. We need to release our child to God and then follow His guidance to raise His child for His divine purposes."[8] They are safest with Him and I will listen so much more intently to what He has planned for them.

But that is scary.

But that is totally different than everything everyone around me says.

I didn't sign up for this.

As Gary Haugen writes, "It sounds uncomfortable, scary, frustrating, exhausting, and probably dangerous—and worst of all, it's unknown and out of our control. This is not why we went to college, bought a nice house in a good neighborhood, put seat belts on our kids, and locked our doors at night. I did these things to *stay out* of the darkness, not to move toward it."[9]

Yet, I can look to all the moms who have entrusted their children to God's call to mission. I see and admire their kids as young adults and I know that I have to follow the trend of the open hand if I want my children to have faith-filled, fulfilling, world-changing lives. Safe-living is not what we want. I am so grateful to read on Lysa Terkeurst's blog (she has older kids that *are* leaving for missions post high-school) about her own take on raising good, safe kids. Lysa eloquently shares, "Maybe God's goal wasn't for me to raise a good-rule-following child. God's goal was for me to raise a God-following adult. An adult just determined and independent and insistent enough to fulfill a purpose He had in mind all along"[10]

Chapter 7

"Why?" Not just Why? But Why Now?

We are too young to realize that certain things are impossible ...
So we will do them anyway.
–William Wilberforce

I am grateful that my children have had exposure to many races and cultures very early in their lives. When my kids were young and we lived in Oregon, my husband and I taught ESL, not only because we loved the people who took the classes and thought it was an extraordinary ministry, but because we wanted our children to be in the childcare with kids of all different colors and nationalities. We knew that our children had to be a part of all of this from the beginning of their experiences of the world. After moving to Connecticut, we sought out an excellent, inner-city magnet school in Hartford, where my son was the minority. I loved that he had a crush on both a little white girl and a little black girl during that year. However, racial interactions can still have unexpected outcomes. Here are two we had that we could not have predicted:

We were at an Ethiopian adoption party with other families that had adopted kids from Ethiopia. Though we hadn't adopted our child/children from Ethiopia yet, we wanted to begin connecting with other families who had, so we went. My daughter was having a shy day with new kids (many of whom already knew each other well). As we were leaving, I asked my Adelaine why she didn't play with the kids. She responded (loudly, of course), "I was just afraid, Mama. I was afraid to play with those black kids."

Surprised by her reaction (and in particular to her choice of words), we had a real "heart to heart" once we got to the car. I dug a little deeper and found out that she was just scared to play with new kids. It had nothing to do with their skin color. She just described them as black … because, well, simply, because they had very dark brown skin and that was how she knew how to describe them as different. Because of how loaded many racial issues are, we are usually pretty instantly uncomfortable with race as a descriptive factor (especially in mixed-race company), though kids will use skin color to describe someone pretty naturally, the same way as describing the color of someone's hair.

Well, flash forward to the next day when I was dropping Lukas off at school. We were walking inside and, surrounded by African American kids and parents, Adelaine ran up and hugged a sweet little African American girl that was in my son's class.

Then Adelaine yelled loudly across the crowd to me, “See Mama, I’m not scared of these black kids!” *Awesome*. Thank you, Adelaine. I had *no way* of explaining that to any of the on-looking parents in five words or less. I just accepted defeat and left with her, acting like I hadn’t heard her and then held my phone to my ear like it had just rung (which it hadn’t).

Our second incident was a couple months later at the same school (where for some unknown reason we hadn’t made many friends … hmm, wonder why). I had found out that Lukas had gotten in trouble for hugging a little boy in his class too much. Surprised that my son was crossing someone’s personal space, I started to drill him with questions. I asked, “Why are you hugging him so much?” He said, “Because he is cute.” Slightly confused how this justified over hugging, I tried to dig further, asking him a series of questions to determine what he meant. Finally, my 7-year old said, annoyed, “Mama, he is just so small. I just want to squeeze him.”

Okay, now I got it. My son had been hearing for months about our adoption and how excited we were to have our little Ethiopian boy in our home, about how we couldn’t wait to hug and kiss and squeeze him. So, my son did what is totally inappropriate and picked the smallest black kid in class and wouldn’t stop hugging him. Again, I could not explain *that* to the boy’s mom. How would I tell her that my son was smothering her child not merely because he was black, but also because he was small? Not sounding really culturally sensitive, were we? Oh dear.

Let me just make a note here: I know that I am still very ignorant of how to approach race well. The above stories could be offensive or inappropriate for anyone, though my heart only wants to love. My good friend, Ruth, has been patient to teach me more about racial issues (and basically enlightening me on not saying outrageous, offensive or white-privileged comments). I don't pretend to know enough yet, and I am still trying to lose underlying prejudices that I suspect we all have, but I do know it is important and I want my kids to do it better than I.

Early Exposure

How does global missions relate to children? I don't mean youth like teens, but children, even very young children. A writer of Children's Missions material, Barbara Campbell, writes:

> *God told the Israelite people to instruct their children to love the Lord with all their heart, soul, and strength at all times during the day, at all occasions (Deuteronomy 6:4-9). God must have thought that children needed to learn in the context of everyday living, at the beginning of their lives. This again goes back to the principle of getting across what is significant at the beginning and the end. Are children too young to understand? Can they have a part? Should they also be concerned? And, if so, how can they learn in the context of everyday living? This area is a weak link in our world evangelism strategy. We need everyone, regardless of chronological age. Too often in our churches we have viewed little ones as a necessary difficulty, a baby-sitting responsibility, so that mature*

> *adult Christians can get on with the serious work at hand ... **Our children need to be taken seriously**.*[1]

Even though some of the racial situations mentioned above may have been as uncomfortable as they are comical, I have known in my soul that my children must be accustomed to interacting with many races and cultures. But, it hardly stops there. All of our family's cultural experience (as a missional family, as a globally-educated family, as a "broken by the hurting" family) can't wait until our kids are older or I've totally missed it. I must be proactive during the short time they are in my direct care while they are young and able to make concrete conclusions about the world. I must be proactive with their early years during which child development theorists tell us children receive information, solidify it, and question it in order to make it their own. I must be proactive with their faith development, including some of God's deepest heart issues in order to show them the entire view of God. They can receive God's global heart as preschoolers, in grade-school serve with us, and then be empowered as teens to live it. They can even live it as children more than we could ever dream.

Yet, why is it that Children's Missions is rarely on the radar with Missions Departments when they are the next generation of missionaries, sacrificial givers, abolitionists, best advocates for the poor, and sharers of the gospel? Why is it that most moms don't engage missions because they want to wait until their kids are older and they can leave them at home? Why is it that I had to write a book about this stuff because there were so few resources out there and so I fumbled around for 4+ years?

To support the idea that young children ought to be included in this global education, I offer three sections:

1. Exposure: an example of how easily and quickly our children make conclusions about things without our intention. I use race and culture as an example since it has been a topic in our life and can either close or open our children different cultures and future missions.
2. Child development: how do children develop empathy in particular? Empathy, as well as worldview, is extremely important as a base for faith in action.
3. Faith development: this correlates to child development but has a twist if we are intentional about the type of faith we hope to instill in our children.

How Young Children Experience Race and Culture

Babies are noted to stare longer at pictures of different races as they try to figure out faces different than their families. However, it is shown that if a child is exposed to many races, people, food, and experiences, they will continue to be open to them. While young, children don't see race the way we do when we're older. Kids use skin color to describe a person just like hair color. As they grow, however, they begin to categorize and qualify races in categories of likes, mostly according to how much interaction they have had with them.

Luckily, I haven't experienced many people being extremely racist so far in this transracial adoption process, but we have experienced some. I'm sure we will experience more. What I am struck with (and what allows me to show grace to those with negative race views so contrary to mine) is that their views are a result of both exposure and decision. Granted, some of how much exposure people have to other races is in fact their decision, but a lot of that decision is a result of whether or not they were exposed to positive interactions of other cultures early on in their lives.

Dr. Phillis Katz has done extensive research on how children developmentally experience race. "When kids turned three, Katz showed them photographs of other children and asked them to choose whom they'd like to have as friends … 68 percent of the kids used race to split the cards, without any prompting. At this time we tend to not talk about race much … yet their minds are deciding about race now."[2] Therefore, based on this research that children were categorizing race so early, a group of children was put in racially mixed classes at different grade levels to see which intermixed naturally and which remained apart. "The researchers found this worked wonders on the first-grade children. Having been in the cross-race study groups led to significantly more cross-race play. But it made no difference on the third-grade children. It's possible that by third grade, when parents usually recognize it's safe to start talking a little about race, the developmental window has already closed."[3]

Isn't that interesting? Many people wouldn't even want to talk about race or expose children to different cultures until mid-elementary, and yet already at grade three kids will tend to not mix with other races if they have not had prior positive intentional exposure to them. Wow! That is a new insight into why it is so hard for adults who have 40 years or more without positive exposure to other races to cross that bridge. It is more ingrained in us than we ever would think to "stick to our own kind." We have to intentionally work to change that for our kids—at the very least to help them empathize with all races.

So, what do you do if you aren't in a multicultural neighborhood or school or church? What do you do if your everyday experience really doesn't bring you near a lot of other cultures or your family hasn't mingled much with other races naturally?

We can choose to intentionally place ourselves with other races and cultures. By the way, by cultures I don't mean that we get our children used to Buddhism or Islam (though knowledgeable at some point), but I mean that we step a little farther into the food, music, and people of other cultures—South America, Eastern Europe, Middle East, Africa, Eastern Asia, and even inner-city culture. Endless possibilities. We can get our kids comfortable watching videos about families in different multicultural contexts and talk about the commonalities of those people with our children.

It is a small step, but any step is a step. Though it may not feel intentional, we influence how comfortable or uncomfortable our children will be with other races and in other cultural contexts by the exposure we provide (or lack of) to multi-cultural relationships, foods, and experiences. No matter what, we can expose our children from a very young age to the heart of God for all people and about God's image in the beauty of all races. The more exposed they are, the more normal it will become. It is the same with their faith and empathy in the early years. I've seen my kids be repulsed by the smell of a Middle Eastern home (different spices and smells) in an initial interaction, asking to leave. By the end of the visit, they are loving the food and truly loving the family and interactions. They ask to go back often. It is a process and it took intentionality.

Empathy Development

Way beyond racial and cultural exposure is the "WHY" of service and missions at *very* early ages.

I am always so sad when I hear that someone is waiting to do service until their children are older. Not only does it seem like it takes the adult away from service they are called to, but it seems almost more tragic that their children don't get to witness it and become part of it as well. The very young child is beginning to process care and identity with what the parent does and believes. They are modeling, making habits, and repeating phrases and actions they see and hear. "The child is a witness; the child is an ever-attentive witness of grown-up morality—or lack thereof; the child looks and looks for clues as to how one ought to behave, and finds them galore as we parents and teachers go about our lives, making choices, addressing people, showing in action our rock-bottom assumptions, desires, and values, and thereby telling these young observers much more than we may realize."[4]

One of the reasons that many give for not sharing missions with young children is that they don't want them to be afraid. I get this. I really, really do. People being lost eternally, orphans, slaves, hunger, disease—it is all scary stuff. It is sad and confusing and heart-wrenching. Of course, every parent has to know their child and each child for their particularities and what information and experiences they can handle, but I also think we can frame their world and how they receive hard information more than we could ever imagine. They gauge their own fears a great deal from us. They are exposed to scary stuff unintentionally all the time. Evening news and its "fear driven media" is more scary then most of the issues raised by caring for others. Young children want to solve the problem; they aren't going into all the whys or whos of the evils of the world. They just want to make it better. If they can learn at that preschool age that they can help make it better, then when they learn more about the scarier realities of global issues, they won't feel quite so powerless, because they have already been part of the solution.

School-aged children are solidifying how their empathy will look for their life. "Concrete projects such as visiting people in a nursing home and bringing a snack to people building a Habitat house make a strong impression on young children … True empathy, the ability to put yourself in a person's place, starts to develop in a child between the ages of six and eight. Mission and service projects can emphasize this growing awareness of empathy. Children can learn about the restraints of having to go through the day in a wheelchair or not having enough money to buy food. Although children are still apt to see the world from their point of view, service and mission projects can help expand their view so they can begin to see the world from other people's perspectives."[5]

If those aren't readily available, stories are helpful. More recently there are more recently many age-appropriate titles (that I list in the last chapter) that engage many worldwide issues.

It is at this age in early through late elementary that the seeds of what they learned in preschool missions have the capability to come to life in a new way, and new experiences, exposure, and teaching can grow deeper roots in the rich soil of early faith. This is when kids want to start truly having answers to problems they see in the world.

Faith Development

In many ways, faith development understandably matches social and emotional development. Children develop their faith based upon how much they can understand what they receive from their parents and environment. Their empathy, ability to absorb information, and level at which they serve is different in different stages of development, but each stage serves its purpose in laying a foundation, and no stage should be missed for missions.

Though there are several people who have researched and mapped out faith stages, James Fowler is probably the most well known expert in this area. I will not go into all the aspects of the faith stages and how they relate to different avenues of faith, but instead will focus on the ones that correlate to missions.

Intuitive-Projective Faith (preschool through kindergarten)

We don't often think of preschoolers as a top market for our mission strategy. I think of them as top of the market for bibs and pull-ups. Yet, it is at this age that our little shadows are truly seeing and modeling us in faith as well. "Preschoolers are sponges; they soak in what they see, hear, and do! When your preschooler observes you praying for others; giving yourself, your time, and your resources to help others; and sharing the love and story of Jesus, he will see and learn from your examples."[6]

It is in preschool, in kindergarten, and a little beyond that children also have extraordinary imaginations. We understandably worry that they will have nightmares (because they do) about bad people or bad things happening, and yet "miracles are entirely credible to these young minds. No problem is too big for their God to handle—they pray in absolute confidence."[7] Therefore, if we can share appropriate information with young children, give them ways to copy after our modeling, *and* help them believe in a *big God* who can redeem the bad, it establishes a pretty ideal stage for missions training.

Mythic-Literal Faith (elementary years)

First of all, on a practical level, these kids have a *lot* of energy. Let's use it for good and get some work done with that energy. I don't know, how about maybe raking an elderly neighbor's yard or shoveling an international family's driveway or cleaning my house (Did I say "cleaning my house"? Oops!)? Just saying. Energy. Lots of it. Tap into it.

In regards to faith stages, from approximately the age of seven to the age of eleven, a child relies on what is real and what is experienced. "As relieved as adults might be that the child has become more realistic, the realism comes with a certain loss. If what is real is what is experienced, then is God real? … Loving God must be spelled out in concrete terms for these students. That's why simple service projects are so enthusiastically supported."[8] Kids this age need to see God's work in action, hear testimonies, see changed lives, and have tangible ways to love God in return. They want to see and touch God in so many avenues. It is this realism and an increasing understanding of right and wrong that also gives children this age a strong sense of justice. We have the opportunity to show them justice carried out through many organizations and through our own actions. We can give them a sense of power (that they too can be part of justice), as well as show them the redemptive effects of justice (like a family that are freed from slavery because someone stepped in to advocate or stop it).

Lastly to note, elementary school kids want to feel like they are good at something. They want to feel successful. We can begin to affirm gifts (even spiritual gifts) now. They are looking for role identity.

Some of this stage is "characterized by conformity, where one finds one's identity by aligning oneself with a certain perspective, and lives directly through this perception with little opportunity to reflect on it critically."[9] It continues on into early teen years and just depends on when or if a child rebels or is disillusioned by a parent's faith. However, regardless of how much a child trusts his parents' faith or has a rebellious spirit, the faith questioning will come.

Synthetic-Conventional Faith (pre-teen years)

Since so much of faith, as well as development, is fluid, and since all kids reach different milestones at different ages, I want to emphasize again here: spiritual gifts begin to come out very early in a person's faith. Though it is easier to do ministry with adult leaders, the truth is that if children have gifts, we either choose to let them use them, know their worth, and empower them while they are in the church, or not. They will find their identity and usefulness somewhere—we just hope it is with the family of God and not somewhere else. Pre-teens can serve well.

They want to be challenged to rise to the occasion. They want to make a difference.

Just thinking about a teenager gives me images of kids with funky clothes who change their style from week to week, all the while questioning their parents with sass. Though that isn't always the case, on some level, teens are definitely questioning their faith as they figure out who they are apart from their parents. Questioning one's faith (especially if it is a faith that one is brought up with) must happen. It is the only way one knows if they ever actually chose their faith for themselves.

So, my question is: do we want our children wrestling with hard global (or apologetic) issues once they leave our home or while they are still in it so we can wrestle with them? Unless they go to a Christian college (which sometimes can do a good job investigating other thoughts, but sometimes just delays the rebellion), philosophy professors will eat our kids alive if they don't know why they believe what they believe and what their purpose is in this world. Though it sounds very hard to wrestle with a teenager on many topics (and global issues can bring up fear, sadness, and anger that I discuss in later chapters), it is actually an incredible opportunity. We can help model how to dive into these topics, wrestle with God on the hard things in life, and search the world to see if there are any better answers than the ones we find in Scripture for this world and our lives. Then, after each tough round, we can, with them, reaffirm even our own faith. We don't have to be scared of any of it—only maybe scared to miss our chance to be a part of it while our children are *still in our home*.

And a Child Shall Lead Them

Let us not ever discount God's view of children and the abilities He has given them. He longs for them to know the fullness of faith, too. He designed them to engage the world from very young ages in every developmental way. We are to include them in His great plan. For even the call to Jeremiah emphasized God's empowerment of those who feel young:

> *The word of the LORD came to me, saying, "Before I formed you in the womb I knew you, before you were born I set you apart; I appointed you as a prophet to the nations."*
>
> *"Alas, Sovereign LORD," I said, "I do not know how to speak;*
> *I am too young." But the LORD said to me, "Do not say, 'I am too young.' You must go to everyone I send you to and say whatever I command you. Do not be afraid of them, for I am with you and will rescue you," declares the Lord.* (Jeremiah 1:4–8)

Even many great missionary heroes, both past and present, were called into their ministry at very young ages. "At only five years of age, Hudson Taylor often said, 'When I am a man, I mean to be a missionary and go to China.' Was it merely coincidence that this little boy grew to become one of China's greatest missionaries? No, this childhood dream was God's purpose diligently nurtured by godly parents."[11] Surely Hudson's Taylor's parents were able to expose him to God's heart and the state of the world in appropriate, but real ways, so that his heart might be both broken and empowered. What a legacy (of immeasurable numbers of Chinese believers) to empower! We, too, can appropriately develop in them an awareness and empathy for the many tragic stories around the globe, and help them to be comfortable with the smells, tastes, and sounds of other cultures. A "walk through the Scriptures shows several times when the perfect tool needed in the hands of almighty God was a child—precisely *because* he or she was a child. The task could not be entrusted to adults. They think too much. They know too much. Or at least they think they know! For sure they doubt too much, fear too much, are too selfish, too eager for glory, too … well, adult!"[12]

There is so much to distract our youth and our children. We want them to give life to others, but also have life themselves.

> *The thief comes only to steal and kill and destroy; I have come that they may have life, and have it to the full.* (John 10:10)

Let us not miss our chance to teach our young ones, to imprint on them God's heart and purpose *now*! But praise be to God for His redemption. We all have surely missed so many teachable moments, or years even, but He still richly blesses those who put effort into this *now* and in the future!

Chapter 8
Introduction to L.E.S.S.

I have seen the Vision and for self I cannot live.
Life is less than worthless till my all I give.
–Oswald J. Smith

At the beginning of 2012, my family of four launched on a month of eating rice and beans. I use the word "launch" because I believe that if it weren't for gravity, we may have launched our home into space with the amount of gas that was emitted from our home that month. (Forgive the potty humor, but it's the truth.)

The month of "beans, beans, beans, they're good for your heart" was started because we were at the beginning of our adoption journey to Ethiopia. We were overwhelmed by the stories of famine coming from the Horn of Africa where 30,000 people (mostly women and children) were dying of starvation (one of the worst ways to die) every month (not year … month)! This was inconceivable to us, and somehow we wanted to enter into it in whatever tiny, tiny (did I say tiny?) way we could. We wanted to remember our blessings, remember that our hopefully future adopted children may already be living in the middle of that famine (or in the womb of a hungry mama with few options). We wanted to take the time we normally used to cook bigger dinners to read and learn about hunger; we also wanted to use the money saved by just eating rice and beans to aid the hungry.

Well, all I can say is that by eating *less* (in variety and amount), we had *more*. We had more awareness of the hungry. We had more awareness of all of our typical food options—when I added fruits and vegetables to my kids' lunches after a week, they learned to gorge themselves on that so they didn't have to eat rice and beans for dinner—the little rascals! However, even if they didn't eat dinner, we had more rice and beans to go around and I had *more* time to spend with my family. We indeed had *more* to give to the hungry (prayers and finances) and we had *more* laughter than we expected. I confess that most of the laughter came at my husband's expense and his gastrointestinal experience during this month of the magical fruit.

But in all seriousness, I think we all know that we are living with *too much*—too much stuff, too many activities, too much stress, too much weight, and too many bills. There are whole shows dedicated to each topic: helping people lose weight, helping people get control of their finances, helping people empty their house of excess, helping people organize their schedules, and so on and so on. We supposedly have more control over our lives now than pretty much anyone in history ever had and more choices than anywhere else the world, yet somehow we feel incapable of changing our dreaded path or choosing from the buffet of options. We throw our hands up in surrender.

I'm not sure why. Do we just listen to the world around us telling us that we deserve that cake or that credit card splurge? Are we merely stuck in a routine? Or do we have too many options? I look at my own life and I can't figure it out either, yet we (I) really can choose (for the most) what we do with that time, body, money, and possessions. Jen Hatmaker dedicates a whole book, *Seven*, to seven things she fasts from in seven different months in order to take the excess out of her life. She lives with extraordinary insight into her heart, our culture, and God's heart, as well as *less* stuff, *less* spending, *less* stress, and *more* time, *more* giving, and *more* intentionality.

If you are reading this book, then you want to be intentional with the youth in your care. I want to start with the basics: what do we want *more* of and thus, what do we need *less* of? I want *more* of God's mission and purpose in the hearts of my children. If I am honest, I want *more* of God's purpose (and the desire to fulfill it) in my own heart, as well. I just want *more* of God for all of us, period. So, what is it going to cost me?

> *The kingdom of heaven is like treasure hidden in a field. When a man found it, he hid it again, and then in his joy went and sold all he had and bought that field. Again, the kingdom of heaven is like a merchant looking for fine pearls. When he found one of great value, he went away*

> *and sold everything he had and bought it.* (Matthew 13:44–46)

I've been thinking about this: so far, what has this journey into justice, mercy, and God's heart for the world cost me? I indeed have *fewer* luxuries (though barely—I live very nicely compared to most of the world), but I now buy *less* stuff. I have *less* "chill" time. I have *less* control over my life and the lives of my kids. I have to teach them the truth about the world and what God has planned for them. I need to offer them up with tears of faith (and sometimes fear) to the God who created the world, will redeem the world, and who may call them into dark places to do it. Sally Clarkson, author of *The Mission of Motherhood,* shares, "When Jesus lived on this earth, he spent the majority of his ministry teaching his disciples, to whom he could entrust the task of reaching the whole world with the gospel. As I have studied his life, I have found a plan for my own parenting. Like him, I have a goal to love and train my children so they will be equipped to reach the world and their families and friends with the message of Christ after I am gone. This is what they were born to do—to truly love God and glorify him and follow him. Thus my goals for parenting must reflect my purpose. Several simple aspects of Jesus's life with his disciples have given me a simple plan for my own home."[1]

So, do you believe all this mumbo jumbo? Do you believe that your job as a parent is to train your children to reach the world? As pastors and teachers, are the kids really going out and ministering to others … to the ends of the earth?

Well heck…then that means a response is needed if we really believe this.

Acronym

Okay, so I confess I mock Christian subculture too much. I pretend it is okay for me to do so because I am immersed in it and actually *love the church* (at least that is my excuse and I'm sticking to it). I love the blog and book *Stuff Christians Like* for this reason. I am not sure if the author, Jonathan Acuff, has done anything on acronyms or our incessant need in Christian circles to have everything start with the same letter. Let me elaborate and see if you don't agree that this happens: if we have a get together with other Christians, we must dare not call it a mere party. No, no dear friend. Heathens have parties. However we may feel called to refer to it as something like F^4 (which could mean: Food, Fellowship, Family, and Fun). Do you get my drift?

It is similar with acronyms. We leave a sermon with goose bumps when the main points of the sermon can magically be remembered in one simple word. In seminary we actually had a whole class on how to use these memory devices to *WOW* your congregation. They taught us how to slowly build anticipation with each letter (kind of like on *Wheel of Fortune*). The brave souls with poor social skills and self control would try to guess what the word was going to mean before the pastor had finished all his points in the letter build up. The truly contrite would wait until the end, in order to watch the magic happen. And then, just when you are giving the last and final point of the sermon, you give the last letter of the acronym. *Amazingly*, the acronym spells a word that sums up the sermon perfectly. How were you to know that the acronym would end up being that word? It's amazing. We were taught to wait an appropriate amount of time during the expected reverent silence as a lot of tears needed to be wiped and were told it was a great time to have an altar call. Later, there would be high fives in the choir room after the service.

Yeah, so maybe we didn't actually have a class like that in seminary, but it would have been a total riot and a good chance for a bunch of Christian leaders to not take themselves too seriously. Regardless, the truth is that some of these memory devices, like acronyms, actually work! Heck, I remember some acronyms very well. So, partially to make myself giggle, and partially because maybe it will help the one person who actually reads this (You are my BFF! Call me every five minutes!) to remember it better, I'm going to use an acronym. I have already introduced it to you, but will now explain it in more detail. There. I said it. I am going to use an acronym for a Christian book. I have now been knighted a Christian author. Drum roll please … the acronym (if you haven't caught it yet) is L.E.S.S.

I must be *less* … less controlling, less confused.

I must have *less* … less stuff, less distractions.

I must care *less* … less about what others think, less about my own agenda.

He must become greater; I must become less. (John 3:30)

The acronym L.E.S.S. highlights how I will structure the rest of this book and how we can go about guiding our children into a life lived with global mission, purpose, and redemption. The main four "How To's" are:

- **L**ive a life worth repeating
- **E**xpose and educate them
- **S**erve together
- **S**end them out

We do *less* that they may be more . . . know God more and live life *more*. Let's begin.

Chapter 9
Live It!—Introduction

A holy life will produce the deepest impression.
Lighthouses blow no horns; they only shine.
–D.L. Moody

At a church retreat, bestselling author, Donald Miller, provided an illustration about living a life of purpose. I'm sure I've tweaked his illustration, but based on what I can remember, it basically goes something like this: Imagine you go to the movies. Now movies aren't cheap, but it is your birthday so you fork out for the two-hour treat that you hope will inspire you in some way. You even get some popcorn and a drink to seal the deal. You settle in to the flick, ready to engage in the story.

The movie you are watching is about a man living a life not unlike yours. He grew up in a pretty average neighborhood, working hard for his education, getting married, and having kids. You feel a twinge of familiarity as you see him argue and make up with his spouse and see him interact with his relatives. He tries to be a good father, good neighbor, and well-liked man. It is all very familiar. Not too far into the movie, the man finally reveals his true desires in life. He has always dreamed of owning a BMW. He just always has. Ever since he was in college (working those two jobs to get an undergraduate degree that did nothing for him … again a familiarity), he wanted a BMW. So now, with a wife and kids, he decided to finally work for his dream. He had to get his family on board because it would require sacrifice for the whole family. They had to sacrifice a few channels on cable for it. He had to skip a few lunches out with colleagues (much to his embarrassment) to save more money. But, on the hard days, when he didn't think he could pull it off and the sacrifice seemed too much, he would drive by the BMW dealer and just sit near it—looking at the cars, deciding that no matter what it took, one day, one of them would be his. He went so far as to deny a chance at a cruise to finally have enough money for that BMW.

At long last, through sweat and tears, the man had enough money for a down payment on the car. He got his whole family together (and the movie soundtrack on the movie amps up, attempting to bring even the hardest heart to tears) and they went to the dealer. He gave the dealer his down payment, and financed the rest of this very expensive car of his dreams. The family hugs (maybe imagine a slow-motion moment with the son running to the father's arms with the keys in hand), gets in the car, and they all drive off. Credits roll.

What? That's the movie? That's what I spent my $50 movie ticket on? (Alright, it was $12.50, but still expensive). The big climax of the movie was to get a BMW? That's insane. Who would pay to watch that? Who would even watch it for free?

Well, if that is true, if this kind of story isn't worth watching, then let's ask the question: *Why are we living this kind of life?* Why would we live and model lives for our children that we wouldn't even pay to watch? Maybe you say you are doing more than just saving up for a car. Maybe it's putting your kids through school, saving for retirement, and building up your local community. These are all good things. Even better, maybe you're really intentional about caring for your neighbors and community. Better than that, maybe you're really involved in your church and have gone on a couple of mission trips! But still, if your life was a movie, would you pay to watch it?

I would never discredit the hard-working person who loves the Lord deeply day in and day out. That is honoring to God—to work hard, love Him, and support your family. We don't have to have lives that people would watch on the big screen. However, the reality is that most of us have the privilege, opportunity, and responsibility to do more because we have been given more financial and spiritual resources than many others around the world. I want to live a life that is worth a movie ticket, even if it is great in just the smaller stuff. I want to live a life that my kids see worth repeating. I don't believe it has to be filled with action and adventure, but it should look different than most. It will reveal sacrifice and it will have a big purpose. If I do, my kids will have the best chance of copying it.[1]

I don't know about you, but I grew up knowing what my parents cared about. I was a witness to their choices, interactions, desires, and values, surely more than they realized. My parents probably told me with words what they value, but I honestly can't remember what they said. I *can*, however, tell you clearly what they value by what their actions showed me...

1. My father values education and dreaming of doing great things. He has a very good salary, but you wouldn't know it by the car he drives or clothes he wears. He puts his money in his kids' and grandkids' education and other opportunities. I have always known that my father didn't value "things" particularly because of how he has used his money (or hasn't used it). My father believes in sacrificing for others. He never considers anything of his out of reach to his children. His car, computer, books … anything was up for use for anyone that needed to use it. He never said some grand statement of "what is mine is yours" or "mi casa es su casa" (the guy doesn't even know any Spanish). I just saw him live it. I learned how to have an open, sharing home because of my father.
2. My mother values frugality and hates wastefulness. We went to thrift stores for clothes, and my mother

> cut coupons for groceries. I grew up knowing that she thought waste (as even a tiny portion of food could go in a Tupperware) was wrong. I also knew that my mother cared about the practical needs of others. She never actually said, "We must clothe all needy kids in our area." However, I know she cared for practical needs because of how she spent her time. She didn't watch soap operas or take up a million hobbies. She spends much of her days sorting, washing, and giving donated clothing to needy children in every public school in the county she lives in. I also know that my mother cares about practical needs because when someone comes over, she makes them meals, cleans up for them, and will make sure they are taken care of. She never formally taught this, but I do many of the things she does simply because I saw her serving others.

Alex and Harris, teenage founders of *Rebellution* (a book, curriculum, and conference movement to empower teenagers to raise their standards of what they can accomplish for God and for others) credit their parents with what sets them apart. They write, "'If our teen years have been different than most,' says Alex, 'it's not because we are somehow better than other teens, but because we have been motivated by that simple but very big idea filtering down from our parents' example and training: *Do hard things*.'"[2]

These boys are not only trying to change the globe themselves, but because they were raised to believe and follow examples of passionate servants, they are empowering a generation for God's glory. I'd love to buy their mom lunch and get a million pointers on how to raise kids like that because we know one thing for sure—these kids learned a lot of it from their parents.

Most Sundays, my family goes to church—probably not unlike yours. Sometimes we have our children attend the service with us and sometimes we have them go to Sunday school. We attend other church events and camps, and do devotions together. Other regular conversations and prayers happen pretty naturally. So my kids know what I *think* about God, faith, and the world … at least in my words. Basically, they know what I believe … at least what I say I believe.

However, as I have mentioned above, my kids also see how I *live* (and therefore I believe they see the basis of my true faith). They see it all:

How much time do I spend with God on my own?

How much do I go to God in prayer and fasting for myself and others … for the lost?

How much do I confess my sins?

Do I care more about what God says about me or what others think about me?

How much money do we put into things that waste away or do we give up those things to put our money into missions, caring for the poor … for the eternal?

Do my kids ever catch me doing good deeds in secret seeing that I believe my reward is in Heaven?

So, I ask, do you *live* the kind of life that you want to share with your children? The next four chapters are about you … and me. They are about us as parents, leaders, teachers, and pastors to children. They are about us as role models—the ones we hope our kids will emulate. Yes, this is a book about missions and children. I haven't forgotten. I'm getting there, I promise. This part is just so foundational that I can't miss it. I'm going to walk through just a few parts of what our children need to see us living out. First comes engaging the issues at hand. We have to dig in, mourn, and truly face the global issues if we are to appropriately teach our children. I'll suggest a few topics to consider learning more about, and the last chapter of the book has a list of resources for you to look into more as well. If you don't really dive into the realities of the lost, poor, and oppressed, then chances are you won't really change your life and you won't have any reasons for asking your children to live differently. A heart broken by God for others can and will do amazing things. It needs no pep talk.

After engaging the issues, we are required to look at our response—I touch on just three main areas (though there could always be more). We need to look into how we are serving, how we are using our voice (in both advocacy and intercession), and how we are giving the blessings God has given us. Josh McDowell reminds us: "You can't take children further than you've gone yourself. When we're modeling true dependence on God with radical faith, and our kids can see the results, they will experience authentic Christianity. If it is real to us, it will be real to them."[3]

Be your own child's role model! The first L of L.E.S.S. is **L**IVE—Live a life worth repeating

Tangible Acts in Response to L.E.S.S.:

1. **Pray about others you can share this journey with. Community is important. Emotions and questions come up in any transformative process and it is more meaningful, lasting, and fun to do it with friends. Pray for spouses to come on board if they aren't already.**

2. **Watch the movie *Isaiah 58* as a good overview (you can often order it free) or World Vision's *Journey to Jamaa* free online. See other resources in Chapter 27.**

Chapter 10
Live It!—Brave the Darkness

We must allow the Word of God to confront us,
to disturb our security, to undermine our complacency and
to overthrow our patterns of thought and behavior.
–John Stott

Me: Lukas, go clean your room.
Lukas (age six at the time): Yeah, I don't think I'm comfortable with that.
Me (in disbelief): Say *what*? You're not 'comfortable' with that?
Lukas: Yeah, I'm really just not comfortable with that.

After my initial confusion, I got to the bottom of this strange interaction. Lukas had used this phrase "I'm not comfortable with that" at swimming lessons to a couple of high school aged swim instructors (who were probably trained not to push kids much beyond their "comfort") and it got him out of having to try the dreaded back float. Seeing the amazing power of the phrase, Lukas thought he'd see if it worked in other arenas of his life to get him out of things he didn't like doing. He (sadly) found out that it does not.

It is funny, though—the things kids say and do to get out of doing what is right. But, if I'm honest about my times before God, especially when I've been confronted with a new and challenging issue that requires me to change my life (like purchasing habits or the amount of time I spend on my knees in prayer), I somehow turn into a six-year-old pleading, "I don't think I'm comfortable with that." Yeah—I don't think I'm comfortable with any of it, to tell you the truth. I hate the things I've learned. Sometimes I wish I had never known the things I know about slavery in the cocoa fields or about the millions (or billions) who are spiritually lost in the Middle East, China, Indonesia, and around the world. Yet, I can never actually say I wish I could go back to a time of not knowing. Though my soul becomes raw and pained in the knowing, it is more alive and aware of God in my life than ever … even though I feel so often like I am barely managing that back float, dangerously close to drowning, desperately aware of my dependence on my teacher, my Lord.

> *But the one who does not know and does things deserving punishment will be beaten with few blows. From everyone who has been given much, much will be demanded; and from the one who has been entrusted with much, much more will be asked.* (Luke 12:48)

As I mentioned earlier about my first true interaction with international missions in college, it was then that I first really felt the weight of my blessings. I felt the responsibility of what my education, faith, and finances require of me. However, it wasn't a one-time thing, something I look back on in the college days. This awareness has only gotten heavier and heavier. Please don't misinterpret it as guilt—it isn't. God's glory and purpose alone are enough reason for me to dedicate myself to a lifetime of missions, but this extra amazement at His blessings on me are almost overwhelming—in the very best way.

This knowledge is heavy and comes with a required response. Some choose to change (in baby-steps or in *big* ways) and some say "I'm just not comfortable with that" and walk away. Jesus had a serious warning for the latter. I'm not saying I have a ton of answers, but I must, at least, engage.

Acknowledge Where Your Heart is

Before we get into this section about *living* (the "L" of L.E.S.S. … modeling what we hope our kids will also live), I ask: How much are you *willing* to change your life, your heart, and your faith for God's purposes?

He is moving in us because He is so good not to leave us where we are and because He wants to include us in His individual and global redemption. Granted, this is a book about children and youth, but again, this section is about *living it yourself* because the greatest gift you can give your kids is to disciple them and to say, "Hey, come alongside me—let me show you."

Know the God of Justice and Mercy

God wants to redeem the world, but He starts with us. Let us not just do justice work, but be just. Let us not just tell others about the mercy of God, but be merciful. When we, at our core, agree with the Spirit in loving justice, mercy, and compassion, these virtues will become a natural desire in us.

I've been confronted recently with the embarrassing reality that to some degree I've been in love with the "idea" of justice, compassion, and mission, sometimes more than the actual work itself. Many of Jesus's dedicated followers have been giving their lives to this work for thousands of years when it wasn't trendy. I admit this because admitting it brought me to my knees before the God who could remind me of who He was. Justice isn't glamorous. It is costly and takes time…our roots must be deep in God's Word and in our communion with Him.

Learn!

You may have many of the books I've referenced, and thus not need to do a ton of learning for yourself on many of the global issues, but regardless, we always want to have a spirit of learning. There are many excellent books about missions and evangelism internationally. I mention many throughout the book, but have a more exhaustive list in the last chapter of books, dvds, music, and more.

Cross Boundaries

Beyond all the books you can read and DVDs you can watch, actually crossing boundaries yourself to experience poverty (tangible poverty and spiritual poverty) is extremely important in this process. We definitely need to approach short-term mission trips with humility and prayer, as it is often wiser to send our money directly to ministries at work in the country, empowering locals to do the work. However, lives that are changed in cross-cultural trips (usually those who are *going* on the trip) are impossible to measure. People who experience these trips tend to give more, pray more, go on longer trips, view God differently, make different career decisions, and raise their children differently. Lastly, cross-cultural experiences give us story and connection. Without the life-to-life contact, it is very hard to truly desire to change our lives or see a sustainable reason to live out these mission imperatives.

My friend, Deborah, got a play-by-play view of her sister's family being changed by such a cross-cultural interaction. But they didn't have to raise a bunch of money and get on a plane to have it happen. Michelle and her family went an hour away to downtown Austin, Texas, with some peanut butter sandwiches to try to find a homeless man they had met the day before at a stop light. You see, when they first saw the man, they did what most of us do, give a couple dollars and drive off without asking his name to simply pray for him. They didn't have big plans beyond getting his name that day, but instead of encountering the man from yesterday, they met another man, Mr. Watkins.

Mr. Watkins was in a wheelchair and was in need of an identification card. Michelle, seeing a man with a name and a story, took his information. When they left, Michelle didn't forget that she had promised to help him. She had to make some phone calls to North Carolina to try to locate an identification card for Mr. Watkins, but in the midst of those phone calls, Michelle found out that a woman on the phone at the Rockingham County ID office in Charlotte, North Carolina, might know someone that knew Mr. Watkins, too. One night, Michelle got a phone call—it was Mr. Watkin's sister and daughter. His daughter had been looking for him for four years. Through this family reunion, Michelle's family became like family to Mr. Watkins and his family as they assisted him. He had reconciliation with many family members and with God, and even flew home to North Carolina shortly before dying of cancer—which he didn't even know he had.

Michelle's family and her sister Deborah were completely changed by this experience. To think that they could have stayed home that day! They didn't have to go out. Who wants to go out and have awkward conversations with homeless strangers? But Michelle got to be part of an extraordinary redemption story before this man went home to be with Jesus. That not only changed Michelle, it changed her whole family! She dared to cross cultures—she dared to go out her front door.

> *But you will receive power when the Holy Spirit comes on you; and you will be my witnesses in Jerusalem, and in all Judea and Samaria, and to the ends of the earth.* (Acts 1:8)

Sometimes it is helpful to view our mission as being witnesses to Jerusalem (our neighbors and cities), in Judea and Samaria (our regions and crossing cultures near and far), and to the ends of the earth! Regardless of how it works geographically, if we live in an engaged manner through our hearts as we follow Christ, this all will become more natural.

Make the Connection

My husband wrote a short story after watching *Invisible Children*. He wrote it as a fictional piece describing something happening in our own country where the economy crashed, different groups were angry, and the government and rebel groups arose in violence. In his story, one of the groups came in our home and did horrible things to us and to our children. Though these things usually only happen in other countries, he could quickly imagine things in our own country getting to the point where a group of people did this, both due to their own sinfulness and fighting the government. Adam actually never finished the writing project. I'm not sure I would have wanted to read it—it may have brought me too close to all these issues that feel comfortably far away in other countries or with other families.

He had written it because he felt like he needed to connect the reality of his own children to these precious children in Africa who were being abducted in the middle of the night and forced to do the most unimaginable atrocities to other people, including their family members. He wrote it because it is easy to keep these issues at a distance, protecting ourselves in ways that we wouldn't worry about them happening to our children. Some of this is reasonable—it is hard not to want to jump off a bridge if we are in constant awareness of these things on every corner. Wisdom is needed when it comes to embracing depressing realities. However, the other extreme of intentional ignorance is shameful.

> *World hunger is a defining daily experience for millions. I can know this, understand it, be worried about it and still hold it at great distance. The phrase starving child becomes different with the addition of the simple word my. The truth of hunger has not been changed by the addition of that small pronoun—but by the addition of one word, the injustice is the same, but the confidence that something must be done is immediate and unequivocal….If all starving children are God's then in some sense all starving children are also ours.*[1]

It is terribly important that we make this jump to connect ourselves with the humanity of others around the world. A father with a little girl living in India loves his little girl just as much as I love mine. His just happens to live in a Red Light district and he has no income because of a disability and cannot keep an eye out for her every moment. A mother in Africa during a famine cares just as much for her newborn as I do for my children, yet she is hopeless in her ability to find food for him and he gets weaker with the water-borne illness he contracted. If I was any of these people, and someone entered into my sadness and helped me, I would marvel at God seeing me in my despair and I might just ask them a question about the God they serve … the God that saw me in my despair.

In the introduction of Michelle Perry's book *Love Has a Face* (about her journey to loving orphans in the thick of southern Sudan's struggles), Heidi Baker (a missionary in Mozambique) writes:

> *I believe that revival does have a face. It does look like something. It looks like love. It looks like stopping daily for the one in front of you and looking into his or her eyes. You have to see the one. If you cannot see the one, you cannot deal with the multitudes. If you see the one, you will understand suffering, because you will see one dying child under a bridge. You will see one baby with AIDS. You will see one widow alone living under a tree. Revival is about looking into his or her eyes and seeing Jesus look back at you.*[2]

Feel It … Deeply

This connection with others, either in the stories of others or in actual relationship, will surely cause you to feel—deeply. Feelings of intense anger, utter hopelessness, and complete sadness will flow in and out as you engage these issues. Kay Warren admits: "I have cried more tears, felt more pain, and experienced more sorrow than ever before. Hardly a day goes by that my heart doesn't break about something. Sometimes I wonder how many times my heart can break and still survive."[3]

Scripture records that Jesus was moved by compassion twelve times. It wasn't warm, fuzzy compassion. The original word usage suggests that it was gut-wrenching, doubled-over pain for the lost and suffering. Our compassion too will twist our insides. May you find a group of others, at your church or among friends, who will brave this darkness with you and engage a posture of worship as you enter this pain.

Live a Life Worth Repeating

So, now comes the response, the *living* it after the learning (though learning is also part of living it out)—modeling to our children that we can learn new things and still be transformed by truth. Our churches are filled with people desperate for vision and yet unaware of the need. We have told them about missionaries and all about the medicine and have never truly explained how sick and desperate people are. We gave them the cure before explaining there was an illness.

> *They just don't realize that there are millions of people crying out every day to be rescued from aching, urgent hunger; from degrading and hopeless poverty; from the ravages of painful disease; from torture, slavery, rape and abuse. The vast abundance and isolation on the Disneyland Island of the world's affluent communities means that many Western Christians miss God's great calling to a life of heroic rescue simply because they are largely oblivious to the need. They just can't imagine that there could really be any great heroic struggle that would need their help.*[4]

If you need to take a break from this book to engage some of these topics head on, feel free. If you want to push forward to the three big ways of responding to what you learn (through serving, using your voice, and giving), then read on. God is with you as you brave the darkness. He is calling us there because His lost and suffering children are there. Know that it will be painful and require a costly response, but also know that it is worth it, that you have others on the journey with you … and little ones are watching, so let's live our lives according to what we know is right.

> *If you say, 'But we knew nothing about this,' does not he who weighs the heart perceive it? Does not he who guards your life know it?* (Proverbs 24:12a)

Tangible Acts in Response to L.E.S.S.:

1. **Find out where you sit within the world's richest: http://www.globalrichlist.com/**

2. **Research one hard issue that you care about.**

Chapter 11
Live It! Get Your Hands Dirty

Sympathy is no substitute for action.
–David Livingstone

I've been challenged a great deal through many recent sermons from the story of the Good Samaritan. At first glance, I can't imagine myself passing by a hurting person on the road and looking the other way. However, if I'm honest, and if I look deeper at the story, I see that I am no better than the judgmental religious leaders that walked by the suffering man, often too busy and unwilling to get dirty (especially if I have a schedule to keep).

We all know that the Samaritans were despised by the Jews. However, this man (though in other situations perhaps shunned by the man he was helping) took it upon himself to care for the beat up Samaritan traveler after two Jewish religious leaders knowingly passed him by. And he didn't just leave the injured traveler at the doctor, but followed up, securing the man's healing. As far as we know in the story Jesus portrayed, he didn't make judgments of the man who was robbed, which could have been tempting to do.

We do that, don't we? When someone is in a bad situation, I can often look to see what they had done to get there. Did the man foolishly travel at night? (I mean, who wouldn't get robbed at night. I'm not paying for that stupidity.) Did he dress in such a way as to ask for this act of violence against him? (Ouch … that has been said about victims of rape, hasn't it?) Was he drunk perhaps or have a history of getting himself into bad situations? (I don't want to make him dependent on me.)[1]

Though we don't know what Jesus' hero of the story might have thought in these situations, we know that no matter what, he *lived* mercy and mercy work is full of lies, addictions, and habits, as well as broken societies, religions, and relationships. Interactions leave wounds and scars, not just on those who are leaving ugly pasts to enter life with Christ, but also on those who help. Mercy and justice are often dirty work … but beautiful all the same. It is also often inconvenient. It comes at the wrong time. It can even get in the way of our other designated "good" and "important" service projects. I've been known to pray for ways to enter into someone's life and then miss the chance because it was inconvenient or I became judgmental about the way I was offered an opportunity. The Good Samaritan story sheds light on the reality that this work costs us in many ways—as we have seen with involvement, inconvenience, and lastly, humility.

Checking off the box of community service by putting in our time once a month at a local shelter doesn't constitute a heart of service. Now, it isn't a bad place to start and we all have to start somewhere, but what about having an actual heart of service. If our heart has been impacted and shaped for serving, then we won't be as easily inconvenienced, we will see people differently, we will *live* our life ready to *respond* … not scheduled to care.

Just Serve

If service is newer to you, or has just found its way out of your confined scheduled yearly to-do list, or if you haven't branched out much in different ways of serving, consider looking around at any and every opportunity. There are *too many* opportunities to serve to even begin to list them here. Either fall in love with one local service ministry or become an expert on all the different ministries in your city. Heck, if you have nowhere to begin, start by picking up trash in any neighborhood. It blesses everyone and none of us are above it. Model willingness and humility. Sally Clarkson writes:

> *Often the parent fails to take the initiative to share his faith or give to the poor or do whatever the pastor was recommending. The children then learn from their parents that it doesn't really matter if you obey God by actually doing good works. It only matters if you can articulate what you should do. God will hold us accountable for the wonderful opportunities we have to minister to others. The*

> *level of materialism in America, combined with the availability of Scripture and the freedom to invest our lives for him, provides us with a heavy weight of stewardship for our own spiritual heritage. He will also hold us accountable for not training our children or, worse, causing them to stumble spiritually (Matthew 18:6)*[2]

Use Gifts and Passions

Once we have a grasp of the different ways we can serve locally and globally, God will be gracious to reveal to us (as He will to our children) the talents and passions He has given to us to exhort the church and be part of redeeming a lost and broken world.

What are your passions? All justice, poverty, and spiritual issues need to be addressed in different ways by the church and by different people, but sometimes we have our personal causes. Is it dirty water or hunger or slavery?

My friend, Lorna, has now been spending years fighting the cancer that continues to find ways to attack her son. He has already lost a leg and part of the other foot to the disease. Having experienced the depths of the destruction of cancer, she is passionate about helping the church see how best to care for the sick—not just in prayers or meals (though those are loving and helpful in their own way), but in supporting life saving research, not just for her son, but for others. It is a message that God has been painfully writing in her. Though I am so sad for their battle, I couldn't be more proud of her family as they continue to fight for healing. I've changed because of the passion God has put inside of her. *Find your passions!*

Next … what are your gifts?

My friend Andrea is a great runner, so she decided to run two insane marathons (over-achiever!) last summer to raise money for clean water for World Vision. Her husband, Josh, climbs mountains, so he uses this gift alongside a passion to minister to youth. Andrea's brother uses his similar gift for mountaineering as part of his ministry to university students in Italy as a missionary to fulfill his passion for sharing the gospel with university students. God has blessed them with these gifts and passions. They have done an amazing job serving Him and His purposes with them.

I look around me at the people in my life (photographers, writers, knitters, builders, medical professionals, etc.) and I see extraordinarily talented men and women who have blessed me already. My friend, Christine, is a wonderful photographer. Though there may be further global possibilities for such a gift, she honors God as she captures beautiful family moments for others, as she raises her kids to know and love God. What a more obvious example from Scripture of handing back our ten talents to our master and showing him what we did with them. Did we bury them? Did we use them for ourselves? Or did we use them to multiply the number in Heaven praising God? I cherish this lady's heart and she will not just hand back ten talents.

Sacrifice in Order to Serve

> *He is no fool to give what he cannot keep to gain what he cannot lose.* –Jim Elliot

> *Whoever tries to keep his life will lose it, and whoever loses his life will preserve it.* (Luke 17:33)

When I met my husband, he was attending a church in Lakewood, Colorado, called Westwoods Community Church. It is a smaller church (compared to the huge ones in which I tend to find myself), and it has rented different meeting locations over the years. The small church had lots of great things to it, but none of them were why I was most moved to serve at the church. We loved the Schmitz family.

The more I learned about this family, the more I loved them. Rick Schmitz could have been a pastor at many large churches, but he felt called to church planting with this small congregation. He admitted in a sermon that he found it hard on occasion to drive up to meet other men in his beat-up old car when they all had nice cars. At one point in the church's history, it found a location that suited the church best, but they didn't have the funds. So, for a season, Rick gave up most of his salary, got a teaching job, and continued on leading his congregation in this new location. Shawna Schmitz worked hard, too, in her job, in her parenting, in supporting her husband, and in loving the church with the open doors of her home. You can see the fruits of this kind of sacrificial labor. Yes … in the church, but man that fruit is *thick* in their home: in their children.

Rick and Shawna have four kids and they are really neat kids … in their own unique ways. Though they are all grown now, when my husband and I attended the church the Schmitz kids were ranging from elementary through starting college. We remember seeing them in junior high as super cool athletes that loved God, reached out to their friends, praying with friends before lunch together. We recently saw a picture of one of their kids' friends, a Colorado University football athlete (that their whole family loved on and led in loving Christ), bowing down in prayer before a huge game—all by himself, still loyal in faith to His God. The Schmitz kids are still spread out across the country and the world serving God and the poor, in their own style.

Unfortunately, even with perfect parenting, all children have the opportunity to turn away from their parents' faith (and everyone has bumpy roads). Still, I don't think it is a coincidence that the Schmitz kids chose a faith they saw preached in front of them and *lived* sacrificially in front of them every day. Rick and Shawna sacrificed a lot to serve the church and serve God's call to missions. Their family was blessed for it. I think about it often. I'm not sure if Rick ever got much of a better car, but I for one am much more envious of his family than any car I've *ever* seen!

Committed to Serving the Soul

Alright, I've put forth ideas about how to meet the needs of the body, but now I need to get more into the soul part … the eternal part, which is not ever the after-thought, but coupled with the other needs. It may, however, appear that I talk about physical poverty more in this book for three reasons:

1. The assumption with which I write is that acts of compassion and justice give credit to us as friends to those with whom we wish to share Christ. They reveal the love and ministry of Christ. Meeting physical needs is often a basis for bringing a person out of survival mode into a place where they can more openly hear the gospel.

   In the same way, let your light shine before others, that they may see your good deeds and glorify your Father in heaven. (Matthew 5:16)

2. In some conservative Churches that I have experienced in the past (and I think this is generally true following the fundamentalism-liberal split in the early 1900s), missions has had its emphasis on evangelism globally. As David Platt writes:

   Anyone wanting to proclaim the glory of Christ to the ends of the earth must consider not only how to declare the gospel verbally but also how to demonstrate the gospel visibly in a world where so many are urgently hungry. If I am going to address urgent spiritual need by sharing the gospel of Christ or building up the body of Christ around the world, then I cannot overlook dire physical need in the process. Frighteningly, though, I have turned a blind eye to these realities. I have practically ignored these people, and I have been successful in my ignorance because they are not only poor but also powerless. Literally millions of them are dying in obscurity, and I have enjoyed my affluence while pretending they don't exist. But they do exist.[3]

3. While Scripture tells us to share about Christ, Scripture also flat out tells us to care for the orphans and widows and feed the hungry. They weren't in passages as part of a master plan of evangelism, as a switch and bait. No, although it is true that caring for physical needs strengthens our witness, it is abundantly clear throughout the Bible that God wants us to care for the poor and outcast.

However, in light of the above and if our churches do *not* successfully emphasize the need for global and local evangelism, let's go ahead and review that for a second. It, like service, must flow from us and become part of our (and our children's) hearts, way of thinking, and way of loving. Let me remind you, the Bible does not say, come and bring the people to the church. It says, *go to them*! So look at some questions … to gauge where we are at:

Do we honestly believe people need to be saved, not just for life, but for eternity?

Do we believe in an eternal Hell?

Do we believe that Jesus can change people's lives and souls?

Do we believe Jesus meant for us to be part of the Great Commission?

These are good questions to ponder in order to verify that we really believe that people need to be saved. If your answer is *no* to any of them, then this isn't the book for you. It is a book about how to live out a calling of loving others that they might know Jesus's redemption now and for eternity. If you have more questions about that, please find those answers—they are essential.

For all evangelism training, consider these Scriptures (and they are good ones to memorize):

> *For all have sinned and fall short of the glory of God.* (Romans 3:23)
>
> *The wages of sin is death. But the gift of God is eternal life through Jesus Christ our Lord.* (Romans 6:23)
>
> *God demonstrates His own love for us, in that while we were yet sinners Christ died for us.* (Romans 5:8)
>
> *Whoever will call on the name of the Lord will be saved!* (Romans 10:13)
>
> *If you confess with your mouth Jesus as Lord, and believe in your heart that God raised Jesus from the dead, you shall be saved; for with the heart man believes, resulting in righteousness, and with the mouth he confesses, resulting in salvation.* (Romans 10:9,10)

My friend, Beth, has these scriptures deep in her heart and her kids have these and hundreds more memorized through Awana. Beth has lived it out though, as she intentionally substitutes in her local schools in hopes of loving on struggling kids. Her husband and she run the Awana program at a local church, serving church and unsaved kids from around Hartford.

I remember being in Mozambique, seeing the cream of community development through World Vision. It wasn't just wells and crops and schools. The whole community was centered around the church. Anyone in need would come to the church in times of trouble. But, I suppose, this could happen in a well-functioning community center instead of a church … but it wouldn't be so successful if it weren't for the undeniable power of God's Word transforming people's lives!

We had the chance to sit in on a Bible study where people shared how God has completely changed cultural practices (men beating wives, etc) because they read His Word. I shouldn't have been that surprised (and none of the World Vision staff were surprised, for they see repentant faith and God's Word transform lives like that all the time). It is true heart transformation that endures. That is what we are after. That is not just sustainable on earth, but will make it through the fire of death into eternity with Christ. Channels of Hope is completely transforming gender equality throughout the world … through *Bible studies*.

So, please, please read my intentions such that "global issues" are an avenue of missions that God not only has an open door to, but has commanded us to respond to. We must hold God's words and acts of love together, not just for this life, but for eternity and for God's glory.

> *As Jesus walked beside the Sea of Galilee, he saw Simon and his brother Andrew casting a net into the lake, for they were fishermen. 'Come, follow me,' Jesus said, 'and I will make you fishers of men.'* (Mark 1:18–19)

Beyond just knowing that we need God's Word for evangelism, as well as transformation, here is another life check. Are you making disciples? If we are following Christ, we ought to be making other disciples who can make disciples. This is more than belief—it is repentance, life change, and an allegiance to Jesus in *Lordship* in a way that costs us our very lives.

We must know Christ in such a way that it is evident in all of our lives, working in a manner worthy of the calling, so that our children see evidence of it all, too. We do them no favors by acting like they can just add Jesus on to their everyday life in fear that they won't accept Jesus's call otherwise. The greatest gift we can give ourselves and our children is this truth, teaching them to serve the world in Word and deed.

My friend Megan Langer writes about her journey to service and justice with her family:

> *It wasn't too long ago that I was living in my beautiful, comfortable suburban home, taking care of my children and saying to my friends, 'I wish that there was something I could do for God now. I KNOW parenting is time consuming and tiring. I KNOW there is a season for everything. I just wish I could be a parent AND make a difference in the world.' My friends would answer back with encouraging words, hoping to make me feel okay about where I was, encouraging me to be content with where God has me now. And then I would go home to my nice house and just live my life for myself. Day after day.*
>
> *God has been awakening my heart to His love for people and His passion for justice in tiny little increments over the last ten years. In 2000 I was part of a group of women who did a Bible study together. One woman in that group told me once that her life goal was to eradicate the world of slavery and human trafficking. Before knowing her, I didn't even realize human trafficking was a world problem! Slowly, from that moment until January 2011, God was softening my heart to justice issues around the world. As I was awakened, however, I felt hopeless and*

stuck. How do you make a difference in a world where slavery is so rampant? How do you help people who live halfway around the globe? How do you do ANYTHING from a suburban house surrounded by some of the richest people in the world? How do you make a difference when you are tired and worn out from educating and parenting your children?

Then I read The Good News about Injustice, by Gary Haugen, Radical, by David Platt and 7, by Jen Hatmaker. These books changed my life.

They were practical, easy to understand books that helped me to recognize not only the problems that we are facing in the world, but what exactly I could do about them. I realized that parenting and educating my children ARE my way to doing my part to end slavery. While living my suburban life, I can set an example for my children by raising awareness of these global issues in my community, and DO SOMETHING with my children. Unless I do something, how will my children learn about justice? Unless I set an example for them with my actions and words, how will they know that God is a compassionate God and cares about slavery, human trafficking, and poverty? If I don't teach them these things, they will waste just as much time as I did not even knowing these problems exist.

So, I started to DO SOMETHING. I had a clothing swap (Jen Hatmaker style). My kids helped me set up the house for the event. Then, my kids helped me pile all the extra clothes into the car to take to ex-prostitutes at Street's Hope. My kids are young, so they don't know the details of human trafficking and prostitution, but they do know that people can be bought and sold. We talked about slaves and slavery. We talked about the value God places on people and His love for them. We talked about how God's heart breaks for people in slavery, and so should ours. We talked about doing something.

I helped organize a winter clothing drive for the Burmese refugees in our area. People that live here in our city that don't have warm clothes to wear and enough food to eat. The kids went through their clothes and as we picked out all the items we could give away (we had a lot), we prayed for the children that would receive these clothes. We prayed that they would be warm this winter, and that they would know the love of Jesus. We practiced compassion, and we did something.

As a family, we decided that instead of filling every little desire of our hearts, we would limit ourselves. For a season, we intentionally spent less money, and gave what we saved to help build an orphanage in Uganda. As we went through this process, my kids would ask for something, or remark that they would like to go out to dinner or to Starbucks. I taught them that when they feel that way, they should pray and thank God for the generosity He has had with us. We talked about being grateful for the things we have, and praying for the people that don't have so much. Still today, my children's prayers are filled with gratefulness for what God has given us and pleas for the people that do not have as much. They still pray for the children that will fill that orphanage in Uganda. We did something.

We've also tried to pay attention to where the things we purchase are coming from. Was there slavery in the manufacturing chain? This is often a very overwhelming thing to think about, but I do the best I can. I talk to my kids about why we don't buy cheap, junky toys, or why I check labels to see where things are made. Since they know about slavery, this is a great way to bring awareness into our everyday lives. I think it's a rare day that I don't buy something, so it's always giving us a chance to talk about and pray for people in slavery. Just making one decision NOT to buy something is a small step toward doing something.

My actions, I've learned, don't have to be big and grandiose. I can do small things and they will add up to enough to mold my children's hearts. Taking a sick neighbor a meal, talking with the children at the local homeless shelter, praying for the people of Madagascar, learning about the challenges of living in a third world country—these are all things that can be done in my community, and used as examples for my children.

A key piece in being able to do something for others is making sure that my life has margin. If we've programmed every minute of every day, how will we be able to respond when a friend needs a ride right now? Or when a pregnant mom who has chosen life is suddenly put on bed rest and needs a meal or her house cleaned? We intentionally fill our days with time to be used to pray, serve and give.

My prayer is that my children will grow up with hearts filled with mercy and love for others; that they will be generous and compassionate individuals who are bold and courageous. I want my children to DO SOMETHING. And I realized it has to start with me.

Tangible Acts in Response to L.E.S.S.:

1. **Find a group that you can serve with as a family and a family location.**

2. **Let yourself be inconvenienced this week. Let your kids know it is hard to be inconvenienced, but meet the need. Pray to be inconvenienced with a chance to share the gospel.**

Chapter 12

Live It!—Raise Your Voice

It is not the violence of the few that scares me,
it is the silence of many.
–Martin Luther King, Jr.

My own son (who was seven at the time) came out of a church with his Sunday School craft and asked me, "Mama, can we please tell the church to stop doing so many silly crafts that just end up in recycling? It seems wasteful to me."

Uh oh.

What do I say to that?

Option 1: "No, I can't, son. Hush, hush. We just don't want to make waves and we like to keep kids entertained as easily as possible, even if it is wasteful." (I'm not saying all crafts are wasteful, BTW.)

Option 2: "Dude—sorry. I'm sorry I put your crafts in recycling so fast. I love everything you make there and will keep it forever."

Option 3: "Yes, I will talk to them. Just so you know … we will shortly be asked to leave the church because we have already made a stink about how much bottled water is used and wasted and because you all like to refer to any chocolate in the church as 'slave chocolate.'"

While I still am trying to fumble through issues like these, the reality is that we all have a voice in our purchases, in our government, in our relationships, and in our prayers. The way we live this out reveals to others and to our children what we believe about God, our world, and what is important.

Raising Our Voice in Prayer

I am going to start where we should all start: prayer. I am embarrassed to admit that my biggest weakness is embracing prayer—both for my own needs and for the greatest source of advocacy that I have for the lost, poor, and oppressed. I am truly humbled by a new understanding of my need for deep supplication, intercession, and listening prayer and asking God to discipline my heart in this practice of prayer before and with any mission work. It is foolish for me to do it otherwise.

> *Is anyone among you suffering? Let him pray … Therefore, confess your sins to one another and pray for one another, that you may be healed. The prayer of a*

> *righteous person has great power as it is working.* (James 5:13a,16)

Bethany H. Hoang's Urbana Onward booklet entitled, *Deepening the Soul for Justice*, is an extraordinary call to prayer on behalf of justice work. Working for IJM (International Justice Mission) in the face of some of the world's most horrific acts of crimes on human beings (even the smallest of human beings), one might think that she couldn't sit still, needing to constantly act on behalf of justice at every moment. However, IJM as an organization has a required 30 minutes of silence in their workday, as well as staff devotional time. Bethany writes: "But when the work of justice is pursued first and throughout, as a work of prayer and an outpouring of our relationship with Jesus Christ, obstacles become opportunities to know the riches of God's glory and great presence in ever-increasing measure. And the victories won through the hand of God will be breathtaking beyond what any of us could ever imagine."[1]

Prayer for Others

First of all, in my attempts to get better with prayer (because I knew I stunk at it), I read books on prayer. Lots of them. That makes sense, doesn't it? If you don't pray much and want to get better at it, then just read books about it, right? Brilliant. After the books I read (though they had great insights), I had to conclude with what most logical people could have told me: if you want to get better at praying, just start praying. Pray! Right *now*! (Seriously, put down the book and do it now!)

> *Prayer reminds us of God's priorities and power when we are dealing with big issues of justice, like poverty. When we pray, we can see the world with God's eyes of compassion and justice rather than being hopelessly cynical, fearful, or naïve about global injustice... As the Lord's Prayer puts it, 'Your Kingdom come, Your will be done on earth as it is in heaven'. This points to the priority of God's control but also the need for us to demonstrate God's Kingdom values on earth.*[2]

This prayer in itself reminds us that our actions must begin with God. He covers all the work we do, sets the stage for our future work, and leads us. Gary Haugen, president of IJM, whom Bethany Hoang works for, writes: "I won't need to be in prayer every thirty minutes in my work if I don't really need God's power to get it done, or if it's work that God doesn't really need done because it has nothing to do with his kingdom.[3]"

IJM's annual conference is dedicated to prayer. People don't only rally to march the steps of the Capitol (though that is important work); they focus greatly on pleading on behalf of the lost and suffering to the King of all nations.

Advocacy through Government

> *Speak out for those who cannot speak, for the rights of all the destitute. Defend the rights of the poor and needy.* (Proverbs 31:8–9)

One thing that I had not known anything about in the past is using my voice in advocacy. I hadn't engaged in it at all.

However, I have begun to change little by little as I make phone calls and write letters suggested by the organizations I trust about justice and poverty issues.

I still feel a bit like a baby in the world of government advocacy work. Luckily, most Christian organizations working in D.C. to advocate for aid or justice work have easy links and directions as to how best to call or email your senators, representatives, and the President about important issues. For example, recently the Trafficking Victims Protection Reauthorization Act (TVPRA) came before our U.S. legislators . It is a bill that had protected the rights of victims of trafficking and it was allowed to lapse. However, with the help of many phone calls and letters, it finally got moved into the House of Representatives. As few as a dozen letters can alert a legislator to begin monitoring an issue or change an editor's mind. And these letters count. Few people take the time to write letters to lawmakers, so a handful of letters can sway an important vote or decision. In addition, well-written letters stimulate debate among politicians and the public.[4]

Esther as an Example

I love the story of Esther. I love Esther and her cousin, the good guard Mordecai. Esther can be quite an example for us in so many ways. For one, Esther felt very much like an ordinary girl. She never had grand plans of becoming a princess, outside of fairy-tale dreams. Once she finds herself married to the king (because of her honor and God's providence), she keeps her identity as a Jew a secret. Perhaps she is being wise, but she may have also just been scared. She knows that Haman is after the Jews. She wants to save her own skin.

May we all have a Mordecai in our life (and may we be a Mordecai to our children and others around us). Mordecai serves to tell Esther the truth, about what injustice is going on, what responsibility Esther has to respond to it, and what it all means in light of her own mortality. He writes to her:

> *And who knows but that you have come to royal position for such a time as this?* (Esther 4:14)

Wisely, Esther is brave in her fear (that's what bravery is, to do something even when we are afraid) and asks Mordecai to have everyone fast and pray for days before she approaches the king. She lays a foundation of fasting and praying before she sees the king. She also does something else: Esther establishes a good relationship with the king and increases it with having him over for dinner. Esther was wise with how she "campaigns" her cause.

It is only then, after prayer and relationship, that she seeks to humbly advocate, in the face of death, on behalf of all the Jews and herself for mercy and justice. God miraculously grants it, receiving all the glory and exalting the Jewish people. What a great model of advocacy, more effective than nasty emails to politicians or prayer-less justice work.

Our Voice in Relationships

I can't push it on others as they have the choice to shut their eyes to it, but I can share what I am learning with others all the time about God's movement in missions, the truth about justice issues, and possible godly responses to it. I need others to share their heart and ideas with me as well. I don't have eyes, ears, and hands in every important issue—there is no way. We need each other. Advocacy in context of relationships can be beautiful.

> *Take up the cause of the fatherless; plead the case of the widow.* (Isaiah 1:17)

The Voice in Our Wallets—Fair Trade and Conscience Purchasing

Our pocketbooks have power. Every time we buy something (whether it is chocolate, coffee, sugar, clothing, or our Florida slave-labor tomatoes), when we buy it and consume it, we are voting for it. We are buying into it. When our churches buy little plastic stuff from Wal-Mart, The Dollar Store, and Oriental Trading Company, we are buying into it (and polluting the earth with more plastic junk that doesn't decompose). I'm sorry if that sounds harsh, but it is true.

Harriet Beecher Stowe was a white abolitionist who wrote *Uncle Tom's Cabin.* That book opened the eyes of a nation (and President Lincoln) to the tragedy of slavery in a new way. She had a lot of other writings, too, but one in particular caught my heart. She said that in regards to slavery "as a Christian, I felt a dishonor to Christianity." They explained it further at her museum: "Deeply religious, Harriet wanted ministers to preach against slavery, but few would. Seeing church-going Northern factory owners buy slave-raised cotton for their textile mills and profit by selling shoes and cloth to plantations made Harriet feel her faith was dishonored."

I just couldn't shake feeling like this quote had been written yesterday because it doesn't feel like we have come any farther. Cotton and shoes are still a source of slave labor, yet stores around us profit from them and we profit from their low prices if we buy them. It is everywhere! I bought into it for so long—mostly not knowing and then as I started learning, I just floundered.

I love a prayer I recently read: "God of the just weight and the fair measure, let me remember the hands that harvested my food, my drink, not only in my prayers but in the market place. Let me not seek a bargain that leaves another hungry."[5]

OUCH!

Consider how scripture warns us not to profit off the poor. I still struggle to live this!

> *This is what the LORD says: Do what is just and right. Rescue from the hand of the oppressor the one who has been robbed....But if you do not obey these commands, declares the LORD, I swear by myself that this palace will become a ruin.* (Jeremiah 22:3a, 5)

> *Look! The wages you failed to pay the workers who mowed your fields are crying out against you. The cries of*

> *the harvesters have reached the ears of the Lord Almighty.* (James 5:4)

So, I've always been a decently thrifty gal. I shop mostly at thrift stores, rarely eat out, make many of my gifts, and don't spend much on groceries. This style of living came first when I married a frugal guy in grad school, but then became a moral decision, as we chose to use more and more of our income to give to God's work here and abroad. As a family, we've decided to include our kids on these decisions to change our purchasing habits and brave a new world of advocacy. It has been slow and sometimes difficult (especially when I flounder back into old ways of buying), but overall, it has been good.

However, I recall when I was at a well-known store and saw a cute discounted shirt that I wanted for my son (seven at the time). Since I hadn't actually *heard* that this store was a producer of clothing with bad origins, I turned a blind eye for the sake of fashion and put it in our cart. Later that night, I brought the shirt out to have my son put it on. I was just *sure* he would marvel at the softness of his new shirt, pop the tag off, and give me a big hug. However, he did not have this response.

He was angry. He was angry at me.

My seven-year-old looked at me and said, "Mom, I don't need another shirt. I have enough clothes. I have too many clothes. There are kids in the world with only the clothes on their body. I shouldn't have another shirt."

I had no response. I couldn't even look him in the eye, yet somehow, because I didn't want the trouble of taking the darn shirt back (or because I needed this shame to be behind me), I convinced him to keep it. I pulled off that tag and sealed the deal. How pathetic is that?

I came downstairs after putting my son to bed, felt sick to my stomach, and cried. My own child had to remind me about kids who have almost nothing. He told me about these children because I had first told him. He saw that I didn't live out what I said I believed … what I told him our family believed and lived.

Bottled Water

Did you know that bottled water is a sham? I had known a little bit, having heard rumors about sketchy companies. I then learned from World Vision about the destruction the water bottle industry has on the poor (as well as on the environment). Industries with clean water bottle it to make more money, rather than making tap water clean for all. Water bottle sources are often taken from the poor. Since learning these truths, we have looked into it more. The facts are sick:

- *100 billion dollars is spent a year on water bottles in the world (10 billion in the US alone) and yet it would take only an estimated 30 billion to bring clean water to ALL the world.*[6]

- "In the past ten years, diarrhea related to unsanitary water has *killed more children than all the people lost to armed conflict since WWII* (Water Supply & Sanitation Collaborative Council)

- An estimated *2.4 billion people lack adequate sanitation and 1.1 billion people are without access to safe water* (UNICEF)

- There are *1.6 million deaths per year attributed to dirty water* and poor sanitation (World Watch; World Health Organization)

- The average distance that women in developing countries *walk to collect water per day is four miles and the average weight that women carry on their heads is approximately 44 pounds* (Water Supply & Sanitation Collaborative Council)

- Over *40 billion work hours are lost each year in Africa* to the need to fetch drinking water (World Health Organization, 2004)

- The lack of clean, safe drinking water is *estimated to kill almost 4,500 children per day*; out of the *2.2 million unsafe drinking water deaths in 2004, 90 percent were children under the age of five* (UNICEF)"[7]

> Did you know that …?
>
> *Bottled water is not safer than tap water. In fact, the federal government requires more rigorous and frequent safety testing and monitoring of municipal drinking water. Bottled water is thousands of times more expensive than tap water. Compare $0.002 per gallon for most tap water to a range of $0.89 to $8.26 per gallon for bottled waters.Bottled water hurts the environment. After millions of barrels of oil are used to produce and ship plastic water bottles, 75 percent of them land in the garbage or our waterways instead of the recycle bin. To make one bottle of water, three times that amount of water is wasted in production.*[8]

Wrapping it up

Clean water, slavery, the lost, and many other issues could take up all of our thoughts and efforts. They will change us and they will change our kids. Whatever issue it is—speaking out about injustice to the government or about what purchases we make as a family—we must make the best decisions we can through the foundation of prayer. God has blessed us with resources, relationships, education, and the opportunity to change things. Check out Shayne Moore's book, *Global Soccer Mom,* and read about her amazing journey into advocating for the poor and oppressed. It started simply, just wanting to help as a mom in these issues, and it exploded from there. Though it is in God's hands, what results come from each of our lives, Mordecai's question spills over again and again in my mind on how we will *live* with the voice we have been given…

> *And who knows but that you have come to royal position for such a time as this?* (Esther 4:14)

Tangible Acts in Response to L.E.S.S.:

1. **Shake hands and say goodbye to those friends you've been secretly competing with in status—confess and mourn it in prayer.**

2. **Research for yourself the top few contributors to slave labor cocoa, coffee, cotton, and sugar. It can seem overwhelming. I recommend the book *Everyday Justice* by Julie Clawson which breaks a *huge* topic into manageable chapters and practical responses for folks like me who cannot change everything all at once.**

I don't want to wear someone else's despair.
I don't want to eat someone else's tragedy.
Ashley Judd in *Call & Response*

Chapter 13
Live It! Looking at the Camel in the Mirror

Not, how much of my money will I give to God,
but how much of God's money will I keep for myself.
–John Wesley

In 1998, my friend Carrie was in Guatemala on a college missions trip. She and her friends were still exhausted from travel, but went in to meet all the people of the town at a local church. Little did they know that the service was going to be a good four hours long … and in Spanish. Nothin' like trying to stay awake in church for an hour in English, let alone four hours in Spanish.

Well, in an attempt to at least act respectfully engaged in the service, they were given some headsets where a woman would translate the sermon for them in English. However, the woman translating didn't always get all the words right in English, but Carrie and the team could catch the drift of the message (when they weren't staring at the back of their eyelids, mind you).

The sermon was about tithing. It always is, isn't it (especially when you visit somewhere new … even on a mission trip)? But apparently the pastor got real heated and excited about the sermon … so the translator did, too. The woman enthusiastically mistranslated, "Give your thighs to de Lord. If you love Him, *give your thighs to de Lord*!"

I don't know about you, but I will hand over my thighs any time, any day to the Lord. There doesn't need to be passages of scripture or strange Weight Watchers BMI offering plates to guilt me into it. He can have them! No ten percent here … let's go 50 percent, heck 90 percent, on *thighing*! However, change that word to *tithing* and I'm sheepish. I'll hand over my backside, but maybe not the money in my back pocket quite as easily.

Henri Nouwen admits that, "Money conversations are a greater taboo than conversations about sex or religion."[1] For those of you I don't know who are reading this, you would have maybe liked me before this, but I may be over the line now. Jesus talked so much about money, how can we ignore it? It ties into our allegiances, our idols, our temptations. In my life, my relationship with God completely affects all aspects of my life, including the kind of parent I am, how much I care about the poor, and how I spend and give money.

I will touch specifically on how much we give, how we give, our possessions, and our spending. Not intrusive at all I'm sure!

How much we tithe … in the Old Testament

So … how much do we give? Most churches preach a ten percent tithe as a rule of thumb. I want to challenge that, but where does that ten percent idea come from? Let's see:

> *Now consider how great this man was, unto whom even the patriarch Abraham gave the tenth of the spoils.* (Hebrews 7:4)

Here we see in Hebrews how ten percent is connected all the way back to Abraham. Surely that is tithing, right? But, what is "of the spoils"? Well, Hebrews 7:4 is referring back to when Abram (not renamed Abraham yet) had repossessed riches from war. But this is not about Abram giving his own possessions or blessings. This is about Abram giving ten percent of his war winnings to Melchizedeck in honor of God, acknowledging that it was with God's favor that they had won the battles:

> *'And praise be to God Most High, who delivered your enemies into your hand.' Then Abram gave him a tenth of everything*. (Genesis 14:20)

However, it is also interesting that Abram didn't keep the other 90 percent though he was given permission to do so, but instead gave it back to those who had originally possessed the items in his land. *None* of this offering was from his vocation (like we'd think of tithing today), and this is the only time it is recorded that he made any sort of tithing at all in his whole life. One time for Abram … yet he was acknowledged in Hebrews solely for the purpose of uplifting Melchizedeck as a great priest, in contrast to the Most High Priest, Jesus. This Hebrews verse is the only New Testament ten percent tithing reference we have, and it isn't even about tithing. Uh oh. But, what else is there?

Well, in an effort to not make a whole new book about tithing, I'd ask that you do your own research … see if what I am writing has any weight at all. A quick rundown of what I found (and have verified with a few Bible scholars I respect):

- Jacob's reference in Genesis 28:20: not tithing—Jacob is making a deal with God.
- Moses' reference in Mosaic Law (Leviticus 27:32, Deuteronomy 14:22, 2 Chronicles 31:5-6, Nehemiah 10:37): all refer to a tithe. Some suggest a tenth and some don't. During this time in Jewish history, after the initial tithe that was required, there were offerings that were voluntary (making the total giving of Levites to the Lord actually closer to 30 percent of their livelihood … not ten percent). These extra offerings were freely given, in love and praise and worship of God. (By the way, I'm pretty sure this is where the fabulous "love gift" term comes from when churches are asking for a little extra giving at Christmas or just the everyday solicitation of most televised preachers. It is a term that has been very misused and humorous in my house, I confess.) Furthermore, I see extravagant giving that God desires outside of normal expected "Mosaic Law tithing," especially for the poor in places like Exodus 35:21, 22, 29, Ex 36:3b, 5–7.

New Testament Teachings

Above, we see that indeed there was tithing in the law to allow for the structure of the priesthood and buildings used for worship (much like we give taxes to our government). There were additional offerings freely given for the poor and for worship. As mentioned, this was well above ten percent with estimates of closer to 22–30 percent of someone's income (not 10%)… so what about Jesus? Did he tithe or teach about it?

Basically, we know that Jesus acknowledged the tithe. Since he was a Jew living under the Law, he probably tithed himself. Jesus also taught that people should still tithe while under the Law (Matthew 23:23 and Luke 11:42). We see life under the Law, but it pertained to the Old Covenant. The New Covenant only came into effect after Jesus was resurrected.

Fortunately, even before the New Covenant came into effect, Jesus taught about what life was to be like with the New Covenant. One of the tenets of this New Covenant between God and us is that our actions are to be motivated by our heart, not by external behavior. In the following sections, Jesus taught about the spiritual dangers for rich men, taught about giving all of it up (not just ten percent), and he knew that a man's wealth and status would hinder many from walking a path to Eternity with Him and doing His work.

> *Go, sell everything you have and give to the poor, and you will have treasure in heaven. Then come, follow me.* (Mark 10:18)

This definitely isn't 10% tithing! It is 100%! So, what does that leave us with? After Jesus was resurrected, we have a whole new covenant. We have a whole new system that gets to the heart of our relationship with everything, including money. In fact (and ironically), the verses about Melchizedeck in Hebrews that seem to point to a tithe actually works up to this:

> *For when the priesthood is changed, the law must be changed also.* (Hebrews 7:12)

Not only did Christ fulfill the Law with Himself as a new High Priest, but we are no longer under the old Law, including tithing. Furthermore, the new Church had no use for all of the different offerings of the Jewish system. Though they had new needs to support apostles and needs of the church, tithes were not needed for sacrifices or many of the rituals. We don't see tithing (in any sort of ten percent variety) *at all* in Acts. Acts is the beginning of the Church, and the epistles are our window into the corrections of the early church's behavior—when it would have been a perfect time to remind people for automatic withdrawal options for their ten percent. But you don't see that. In fact, there is no statement to New Covenant believers to "tithe" at all. If anything, we see evidence of a whole new giving system. The new giving system is reminiscent of Jesus's teaching about the heart of our relationship with money. Example:

> *Joseph, a Levite from Cyprus, whom the apostles called Barnabas (which means 'son of encouragement'), sold a field he owned and brought the money and put it at the apostles' feet.* (Acts 4:36–37)

If Barnabas was still following the law as a Levite, he would have given ten percent, but he didn't! He gave it *all* to the growing church. Not what you wanted to hear, huh? But, remember what we read in Acts. The people of the early church, including Barnabas, saw and knew that their generosity was changing lives, and if I had been with them, I wouldn't want to miss out on God's work either. For example, we are all ready to give anything after an incredible mission trip experiencing God in a new way and seeing physical needs. This is why giving, generosity, and sacrifice can't be sustained outside of a deep relationship with Christ and *relationships* with the suffering.

Why is it so hard for us to get our minds around the idea that tithing in the 10% sense has nothing to do with us in the New Covenant with Christ? Sadly, when we bring our congregations, families, and bank accounts back under a rule of the Law—even if it feels safe, almost comforting at first—we are in fact binding ourselves back into the Law. I believe that giving 10% of our income as a tithe and then "checking that off our list" of Christian things to do is going back to the Law and opening ourselves up to legalism in this area of our life. If you look at the tithing rules, they require our 10th child as well, and I don't see people lining up to offer their children to the servant-hood of the church in that way (except when I run out of ideas for punishment, as I am tempted to on occasion).

I honestly don't have any historical view of why churches let us believe that ten percent is what we should give. We can certainly acknowledge that it is tricky to interpret the whole of scripture in light of the New and Old Covenants. It seems that whenever there are questions between the two, we like to lean on the side of rules, because it feels safer. However, I wonder if under it all that the reason churches don't teach a freedom of tithing is just simply fear. Fear that if churches free up their congregations to give what is on their heart, that they will give less—or not at all. I get it, but I think the alternative is worse. We have generations of Christians (many rich) who feel safe in how much they give. If the Holy Spirit nudges them, they can just put their hands up and say, "Hey, I already give my share."

I say this all so harshly because I'm also talking to myself. I like to know what is God's and what is mine. I can give God His amount, then count on His blessing. After that, I could kind of figure (so long as I'm not immoral or anything) that it is kind of up to me and my priorities how to spend the rest. Right? I'm seeing more and more that this isn't what God has in mind for me. He wants more than that of me. He doesn't want a cheap (literally and figuratively) relationship with me. He has bigger plans.

Craig Blomberg, a former seminary professor of mine (who is an incredible theologian and respected author of many New Testament theology books, including *Christians in the Age of Wealth*), explains:

> *In the era of the new covenant, however, no command to tithe ever appears. Instead, we read of models of generous, even sacrificial giving (see esp. 2 Cor. 8:1–5). The problem with ten percent for most middle-to-upper-class Westerners today is that it is often too little to truly qualify as generous and sacrificial, given all our assets. The 'graduated tithe,' by which one gives away a higher percentage the more one makes may well better reflect biblical priorities. That at least is what my wife and I have attempted to do in our twenty-five years of marriage. Starting with ten percent to our church and to other Christians and Christian organizations particularly concerned with ministering a holistic gospel, addressing people's physical as well as spiritual needs at home and abroad, we have increased that percentage by one or two percent every year since. And yet our comfortable middle-class lifestyle suggests to me that we still have much more to learn in our lifetime about truly sacrificial giving.*[2]

Russell Earl Kelly, author of *Should the Church Teach Tithing,* supports freewill offering as a response from the heart as motivated by love from the Holy Spirit. He is convinced that a mandatory ten percent (so-called tithe) of gross income, regardless of circumstances, is unscriptural and causes more harm than good to the body of Christ. Churches that teach tithing often scorn those who disagree with them, denying positions to pastors, deacons, and teachers because they won't teach tithing, even though they may be excellent soul-winners.[3]

Though we long for rules, C.S. Lewis in *Mere Christianity* also gives another confusing standard for giving: "I am afraid the only safe rule is to give more than we can spare … If our charities do not at all pinch or hamper us … they are too small. There ought to be things we should like to do and cannot do because our charitable expenditures exclude them.[4]"

New Reasons in Scripture to Give Generously

Christians are free to give now in a new way. Why would we go back to the old Law? God has instead enabled us by His Spirit to be led to use all of His resources that He has given us for His Glory. Wow! That is tough. After the ten percent, can I say that I use the rest for God's glory? That's harder, but sounds a lot more like God, huh?

There aren't guidelines on exactly how much to give in the New Testament, as much as we crave guidelines. So, if you want off the hook to even giving ten percent … I guess you have it. There is no rule to give ten percent of your income. But we are warned: we also now know that God has asked even more of us—our time, possessions, heart, and money. He has asked for *all* of us for much richer reasons:

It shows God's righteous work in us**:** *They have freely scattered their gifts to the poor, their righteousness endures forever; their horn will be lifted high in honor.* (Psalm 112:9)

Rightful understanding of what you have been given: *Freely you have received; freely give.* (Matthew 10:8b)

Living Compassion: *Jesus called his disciples to him and said, "I have compassion for these people; they have already been with me three days and have nothing to eat. I do not want to send them away hungry, or they may collapse on the way.* (Matthew 15:32)

Reward in Heaven: *Then Jesus said to his host, "When you give a luncheon or dinner, do not invite your friends, your brothers or sisters, your relatives, or your rich neighbors; if you do, they may invite you back and so you will be repaid. But when you give a banquet, invite the poor, the crippled, the lame, the blind, and you will be blessed. Although they cannot repay you, you will be repaid at the resurrection of the righteous.* (Luke 14:12–14)

Example of Jesus: *Walk in the way of love, just as Christ loved us and gave himself up for us as a fragrant offering and sacrifice to God.* (Ephesians 5:2)

Obedience: *This service that you perform is not only supplying the needs of the Lord's people but is also overflowing in many expressions of thanks to God. Because of the service by which you have proved yourselves, others will praise God for the obedience that accompanies your confession of the gospel of Christ, and for your generosity in sharing with them and with everyone else.* (2 Corinthians 9: 12–13)

We reap what we sow: *Whoever sows to please their flesh, from the flesh will reap destruction; whoever sows to please the Spirit, from the Spirit will reap eternal life.* **9** *Let us not become weary in doing good, for at the proper time we will reap a harvest if we do not give up.* (Galatians 6:8–9)

Avoid love of money: *For the love of money is a root of all kinds of evil. Some people, eager for money, have wandered from the faith and pierced themselves with many griefs.* (1 Timothy 6:10)

Use what is given by God: *Each of you should use whatever gift you have received to serve others, as faithful stewards of God's grace in its various forms.* (1 Peter 4:10)

Showing Christ's love to others: *This is how we know what love is: Jesus Christ laid down his life for us. And we ought to lay down our lives for our brothers and sisters. If anyone has material possessions and sees a brother or sister in need but has no pity on them, how can the love of God be in that person? Dear children, let us not love with words or speech but with actions and in truth.* (1 John 3:16–18)

Those are some great reasons to give and give generously and have LESS. I believe that this actually sets us free to give more than ever before, and to bless others more than ever.

One of the chapters in Jon Acuff's hilarious book, *Stuff Christians Like*, that made me giggle recently was entitled "Being Slightly Annoyed when God asks for More than 10 Percent of Your Money." It is ridiculously funny as the main character Christian is trying to barter with God in this tithing debate and emphasizing his "set in stone" Quicken financial software:

> *See right here, this column that says, 'tithe'? It's automatic. I am automatically firing off a direct deposit to church every month for 10 percent of my salary. Pretty nice, right? But I could just swear I just heard you ask me to give more than 10 percent which is weird because you and I are kind of locked into this 90/10 contract. I keep 90. You keep 10. I'd like to change that, I would; that sounds great, in theory. But 10 percent is in the Bible. And I'm not ready to go against the Bible, soooo let's just stick with our current agreement.*[5]

Extraordinary writing, really funny, but also so close to home. Another funny chapter, called "Refusing to Tithe until You have the Proper Amount of Cheerfulness in your Heart," is worth the read and chuckle.

So, where do we go from here? If we chuck the ten percent out the window, what standards for giving do we have? What do we teach and model to our children? Well, that is the tricky, but amazing, part. It is between you and God. Rich Stearns suggests:

> *What about your giftings? Are you entitled to them to do with as you please, or were they entrusted to you for a purpose, God's purpose? If we see them as God sees them, we must think differently about how we use them: Should I buy this new car? take this vacation? add this new insurance policy? increase my savings account ? Maybe, but not until I prayerfully consider what God would have me do with His money. It's not easy being a steward.*[6]

It isn't easy. If everything I have is really God's, then I actually need to start consulting Him on how I use everything … the other 90 percent as well as my time and my possessions and my talents. That is scary because He might ask something hard. But that is extraordinary because if you think about it that means we mean more to Him than just wanting our money at church.

I want to go back just a little and make sure it is clear that though I do believe that New Covenant Christians are free from "tithing" in a ten percent contract way, that doesn't mean that God's church isn't worth our financial investment or that somehow being free from a tithe means that Jesus should get less. Matthew E. Narramore sums up:

> *Jesus is certainly worthy of a tithe and much more, but his kingdom and priesthood are not based on the tithe. The tithe has no place in it. Everything about tithing is inferior to New Covenant life in Christ. Jesus never called anyone to a ten-percent commitment. His call was to absolute abandonment of all things for him and absolute commitment of all things to him. He never sanctioned the tithe as a standard of giving in his new kingdom that would begin with his resurrection. He required his*

> *followers to forsake all, to give all, and to use all for the accomplishment of his purposes. Paradoxically, he entrusts all things to his disciples to jointly possess with him and use in his service. And the Holy Spirit is now the leader in all matters, not the tithe principle.*[7]

Give As Led by the Spirit

Now that we've torn down the infrastructure that we all felt comfortable with (which I am still mourning, by the way), let's talk a little more about what God desires for us in giving, in contrast to the contract methodology: that we would be sacrificially generous and give willingly as led by the Spirit, give wisely, and give humbly. So what might it look like to be led by God?

> *Now this I say, he who sows sparingly shall also reap sparingly; and he who sows bountifully shall also reap bountifully. Let each one do just as he has purposed in his heart; not grudgingly or under compulsion; for God loves a cheerful giver.* (2 Corinthians 9:6–7)

We can give what we feel God intends for us to give in worship and in joy. Sometimes it may not look very sacrificial because we are using our finances to minister in other ways that God leads, but other times it may look like a big leap of faith. Whatever we do, if we are led by the Lord, joy, hope, and even cheer will follow (even when it hurts a bit).

> *Jesus sat down opposite the place where the offerings were put and watched the crowd putting their money into the temple treasury. Many rich people threw in large amounts. But a poor widow came and put in two very small copper coins, worth only a few cents. Calling his*

> *disciples to him, Jesus said, "Truly I tell you, this poor widow has put more into the treasury than all the others. They all gave out of their wealth; but she, out of her poverty, put in everything—all she had to live on.* (Mark 12:40–44)

We aren't giving under compulsion. The hope is to be *willing* to give everything, if needed, in a spirit of sacrifice and generosity in our giving to three main places: our place of worship, the furtherance of the gospel, and the poor (the second two will often and sometimes ideally be together). It is in this generous giving to these places that we seek wisdom.

Give Wisely

> *If we have sown spiritual seed among you, is it too much if we reap a material harvest from you?* (1 Corinthians 9:11)

We see many examples of giving to the church in the epistles where churches are instructed to give to those who teach them the Word of God. Basically, for us: give to those who spiritually nourish you. Does that just mean your local church? Usually, but not always … and not necessarily exclusively. If you are fed by Compassion Radio or by a parachurch ministry, we are to give there too, or perhaps instead … *as God leads you.* Personally, our family has offered our time and money often in several different places according to what we think is wisest and most efficient. Sometimes we feel led and sometimes it's more just what makes sense to us. God will correct us if we get off track.

> *Because of the service by which you have proved yourselves, others will praise God for the obedience that accompanies your confession of the gospel of Christ, and for your generosity in sharing with them and with everyone else.* (2 Corinthians 9:13)

Other giving, beyond the regular giving to where we are spiritually led, is to the furtherance of the gospel, in word and action, to the ends of the earth. We give both so that people can know Jesus through Scripture, in order to confess His name and be saved, as well as that they might be physically released from the poverty, chains, and sickness that plague their lives and always burdens God's heart.

Give Humbly

> *But who am I, and who are my people, that we should be able to give as generously as this? Everything comes from you, and we have given you only what comes from your hand.* (1 Chronicles 29:14)

I love being the giver. Gift giving is, in fact, my love language, and my friends know that I have a gift for them quite often when I see them (a picture my kid drew, a used book, silly pencils for their kids, whatever). That gift giving comes from me literally thinking about them and wanting to express it.

However, if I can view myself as I ought to in light of God, I am quickly humbled, embarrassed by my false pride. If I remember that everything—I repeat: *everything*—I have is from God, then I not only can give more freely (for it isn't mine to be selfish with), but I see myself on more of a level playing field with those I am giving to.

What *Too Much* Does

Having so much in America is a blessing—no doubt. We have opportunities, warm homes, education, and the ability to give a lot to God's work. However, having too much has quite possibly hurt us. We have too much stuff, too much control over our lives, too much money, too much on our calendar. Too much! Our churches have too much sometimes, too, with our desire for the newest technology, products, etc.

Quickly, let me clarify: Being rich obviously isn't bad. Ronald J. Sider writes:

> *Prosperity and wealth, on the other hand, are good and desirable. God repeatedly promised his people Israel that obedience would bring abundant prosperity in a land flowing with milk and honey (Deuteronomy 6:1–3) ... But the threat of curse always accompanied the promise of blessing (Deuteronomy 6:14–15; 8:11–20; 28:15–68). One of God's most frequent commands to his people was to feed the hungry and to seek justice for the poor....biblical texts warn of God's punishment of those who neglected or oppressed the poor and tell us that material abundance results from obedience. The two statements, however, are not contradictory. Both are true. It is the biblical balance that we need.*[8]

I know some rich Christians who are incredibly generous with their money, outrageously blessing others with the gifts God has given them in wise, glorifying, and sacrificial ways. I know it can be done. Those people amaze me, and I ask God's continual blessings on them because I think He knew that they could handle their finances wisely, where I would possibly struggle. The issue is our hearts and our response to wealth, not the money itself. It is our desire for it, our selfishness with it, our control over it, and our obsession for it that is the problem.

What L.E.S.S. Can Do

Besides just living a life God might have planned for us, I want to suggest a few more impacts that being a generous giver and wise spender can have on your life:

First, when you give your money over to God or write a crazy-big check to a charity, you can feel an instant surrender to the Joneses. I don't mean "Jones" literally, but figuratively as those around us we try to keep up with. If you are like me, it is rarely one person in particular, but a collection of people in our lives meshed into one illusive, impossible person that we will never match. So I shout, "I give up. They win." I choose (at least I try to choose) a different path.

Second, making a life change toward giving more and spending less means a life change to simplicity. You may find that giving away your money and your stuff is actually remarkably freeing. Seriously, the less stuff I have, the less I have to dust, keep track of, keep in good condition, get mad that the kids ruin, wonder if a friend ever returned to me, etc.

My friend, Mandy, seeks to live by a principle: "*Live simply so others can simply live.*"

I have seen her intentionally try to wrestle with this idea because of her family's love for God and for His hurting people all over the world. She thinks through if she should cover the cushions on her chairs because they surely are good enough for a while longer because people around the world don't have chairs at all. Mandy uses her amazing talent of crocheting to raise money for a missionary friend or to give incredible gifts freely to those around her. She acknowledged that making a "mission" as a family (a goal for what their family was about) was an important step for making all their other financial and time decisions. If the extra items or activities (though so many things are neat and great) didn't fit in their mission as a family, then they don't do it. Simplicity. I love it and am trying it myself now.

I have gotten a plaque of this quote and put it in my home so it stares back at me: "*Live simply so others can simply live.*" (…because you know, that makes sense right? Spend money to buy the plaque to remind me to not buy things. Hmm. I'm learning). The quote's bluntness and challenge on my multi-tasking, over-extended life is painful at times and it (along with my friend Mandy) has caused me to re-evaluate many previously perceived priorities. It has recently caused me to choose to forgo a family vacation to give to the relief of those in Iraq and Syria. It was costly not just to me, but my kids, but we can never truly regret it. So, miracles do happen – even in our own hearts.

Lastly, if I can live on less, I am doing my children a huge favor. Honestly, this may not be a giving motive at all, but in terms of parenting, our generation's recipient of giving is our children (of toys, activities, multimedia, everything). If I can help my children to be joyful with little (which means I have to be the same), work hard, love God, and share what they do have with others, then I believe they will do well in whatever economy they find themselves. If they do find themselves in a good economy with a good income, all the better because they won't have as many wants and can give more.

Thank you for reading this chapter of the book. The foundational purpose of this "awkward conversation" chapter is simply that I am passionate about my kids serving the poor in obedience to God. Money needs to be discussed because it occupies so much of our heart and can be a great blessing or barrier to God's best in ourselves and children. I want *life* for our kids and nothing less than that.

> *Command those who are rich in this present world not to be arrogant nor to put their hope in wealth, which is so uncertain, but to put their hope in God, who richly provides us with everything for our enjoyment. Command them to do good, to be rich in good deeds, and to be generous and willing to share. In this way they will lay up treasure for themselves as a firm foundation for the coming age, so that they may take hold of the life that is truly life.* (1 Timothy 6:17–19)

Here are some finely written words from Jen Hatmaker:

> *Jesus never utters a positive word about the wealthy, only tons of parables with us as the punch line and this observation: IT IS terribly hard for us to receive His kingdom, harder than shoving a camel through the eye of a needle. That's really hard. If this is true, then more than*

> *fearing poverty or simplicity, we should fear prosperity. Shall we stop imagining these sad, sorry, rich people belong to a different demographic? A brave believer admits, 'He's talking about me.' Look at our houses, cars, closets, our luxuries; If we are not rich, then no one is. If we aren't swept up in entitlement, indulgence, and extravagance, then Jesus is a fool, and let's get back to living. If tithing the minimum and consuming the rest is okay, then we can dismiss Jesus' ideas and act obsessed about other stuff He said. But what if? What if we are actually called to a radical life? What if Jesus knew our Christian culture would design a lovely life template complete with all the privileges and exemptions we want, but even with that widespread approval, He still expected radical simplicity, radical generosity, radical obedience from those with ears to hear, eyes to see? What if we are camels, on this side of the needle, dangerously content with our fake gospel and avoiding the actual Christian life described in Scripture?*[9]

It requires sacrifice and less frivolous living (fewer activities and things) perhaps, but that is worship to my God. I won't make decisions out of guilt though either, but seek the Spirit's leading with my family. I want to look my God in the eye with my whole life and not fear being the camel looking in the eye of the needle.

Tangible Acts in Response to L.E.S.S.:

1. **Clean your house out!**
2. **Make a big donation in response to God in love!**

Chapter 14
Exposure and Education—Introduction

The truth does not change according to our ability to stomach it.
–Flannery O'Conner

I need to warn you that once you teach your kids about global issues, you become a target for awkward social situations. Luckily for me, it's mostly my husband who has been with the kids when misfit moments occur. They look something like this:

My husband took our daughter to her kindergarten soccer game because I was working. Unfortunately, she had forgotten her reusable water bottle. Seeing Adelaine dramatically thirsty, a sweet little Indian girl on her team offered her bottled water. My son, Lukas (who was appalled by the bottled water info we had all learned), yelled to Adelaine, "You can't take that bottled water! It is taking water from the poor!"

Well, my son meant that drinking bottled water "votes" for it and perpetuates an industry that is literally taking clean water from the poor (see the end of the last chapter). However, no one would *ever* think that that was what he meant, and it looks really random and awkward that my son is telling my daughter not to take the water from the poor (when she is literally taking it out of the hands of a little Indian girl). So, the Indian family wasn't understanding what was going on and why my son seemed to be calling them poor (when I think they had way more money than we did) and *no one* could understand why Lukas would not let Adelaine take one tiny drink of water, mumbling pathetically in repetition "taking it from the poor" as Adam is trying to box him out of the interaction, threatening punishments if he doesn't keep his mouth shut. Can you picture it? Cultural confusion and parental heroism on so many levels, yes?

My children may be demented, but it makes for some humorous moments (especially when my husband has to cope). Those are my favorites!

But in all seriousness (though the above story is true), my daughter is very passionate about water. She did her science experiment on it and presented on the global water issues to a large Science Fair (and she is 5!). No need to mention that my son's experiment that time was called "How best to hit my sister with a marshmallow," rating different sling shots, catapults, and blowguns for nailing his sister with a marshmallow.

While we all want our children to have empathy and convictions; we definitely don't tend to run toward teaching our children about painful topics. However, the reality is that our children cannot know about these R-rated topics in a G-rated Christian culture unless we bridge it with them. Tim Kimmel writes, "We need kids who challenge entitlement and develop strong empathy—the ability to *feel with* and *feel for* others, even who those are drastically different from themselves."[1]

Developing this in our children is challenging our youth in America are the richest in the world. Their problems and concerns are so separate from the majority of the world—particularly anyone living in poverty, *we have to go to extra effort for them to learn about and enter into any experience of poverty.*

Experience

My friend, Kerrie, had her kids do a walk for water down to a local river every day throughout Lent one season. It was impactful for their whole family and for those who asked them about it while they were on their walk.

My friend, Barbara, used to lead an experience focusing on the Underground Railroad as part of a historical camp. Though some may be uncomfortable with the idea, there is something profound about having youth participate in an experience where they are yelled at by slave traders, have to track a trail at night to escape to freedom, and hide huddled up in the dark from someone knocking on a door. Yeah, they would be scared, and we don't like when our kids are scared, but *those* are the kids who will stand up next for someone else who is scared and who will sacrifice for the freedom of others because they have felt it. A great quote from Atticus Finch from *To Kill a Mockingbird:* "If you can learn a simple trick, Scout, you'll get along a lot better with all kinds of folks. You never really understand a person until you consider things from his point of view, until you climb inside of his skin and walk around in it."[2]

After I saw Barbara lead youth in a similar experience as part of an understanding of the modern underground church, I haven't been able to read *Voice of the Martyrs* magazine the same A mere 30 minute game changed me because I experienced a little bit more, for a moment.

> *"The word compassion is derived from the Latin words pati and cum, which together mean 'to suffer with'. Compassion asks us to go where it hurts to enter into places of pain, to share in brokenness, fear, confusion, and anguish. Compassion challenges us to cry out with those in misery, to mourn with those who are lonely, to weep with those in tears. Compassion requires us to be weak with the weak, vulnerable with the vulnerable, and powerless with the powerless. Compassion means full immersion in the condition of being human."*[3]

Compassion changes us. We aren't so judgmental. We do feel things deeply—sadness, anger, sometimes fear, but compassion moves us into action. "Scripture scholars connect the word to the entrails, to the bowels, from the deepest part of the person. This was how Jesus was moved, from the entirety of his being."[4] Empathy and compassion occur in inward struggle.

Mary Gordon (founder of Roots of Empathy, a children's program about modeling empathy) grew up in Newfoundland in a multigenerational family with a mentally disabled uncle and was always taking in strays (unwed mothers, homeless):

> *"Young Mary often tagged along as her mother visited the poor, bringing food, clothing, and coal to heat their houses, which were often dark, damp, and cold…On some weekends, she'd go with her father to visit the sick in the hospital, often reading aloud to them … And although all this charitable work might sound grim or self-sacrificing, Gordon's family infused it with pleasure and humor so that's how the children perceived it, too. The visits were enjoyable social experiences—they liked accompanying Mom or Dad somewhere; it was fun, not a dull duty…all five of the family's children carry on their parents' mission in some way."*[5]

Relationship

Through struggling with others, "issues" become personal. "Rather than look away from such ugliness, Christians have to actually go looking for it."[6]

Where do you start? In your own city there are loads of ministries to join (nursing homes, homeless ministries, battered women's homes, inner-city kids' camps, ESL for refugees or immigrants). There are others that can come to you (foster children, your dinner table guests, opening a food or clothing ministry in your home). Get their names, learn their stories, make room in your lives for this.

Internationally, I can't express how much I love child sponsorship. I remember growing up and seeing commercials on TV from other organizations for sponsorship and I didn't really understand it. The sad pictures of kids playing in the dirt, wiping their runny noses with flies around were depressing for sure, but I didn't understand how sponsorship went from that to community transformation. Now, sponsorship is my weakness, the kind of shopping that I don't feel guilty about when I come home with another sponsorship packet, even if I have to adjust our finances.

What is crazy about sponsorship is that it isn't just about the children sponsored—or even whole villages changed with ripple effects that make sponsorship just smart giving and smart stewardship. No, that isn't all. Like so many things that God asks of us, like giving, we are *so blessed* ourselves in return.

For the past four years (since my daughter was three and my son was five), both children have had sponsored children their exact ages born on their exact birthdays. At the time, I just thought that it would be good for them to grow up with a minimal pen-pal relationship with someone who was born in a very different situation. I longed for them to have perspective, but it has turned into so much more.

They indeed started writing … my daughter drew pictures and even at the age of three wanted to send packages to Yinith in Honduras (I had to convince her that that we didn't need to send her some bugs at one point and often have to deter her from thinking we can send huge boxes of her toys and dolls).

Then the responses came: letters and pictures that made connections for my children that I cannot quite explain. Morapeli held the matching shirt we sent that Lukas also was wearing. Adelaine held a picture of Yinith who in turn was holding a picture of Adelaine. Thus the cycle has continued. These were real friends, real kids, that they wrote to and cared about.

Lukas once wrote about his sponsored friend: "I care about Morapeli. I hope to meet him someday. God loves him. We are the same."

While clearly there are so many things that make my children and sponsored children worlds apart and in many ways *not the same,* it is that fact that God *loves them all* that makes them the same.

A teenager named Jenell Giannini, part of *The Zambia Project*, writes about his experience of a relationship. "Meeting Leviticus made poverty a personal issue. I cannot live as if his problems have nothing to do with me. Those problems are my problems."[7] When numbers or issues are translated into one story, person, life, and friend, not only is it personal and approachable, it is necessary. It requires our response. Kay Warren bravely asks:

> *You can watch a news special on TV, read an article in a magazine, or download a video from the internet and become disturbed by the suffering in our world. But to become ruined, you'll have to actually do something ...anything that puts you in direct contact with hurting people. As long as suffering people are a mere statistic to you, you will never become ruined for life as you know it.*[8]

Our good friends, Todd and Thao Green, attended a food-packing event and reflected on conversations later about it with their six-year-old son. Todd writes in a reflective email:

> *We took the kids to help with an organization called 'Kids Against Hunger.' Here we received some information*

about poverty and hunger and then did some hands on work helping to pack bags of dehydrated chicken, vegetables, soy, and rice, that were boxed to be shipped to a poor country; I think it was Haiti. Johnathan got into the action; Amelia (a toddler) just enjoyed running around the room.

For dinner, Johnathan and I cooked hot dogs and marshmallows over an open fire. Then Johnathan went walking around in the woods behind the house. He found the old dug well that the house originally used that was abandoned long ago.

He asked: 'Do all people live in houses?'

(I was pretty much done with wanting to think about poverty for the day) so I said 'no some people live in condos or apartments'.

He said: 'No I mean do all people have a roof to keep the rain off their head?'

I said: 'No, some people have tee-pees or igloos. Do you know what an igloo is?'

'No Daddy, do some people not have any place to keep the rain off their head?'

'Well yes, some people have no place…maybe they live under a bridge or something". 'But I don't think the bridge will keep all the rain off'

'Yeah, you are right'

'Do these people know anybody?', he asked.

'I don't know'

'Well if anybody knows them they should have them come live in their house', he concluded.

'That would be very nice, wouldn't it?'

While children may be very naïve, perhaps….Johnathan is a teacher to me. Jesus said 'unless you turn and become like little children, you will not enter the kingdom of heaven."

We can learn so much from our kids. We are also so blessed by the resources available today to empower and engage youth to change the world *now*. Most I have read or heard about somewhere, though I can't recall them all. I have a much more exhaustive list that I am happy to email personally (annagoodworth@hotmail.com), but here is a starter to show some of the range of avenues to expose our kids in home and church settings to both of these hard topics and God's heart of redemption.

Organizations with Specific Curriculum for Kids:
RedCardKids (8 week DVD interactive curriculum).
Weave (A Blog with ideas on it)
Justice Kids (Activities/teaching to buy)
Harvest Ministries
- free downloadable curriculum

Compassion International and World Vision resources
YWAM and Kids of Courage (under Voice of the Martyrs)
- free and purchasable resources

Slavery:
DO: Underground Railroad Re-enactment or visit a historic trail
GO: Go to representatives and senators to advocate for those in slavery with petitions
WATCH: Stolen Childhoods DVD
READ: Iqbal or The Carpet Boy's Gift

Poverty:
DO: Go barefoot for a week (feel for those without shoes)
DO: Build a community development project with Legos
DO: Wear the same clothes for a week…wash by hand
GO: Visit an AIDS clinic here. Contrast with AIDS in Africa
CRAFT: Make soccer balls out of plastic bags like in developing world countries (GAME—play soccer with it)
CRAFT: Give kids a bunch of recyclables that they have to make toys out of (Recycled magazine bead necklaces are really fun, as are cardboard box cars with bottle top lids as wheels.)
LEARN: Where you are among the wealthiest in the world:
GAME: Tribe by World Vision
WATCH: Journey to Jamaa at www.jamaa.worldvision.org or 58

Water:
DO: Do a Walk for Water
DO: Don't use water in your home for a week. Walk to a friends' house for a week for your water supply for all your needs.
Chart Water Use in Your home & compare it to other countries.
LEARN: Learn about bottled water (*The Water Project* website has a great deal of resources).
READ: A Long Walk to Water
WATCH: Sabina's Shoes on YouTube

Girls:
DO: Host a WAR (Women at Risk) party to purchase these items made by women at risk while learning about them
WATCH: Girl Rising
READ: Beatrice's Goat
GAME: Play a game (maybe a scavenger hunt of needed items), but give all the girls their instructions in a gibberish language

Hunger:
WATCH or DO: 30-Hour Famine Videos through World Vision
GAME: Split up kids and give some lots of animal crackers, some a few, some one or none to represent the distribution of food. Let them discuss their reactions to their differing food amounts and then reveal the hunger levels of different countries.
DO: Rice/Beans for a Month or Famine meal of Cornmeal/Soy Mush
READ: The Good Garden
DO: Digging out of recyclables for money or food tokens

Refugees of War/Immigrants:
GAME: Pack up a suitcase quickly as if having to flee in war
DO: Visit and serve a refugee family that recently moved here
GAME: Blindfold a child. Put balls on the ground in front of him/her and a prize somewhere around too. The balls represent mines that could kill or injure the child, but the prize is food (that the child's family desperately needs).
READ: Four Feet, Two Sandals
WATCH: Under the Same Moon

Homeless:
DO: Eat out of can of beans/sleep on cardboard
GAME: Building a home out of different trash-like materials
GO: Sleep in a hostel downtown somewhere, visit urban ministries down there, and prayer walk!
CRAFT: Make homeless packs of food/toiletries with cards for homeless you might meet
WATCH: Pursuit of Happyness
READ: A Shelter in Our Car

Persecution/Faith:
GAME: Underground Church Service—Make secret signs to find the church, share small verse during the quiet, Have it get interrupted by the "police".
CRAFT: Make parachutes for Bibles dropping down in closed countries—Voice of the Martyrs
DO: Write to prisoners from Voice of the Martyrs to see how precious and costly faith is.
READ: Window on the World Book about people of the world or Voice of the Martyrs Magazine
WATCH: Voice of the Martyrs animated movies

Exhibits around the country that allow you to walk through the stories and sights/sounds of poverty and oppression:
World Vision AIDS Experience Exhibit (traveling)
REAL Life Exhibit with Medical Teams International in Oregon
Traveling Compassion Int. Experience
Wayumi in Pennsylvania – a retreat center of New Tribes Missions teaching about indigenous people

We also can continually engage all of these issues in a powerful way by supporting missionaries through letters, emails, prayer, money, and care packages. Also, by hosting missionaries on furlough and interacting with them and their children, we make another channel both into different lands and lives spiritually that

God can use to work for His Kingdom, for ourselves, and for our children. A man who was raised in a missions-loving family recalls:

> *I remember even at that young age seeing the poverty and wondering how the people lived with it. That memory has stayed with me throughout my life. Another thing I remember is that we had people from other countries in our home all the time. The stories I heard, especially around the dinner table, were fascinating. I would sit there as long as our guests did, not wanting to miss anything. Those times taught me at a very early age to accept cultural diversity. More importantly, they made me realize that not everyone in the world knows about Jesus, but they need to. When they learn about him, their lives are transformed.*[9]

My friend, Eve, includes the missionaries they support in their homeschooling, doing unit studies on the places their missionaries live. This way they can pray better for the gospel to be preached and received. They are reaching out more to the missionary and these relationships with their families are becoming richer.

We've sent packages to missionary families we know in the field, and it is a blast to put those together specifically according to their needs and desires (along with some extra treats). We were blessed recently to host dinners for missionaries who were home. In this case, I don't know how much it affected my kids, but the experience humbled and blew me away.

Raise a Fighter

When my close friend's son, Grant, was six he attended a Christian kindergarten. The teacher ritualistically and graciously asked the kids if anyone had prayer requests each morning. One day, she asked just like normal if they wanted to share any requests with the class, so she could quickly pray and get on with the days' busy lesson plan. She understandably expected the normal such as "Please pray for my grandma. She is sick" from the sincere kid and maybe "I pray we learn a lot today" from the teacher's pet or "I pray that we'd all know Jesus more today" from the over-spiritual kid that is punching the kid next to him. On this day, Grant raises his hand with a *very serious* prayer request. He announces that he really needs prayer for something. He asks (with total sincerity and passion for the entire class's prayers) that others would intercede that "Jesus would help my Jedi Skills." Love. That. Kid.

Our boys have an innate desire to fight for justice. You see it on the playground. You see it in their imaginative play when they're alone in their rooms and some Lego mini-figure heads fly off. They always want to know which side are the heroes and which side are the bad guys to be destroyed. We sometimes like to act like we don't give in to violent toys or movies for our kids and yet somehow mysteriously our kids totally still dress up as Spiderman for Halloween. We secretly love the hero play!

We know there is a spiritual battle out there. We understand that our kids need heroes. We love seeing them excited and with capes on. We want to empower them to be heroes. Who are they to fight if we don't tell them who the bad guys are? If we don't tell them who the ultimate bad guy is? It seems sometimes like we are so scared to talk about Satan (for fear that they'll have nightmares … as if they don't already come up with things to have nightmares about) or talk about bad things, like disease, natural disasters, sin, and sinful people. Our kids are not as naïve as we sometimes think; they already know this world isn't right! If you ever have the news on, if you ever let them watch any Disney movie, if you ever let them hear about missions at church, if you actually allow them to read the Bible (even the Easter and Christmas story), or heck, if you ever let them walk out the front door, they *know* that something isn't right in this world. Their soul tells them it isn't right here. Their soul tells them there is something they must fight. Let's give words (yes, of course, age-appropriate words—I'm not psycho) to what they see and be empowered to do something about it.

It isn't just our boys. Our girls have the same desire to fight and also often a desire to teach, take care of the sick, be motherly, etc. With girls, whether it is giving a bigger glimpse into how taking care of a little baby doll now could someday be a little orphaned child, or how tending to the "owie" of a stuffed puppy dog could someday be tending to the wounds of people in a country they can't spell, or how wanting to fight with swords against the bad guy now is part of a good desire to stand for good ideas in days to come, let's give our little girls a strong voice *now*!

Why not? Or they could just instead spend the days dreaming of being Snow White, waiting around to be kissed, for some guy to be the hero of their story.

I know these are big topics and hard things to share with our children. But, we *don't* need to be scared of their response. Their response is actually the most important part! In the following chapters, I will approach the possible reactions that we are nervous about as our children could experience fear, sadness, anger, or, worst of all, apathy about these hard global issues. Read further about each in the following chapters.

Tangible Acts in Response to L.E.S.S.:

1. **Experience missions through sights, sounds, smells, and tastes. Go to restaurants, get some CDs from the library, and read about people of the 10/40 window or places your family supports. Make connections!**

2. **Decorate your home missionally with time zone clocks, a huge map (with locations of people you support in prayers, finances, etc.), items from cultures (that don't have anti-Christian spiritual components (i.e., probably not the Buddha statue), with kids of other races/countries in your pictures/movies, etc.**

Chapter 15

Exposure—Scared of the Dark

Courage is not the absence of fear, but rather the judgment that something else is more important than fear.

–Ambrose Redmoon

When my son was going to a public school a couple of years ago, he experienced some extreme anxiety over a number of issues, exhibited mostly in stomachaches at night and in the morning on school days. Not only did his speech delay make him scared to speak in front of others, but he was awkward socially *and* he had gotten lost in his school several times.

We tried a number of different strategies to ease his anxiety: prayers, talking with him, imagining how his day could go well, or just plain distraction. One of our favorite distractions in all circumstances is in the form of stories, particularly *Adventures in Odyssey* audio stories.

One morning, when Lukas's stomachache seemed particularly bad, we happened upon a story about Joshua. It was a story about courage, but somehow in all of my readings of that story, I had totally missed one of the glaring themes of it. It wasn't about Joshua being brave, it was about God assuring him that he could have confidence because *God* was with him. He didn't just say "Be brave" for bravery's sake. He said, "Have courage for I am with you." He didn't just say it once (to this big Bible hero we esteem in our minds), but several times! It wasn't that the angel had a social disorder problem of repeating to himself or that the scribes wanted to use up precious papyrus space in writing more of the story. Therefore, the truth must be that Joshua needed to hear it several times! He had either forgotten to have courage or remained afraid after the first encouragement. Perhaps, just perhaps, he was like all of us where he hears something and believes it for a moment, but then doubts it or questions himself. So, I find God is kind to say again and again:

> *Have I not commanded you? Be strong and courageous.*
> *Do not be afraid; do not be discouraged, for*
> *the LORD your God will be with you wherever you go.*
> (Joshua 1:9)

We don't need to be afraid of the darkness of the world. That doesn't mean that we walk into dark alleys without precaution or that we don't use wisdom when taking international trips to dangerous countries. What it means is that we can have courage—not some fake confidence that we muster up or some superhero strength that we can never achieve, but confidence that *God is with us*. And guess what? He is with our kids, too. But that one is harder, isn't it?

In our battle to release our fears to God, we can model our faith and courage to our kids—not because of anything we or they can do, but because of who *God is*. Because *He is with them*. In all of these hard topics of orphans, hunger, disease, and war, it is understandable to be nervous that our children will have reactions of fear. However, I believe that we can model to our children at a very young age how to respond to some of those fears.

Parents can downplay hurricanes and plane crashes and diseases, fearing that their children will be scared. Every parent must decide what is right for their own child's emotional coping skills. However, sometimes I also think that these moments are precious opportunities to model how we can pray and ask God for protection and then after that to thank Him for it. Well, you ask, what if someone they know does die in a hurricane? What if something bad does actually happen? Will it mess up their view of God? Maybe. I guess, personally, I just figure it is better to acknowledge and engage those hard realities slowly as they grow than in one big swoop of a crisis of faith outside the home in college or during rebellious years when many are confronted with the reality that evil exists in God's good creation and that God does allow bad things to happen to good people. I want my kids to see that it is safe, appropriate, productive, and even good for me to struggle before God, cry out before Him as they grow up—and that they may do the same as they need to.

The Butt-Kicker

When my son was six, he went through the typical fear of being scared of the dark, thinking he heard something in his room. I've heard many strategies for handling this, but the one that seemed to work the best for us was telling my son that "God kicks Satan's butt." Due to the amount of giggling this produced (which also alleviates fear), this has become a common term in our home. The kids have learned that they can yell into the darkness that "God Wins," that "Jesus's blood covers our home," that "Evil must leave because Jesus is with me," that "Satan is a stinky face and has to leave," and yes, that "God kicks Satan's butt." He is the ultimate Butt-Kicker and *victor*! We do not need to be afraid, for *God is with us.*

> *I have told you these things, so that in me you may have peace. In this world you will have trouble. But take heart! I have overcome the world.* (John 16:33)
>
> *For I am convinced that neither death nor life, neither angels nor demons, neither the present nor the future, nor any powers, neither height nor depth, nor anything else in all creation, will be able to separate us from the love of God that is in Christ Jesus our Lord.* (Romans 8:38-39)

After the shooting at Sandy Hook elementary school, Ann Voskamp gave one of the best explanations of evil in this world I've ever heard. As my daughter asked (at the age of five), "If

Jesus died on the cross, why is there still sin and evil?" Great question, Honey! This analogy, I think, is excellent:

> *I remember it—how a missionary told of this snake—longer than a man—that slithered its way right through their front door and straight to the kitchen. How she had RUN outside screaming and a machete-wielding neighbor had calmly walked into her kitchen and he sliced off the head of the reptilian thing.*
>
> *But a snake's neurology and blood flow make it such that it slithers wild even after it's been sliced headless. For hours the missionary stood outside. And the body of the snake rampaged on, thrashing hard against windows and walls, destroying chairs and table and all things good and home.*
>
> ***A snake can wreak havoc until it accepts it has no head, that it's really dead.***
> ***The answer to our suffering is so incomprehensible that it has to be incarnated, the Word must come to us as flesh.*** *The Truest Answer always comes in Story. And that Story that begins in Genesis 3:15 with God's promise to the snake: "he will crush your head, and you will strike his heel," it ends in Revelation with nothing less than Christmas.*[1]

This victorious perspective is not only accurate, but also a huge help in alleviating fear of what the end of this hero story is.

Essentials We Often Overlook

Our kids have spiritual power. We can train our children to *pray*! We want to raise children to be adults who know how to pray, but about what? The early church wasn't a world of peace and sheltering of children. Faith and strong believers grew out of experience and usually out of trial. The early church in persecution grew quicker than it ever did after it was legal. Still does. Let us teach them to pray and be aware of the spiritual world (ignorance is not innocence always) "*in order that Satan might not outwit us. For we are not unaware of his schemes.*" (2 Cor. 2:1). These tiny people or crazy teenagers, if followers of Christ, have spiritual power! "Taking authority simply means commanding, out loud, any actual or potential activity of the Enemy to be shut down, as seen in Matthew 4:10; Luke 10:19; Acts 19:18; James 4:7; and 1 Peter 5:9."[2]

There are plenty of youth in the Bible that did brave things, like David, Daniel, Mary, and Gideon, that can be spiritual examples of facing evil. There are so many kids in other countries still today through Voice of the Martyrs and other mission organizations that could be unbelievable role models of faith, struggle, and courage in the midst of spiritual or actual war.

So in light of the response of fear, with the reality that God wins, we can remind and reassure our children also that God *will make things right*. These hard realities are not the end of the story, and our children have a part to play to make things right again. We love talking about the beginning of the Bible, the creation story (we Christians certainly love to argue about exactly how and how long it took for it all to happen), but the end of the story is some of the best stuff! This is amazing and gives me great courage: both the role we play and, most of all, God's promise to redeem! He will wipe away every tear, give justice for evil, heal our bodies, and restore families. It is the middle that is the hardest to cope with. Contemporary theologian, Os Guinness, sums it up perfectly (please read it all):

> *Facing up to human evil—and especially the magnitude and malevolence of contemporary evil—is disturbing....Finding the words to come to terms with the unspeakable is crucial to facing up to it and to overcoming the fear that is so widespread in today's world, but exploring the challenge of evil need not be depressing; indeed, it may be bracing, even inspiring. For some people, evil is the rock against which their faith stumbles, never to rise again. But for others, and probably for the majority, it simply is not. The stumbling block becomes the stepping stones to real and deeper faith.*[3]

God is so gracious to include us in His redemption of this earth. If we can model, train, and send our kids out in ways that help them change the things that we find so horrible, they not only may rely more on God, but also find their purpose in life and fight fear with the abilities that God has given all of us.

Tangible Acts in Response to L.E.S.S.:

1. **Memorize verses on God's Providence and protection like *"When I am afraid, I put my trust in you." –Psalm 56:3***

2. **Put it into practice! Share fears you have with your children. Ask them theirs. Pray with your kids in spiritual power about those fears.**

Chapter 16

Exposure—Love Hurts

In suffering with somebody, we take it into our own hands to suffer. We choose to do what we do not have to do, or even want to do; we walk, eyes wide open, into the pain of another human being and claim it as our own.

–Lewis Swedes

One night when I was visiting my family, of which only some express a desire to follow Jesus, my son (six at the time) was going to bed. He called me into the room he was sleeping in and asked me some hard questions about my family and their faith. Though I was very uncomfortable, I felt I should give him honest answers.

"But Mama, they have to know how much God loves them. We have to tell them Jesus died for them. It will change everything." I tried to explain to him that not only would that appear very judgmental, but that I had in fact done that before and they had been angry with me for it.

My son began to weep, pretty uncontrollably. I felt very conflicted at that moment. Should I have not told him? Any non-Christian would condemn me for sure and many Christians would have softened and clarified it more. I felt *extremely* self-conscious being at my parents' house, while they were so generous, loving them so much, and now burdening my son with some of the hard things about my family, especially their relationships with God.

After sobbing, he asked, "Do you pray for them, Mama?"

I was a little stumped. I mean, I *do* pray, but it is hard to pray in angst over and over on things that you are too scared to hope about. I'm embarrassed to say that I am not consistent in my intercession for them, but it is true. I said, "I do, Lukas, but not all the time. It's just hard."

He just took a deep breath and said, "Fine, Mama, then **I** will pray."

So there in a dark room, I held my 6 six-year-old son as he began to pray one of the most extraordinarily deep prayers I've ever experienced in my life. He wept and I wept. He gave words to desires in my heart that I have lacked the faith to pray. I was so humbled by him as he uttered the groaning of my heart for the family I love so deeply and would die for.

It was a hard night, but a beautiful night. I was grateful for it, but still had a hard time whenever I tried to explain it to others who questioned how much I should "burden" my kids.

However, a few months later we found out that God had done something remarkable in one of my family members that we hadn't known about … that this answered prayer had actually happened shortly after Lukas' prayer. I truly believe God responded to my son's prayers. When we told Lukas about the effect of his prayers, he was so grateful and had a newfound desire to pray (as did I).

There is no way around it: the burden of sorrow is hard, especially if we think about it for the kids in our life. But that "burden" can be a gift. It is a gift of love, an entry into prayer, and a communion with God that I would never take away from my son's story. Ann Dunagan summarizes it perfectly: "We must realize that the prayers of a child—even the prayers of *our* children—could change lives and impact nations! A child's simple trust may even challenge and encourage us to rise to a higher level of faith."[1]

One verse we have on the wall in our home overwhelms my soul:

> *He has shown you, O mortal, what is good. And what does the* LORD *require of you?To act justly and to love mercy and to walk humbly with your God.* (Micah 6:8)

What does it mean to "love mercy"? Isn't that extraordinary? To actually "love mercy." How do we begin to teach that? It may be allowing God and the suffering of others to shape it in them.

Usually when our children cry, we want to help them find a way out of their tears. Therefore, it seems absolutely cruel and almost unmotherly to walk with them into something that we know will hurt them, yet we are told that we are to "love mercy." We are to love mercy like Jesus did. But mercy hurts.

Mercy isn't just giving a cold drink to someone or bandaging a wound. Mercy costs us. Cory Trenda writes: "In many ways this same ministry, the ministry of touch, of tears, and of blood, is the ministry to which we are all called. It is the way Jesus ministered in His compassionate identification with the broken and suffering. He came, He touched, He wept, and He bled. And He calls us to do the same. It is the way of the cross."[2]

Love Mercy

Jesus's example of loving mercy is kind of shocking, actually. At least for me, as I don't usually think of Jesus crying. We all pretty much know he wept for Lazarus (I mean, it is the shortest verse in the Bible and we all memorized it for an easy Sunday School out, right?). But do we understand that he didn't necessarily weep for his friend whom he knew he would soon raise up, but for the human condition of death and suffering? But what else? Jesus's compassion over Jerusalem is noteworthy:

> *As he approached Jerusalem and saw the city, he wept over it and said, "If you, even you, had only known on this day what would bring you peace—but now it is hidden from your eyes*. (Luke 19:41–42)

Very much like when we are overwhelmed by the lost and suffering in the world and crumble up in a ball of tears, Jesus—both man and God—wept. He wept for sin and darkness, for our whole human condition. But the sorrow burdened him … all the way to the cross.

> *He himself bore our sins in his body on the cross, so that we might die to sins and live for righteousness; 'by his wounds you have been healed.'* (1 Peter 2:24)
>
> *Surely he took up our pain and bore our suffering, yet we considered him punished by God, stricken by him, and afflicted. But he was pierced for our transgressions, he was crushed for our iniquities; the punishment that brought us peace was on him, and by his wounds we are healed. We all, like sheep, have gone astray, each of us has turned to our own way; and the LORD has laid on him the iniquity of us all.* (Isaiah 53:4–6)

So when we see our broken world, do we weep? Pastor Tom Davis, author of *Fields of the Fatherless*, asks:

> *Do we cry for the child in Honduras whose only source of sustenance is the trash heap he lives on? Does our soul ache for the infant who is abandoned on the side of a drift trail in India, screaming for a meal from her mother, until she screams her last scream? Why doesn't our heart hurt more for those who are starving to death by the thousands, for children living in the slums because they have no parents, for young girls in Thailand sold into prostitution by their fathers for only a month's wage?*[3]

Our children don't need to know the full depths of these horrors when they are little, but some sorrows of the world are inevitably around us. The question is: do we believe that the call to love mercy through suffering is worth it for our kids? John Piper shares, "The call to suffer with Christ is not a call to bear our sins the way he bore them but to love the way he loved. The death of Christ for the sin of my selfishness is not meant to help me escape the suffering of love but to enable it."[4] Consider the calls on the church and prophets to be burdened for the lost and suffering … these are our heroes:

> *Yet when they were ill, I put on sackcloth and humbled myself with fasting.* (Psalm 35:13)
>
> *Oh, that my head were a spring of water and my eyes a fountain of tears! I would weep day and night for the slain of my people.* (Jeremiah 9:1)
>
> *Rejoice with those who rejoice; mourn with those who mourn.* (Romans 12:15)
>
> *Remember those in prison as if you were their fellow prisoners, and those who are mistreated as if you yourselves were suffering.* (Hebrews 13:3)

In another story where I appeared as the torturous parent, I let my children watch *Kung Fu Panda 2*. Now, while some may raise an eyebrow at the fact that I let them watch an animated movie that turned out to be quite violent (lay off the judgment!), fear wasn't the unexpected suffering. I was in the kitchen making dinner and I suddenly heard Lukas (age seven at the time) wail like I had never heard him cry. I swore he must have just severed his leg off with a cry like the one I heard, so I dropped everything and darted into the living room. For what felt like an eternity through his hyperventilating sobs, I tried to figure out what happened. I *finally* got him to explain that it was the movie he was crying about. He kept saying that "Po" the panda was left as a baby. To understand what he meant, I rewound the movie and watched.

(Yes I'm going to explain a scene from *Kung Fu Panda 2*). Po is having a memory about how he became an orphan. Some wolves (I think) were doing awful things in his village and his mother was running to safety with Po. The wolves got close, so the mother hid Po in a cart with vegetables and then ran in the distance, calling the wolves in her direction (to sacrifice herself in order to distract them from finding Po). You don't hear from her again. Unbelievably sad. Totally scary—even for an adult. It's scary because this stuff actually happens. But, still, my son was absolutely destroyed, and I was honestly surprised by the intensity of his reactions, reminding him that it was just a movie.

He kept saying, "Mama, I didn't know. I didn't know."

He didn't know what? What was he talking about? But then, as he buried his cries into me, I understood.

We had started our adoption journey a few months before, and though our son expressed interest in our adoption, he wasn't as obviously enthusiastic about it all as our daughter was. Knowing it would be good for him to reflect more on the upcoming adoption, I had actually prayed that God would help him "get it" a little more. Well, I guess God answered that prayer, though who knew Dreamworks would be the mode?

"I didn't know. I didn't know," he cried.

Then he asked, "Mama, is that happening to my little brother? Is he left all by himself?"

"Maybe. Maybe not. But, Lukas, this has happened to orphans before and to different children in horrible situations around the world. God never intended this kind of suffering. It is good to cry about it."

My son spent the rest of the night wailing. He went up to his room and cried and cried for *hours*. When I visited him in the lull of his cries, he just quietly said, "I'm glad we are adopting." I knew God was active in this. He also asked that night how he could help. I told him that we could think of some ways the next day, but for now he could pray for all the orphans in the world.

He said that he didn't know how to pray about it, but I assured him that his cries could be his prayers to God, that his wails could be wails on behalf of countless suffering children around the world. Man, did that kid wail and pray that night! If anyone had heard him that night, they would have thought we were total jerks and torturing him with information too heavy for a child. But I believe with all my soul that his tears and prayers were an offering to God, served others, and did great work in him. Who knew *Kung Fu Panda* could throw such a punch, eh?

In the rest of this chapter, I will try to further outline how intentionally taking on sorrow is worshipful to God, purposeful in caring for others, and refining in our children.

Our Sorrow is Worshipful and Biblical

Whether suffering for the sake of a group, or out of obedience, or to know Christ better, it is clear that Scripture values intentional sorrow and suffering in this world. *Justice Kids* organization does a good job setting up God's characteristics first – His Mercy, His

Justice, etc. Then as we know and love Him, we follow who He is into these hard issues. These issues break His heart and He is honored by our hearts following suit.

> *When I heard these things, I sat down and wept. For some days I mourned and fasted and prayed before the God of heaven.* (Nehemiah 1:4)
>
> *I want to know Christ—yes, to know the power of his resurrection and participation in his sufferings, becoming like him in his death.* (Philippians 3:10)
>
> *Carry each other's burdens, and in this way you will fulfill the law of Christ.*
> (Galatians 6:2)
>
> *So that there should be no division in the body, but that its parts should have equal concern for each other. If one part suffers, every part suffers with it; if one part is honored, every part rejoices with it.* (1 Corinthians 12:25–26)

When we cry for the lost and suffering, we glorify God. "This is the first purpose of missionary suffering; to wean us from the world and set our hope fully in God alone."[5] We can't fix the majority of the greatest sorrows in this world, and neither can our kids. Though I love to tell people how they can tangibly get involved in hard issues, I know that it is truly God's work that needs to be done. He needs to speak to the hearts of my family, as well as those in the 10/40 window. He needs to lead to the prosecution of the oppressors and deliver the suffering. We beg Him for that. We will praise Him for it. That reliance on God is a great place to start… for us and for our kids. Not only is it worshipful, but it takes some of the unrealistic burden off our children—still keeping them involved, but with the knowledge of a mighty and active God.

Our children worship God when they see and acknowledge that He suffers for the hurting. Suffering for others starts and ends with God. Henri Nouwen writes, "Compassion, to be with others when and where they suffer and to willingly enter into a fellowship of the weak, is God's way to justice and peace among people. Is it possible? Yes, it is, but only when we dare to live with the radical faith that we do not have to compete for love, but that love is freely given to us by the One who calls us to compassion.[6]"

Sorrow is an Avenue to Loving God's Suffering Children

Not only is bearing the suffering of others through the gift of tears worshipful to God, but it honors those who are suffering.

> *Have I not wept for those in trouble? Has not my soul grieved for the poor?* (Job 30:25)

Simply put, carrying one another's suffering is a way that our children live out their faith. Though some have the spiritual gift of mercy (often literally feeling like they are taking on the illnesses, sins, and sadness of others), as Christians, we are all called to "love mercy." Sometimes we may even just cry out to God without words:

> *Weep with moaning—praying. In the same way, the Spirit helps us in our weakness. We do not know what we ought*

to pray for, but the Spirit himself intercedes for us with groans that words cannot express. (Romans 8:26)

Even though the honor of weeping is a repeated theme to those who read the prophets, our world hides from crying. However, I read on a blog a while back about the extraordinary idea of providing intentional times for weeping:

> *Regular, disciplined weeping gives us a place from which to speak and act. As we work and pray and give on behalf of this cause, we do so with traces of tears that recall names and faces and places. We speak out about such situations not with the voice of a do-gooder but from a broken heart—one that has fellowshipped with God's broken heart. This keeps us away from vengeance, fuels our work for justice, and bonds us to the heart of our weeping God.*[7]

If our children are burdened by the suffering of others, let them weep … even regularly. Affirm their sweet, God-given, broken hearts. Which will it be: sadness over not getting a new videogame or the reality of street children in Brazil? The first may happen either way; if we aren't intentional about the second, it might never happen.

Sorrow is the Refining of Our Children

To enter suffering with our children not only worships God and serves others, but also actually benefits our children. Take a look at another verse and the following reflections from writer, missions speaker, and mother, Ann Dunagan:

> *'Thus says the LORD of hosts: 'Consider and call for the mourning women, that they may come; and send for*

skillful wailing women, that they may come. Let them make haste and take up a wailing for us, that our eyes may run with tears, and our eyelids gush with water.' (Jeremiah 9:17–18)

Isn't that kind of strange? God was calling for the professional criers and the wailing women. There was a need for tears, but a total lack of mourning and grief. Then in verse 20, Jeremiah 9 says, "Yet hear the word of the LORD, O women, And let your ear receive the word of His mouth; Teach your daughters wailing . . ."

Wow. This verse really stopped me.

I'm a mom with daughters, and I'm always on the lookout for what God tells me to teach my girls. So here, God is saying to teach my girls to cry . . . to shed tears . . . and even to wail. God is talking about big stuff, like rebellion against God, and not caring about sin.... All across the globe, and in our own nation, and right down the street, and (sadly) even blaring into family rooms through televisions and movies, there's horrible stuff going on. It's stuff God calls SIN and INJUSTICE. Even while living in God's joy and peace, there should be seasons when the needs of this world should make us so sad, and so shocked, and so ashamed (especially as mothers who deeply care for the next generation). At times, we should be compelled to our knees, where we should cry, and even weep.

...Our little girls don't need to know all the nitty-gritty details of the world's horrible evils; but as they're old enough to understand, we need to teach our daughters to pray, and to pray HARD! Our daughters can be radiant pure lights . . . to reach a very dark world.

We need to teach our girls to cry.[8]

I love these words. Ann is a mother to seven children, has done ministry on six continents, wrote two awesome books on missions, and started the Daring Daughters ministries (which is specifically for mothers and daughters to connect with God, each other, and the hurting world together). Obviously our boys benefit from crying as well, but in this verse it tells us specifically about girls, whom we usually try to shield the most.

Sorrow is Not the End of the Story

In conclusion, as I discussed in the previous chapter with Fear, I want to remind us all (so we can appropriately remind our children) that this grief-stricken world is not the end of the story. We read in Revelations that the end of the story is quite different. We don't even have to wait until the end of time for the redemption of suffering, because God promises redemption even here on earth:

> *Those who sow with tears will reap with songs of joy.Those who go out weeping, carrying seed to sow,will return with songs of joy, carrying sheaves with them.* (Psalm 126:5–6)

Not one tear will go unnoticed by our Lord. I don't know about you, but that means so much to me, and at moments, it has meant a lot to my children to hear. We read the psalmist cry out the same desire:

> *Record my lament; list my tears on your scroll--are they not in your record?* (Psalm 56:8)

Teaching our children that God honors weeping is a wonderful thing. It will carry over to all areas of their lives. Their God sees and knows them completely and is there for them. God will bottle up the tears of our children. They may cry for themselves, but they may also cry for children who cannot cry for themselves. Hallelujah! They will honor the lives for which they weep, and they will bless the world with the watering of their tears.

May our children learn to love mercy, even if it hurts.

Tangible Acts in Response to L.E.S.S.:

1. **Get a large bottle, put a small map in it or put pieces of paper with global issues written on them for which your children weep.**

2. **Pray through a book about other cultures. Pray with a blow-up globe with fingers on different countries of prayer focus.**

Chapter 17
Exposure—Raised Fists

While women weep, as they do now, I'll fight; while children go hungry, as they do now, I'll fight; while men go to prison, in and out, in and out, as they do now, I'll fight; while there is a drunkard left, while there is a poor lost girl upon the streets, while there remains one dark soul without the light of God, I'll fight; I'll fight to the very end!

–General William Booth (founder of Salvation Army)

My son was having "a moment" in the car, one we had seen far too many times during a hard developmental season during his sixth year of life. I can't remember exactly which dialogue we were repeating (if it was him being too sassy or if he was being a bad sport or just being mean to his sister). During that season, we felt like we were finding random consequences and having discussions with him daily, sometimes hourly, as we continued to tackle some bad habits and heart issues. Fortunately, that day it seemed like we had an easy consequence for my son's poor choices.

He was holding a toy. We can hold toys in the car when we are kind and respectful, right? Well, we took the toy because he wasn't being kind. Normally, that is a great and easy discipline tool and things change. But for some reason today, whether it was that particular toy, the time of day, or whatever, my son *lost it*! He began screaming at my husband, crying hysterically, and saying, "You are mean."

Many parents face this, but this was the first time our young, quiet son had acted quite so extremely in response to something so minor. Not knowing what to do, we just told him that he was welcome to respectfully say he was angry, or to say he was mad, but that we won't listen to him calling his daddy mean names. He said, "I can't say I'm mad. I'm scared to say I'm mad." It was then that we realized something not necessarily common to all kids. We realized that one of his anger issues was that anger scared him. I understood this because I, too, am embarrassed by anger. Anger can be terrifying. Yet, we know that Jesus was angry. We feel anger whether we like it or not. It is important to identify it. My husband clued in to my son's struggle with anger, and decided his "consequence" for this behavior was to write a letter. It started with "Dear Dad" … and in the letter he had to use the words "angry," "mad," "sad," and "hurt." He wrote the letter and it was such a sad, beautiful little letter from a six-year-old that loves his daddy, but was angry at him for taking his toy away. It felt like such a strange victory in the life of a kid who needs to express his angry feeling in a productive manner and not be scared of his feelings only to let them fester inside.

In this short chapter, I want to offer just a few thoughts on how to deal with anger, since it is a response our children may have as they learn about some of these hard global poverty or justice issues. I believe it is important not to be scared of anger—and possibly at times, to affirm it:

> *Be angry, but do not sin: Do not let the sun go down while you are still angry.* (Ephesians 4:26)

There is an assumption that one will be angry. We kind of know that, but still it sounds strange in the Bible, right? We usually avoid anger, don't we? There are actually two different kinds of anger described here and elsewhere.

There is the "anger of man," which "does not achieve the righteousness of God" (James 1:20) and the anger that is an expression of God's righteousness. We are commanded in our text to be angry in a way that is righteous, which is a reflection of God. Anger is often not wrong. Anger that is righteous has certain earmarks, by which it can be distinguished from sinful anger. Consider the following characteristics:

1. **Godly anger is God-like anger. It is an expression of the anger that He has toward the actions of men.** Godly people are angry when God is angry. It is anger that is consistent with the holy and righteous character of God.

2. **Godly anger is legal anger.** It is wrath based upon men's violation of God's law and against His holiness, and it is anger that is lawfully expressed. Godly anger is not vigilante justice, it is legal justice.[1]

So we don't have to feel bad about getting all fired up about things that we hate like abortion, slavery, poverty, cowardliness, selfishness, laziness, etc.

But what about our kids? First, let's allow and encourage our children to *be angry* at times. If this is their response to any global issues they learn about, it is actually evidence of taking a moral stance and even a love of justice, which together suggests God is working in their heart. They can, even in the roughest of terms, see what is right/wrong and holy/unholy. That is something to *praise God* for!

> *On reaching Jerusalem, Jesus entered the temple area and began driving out those who were buying and selling there. He overturned the tables of the money changers and the benches of those selling doves.* (Mark 11:15)

Let us also not forget the God that we worship and the Lord that we model ourselves after. Jesus was angry in the temple, not just because His temple had been made into a marketplace, instead of a place of worship, but also because the Gentiles (those the "chosen people" where supposed to bless) had no place to enter and interact with God. He was ticked off. I love that He was! It tells me that He loves me and wanted me there to worship Him with the Jewish people.

> *He is not only a God of compassion, he is also a God of wrath ... God does not respond to injustice or abuse with mild interest. He responds with vigor, with wrath, with judgment ... And, frankly, when children are raped, when innocent people are murdered, I am glad to know that God responds with righteous anger.*[2]

So, since we know that our children will deal with anger in their life anyhow and since we know that the injustice of the world is far more worthy of anger than not getting the Nintendo game they want, my suggestion is that we offer our kids some hard truths and walk them through feelings of godly anger. We can offer topics that will make them angry (or should, for that matter) and then guide them through constructive uses of anger, which are: prayer, standing up for others, acting to change the situation, and telling others about injustice. "The poor teach us to embark on the sacred search for indignation: to discover our anger in the face of greed, malice and human indifference that give birth to suffering and to speak to it."[3] Those are life, faith, depth of character qualities that I would never want to rob my children of. Anger can, in fact, be beautiful. Our child's anger that there are kids in the world in slavery can fuel prayers and action that might transform the world … if we brave it with them.

Even if our children choose to wrestle with God (even question Him), it is probably better that they do it in our home than amongst the council of our present culture. God can handle our wrestling with anger … even if we are angry at Him for what He has allowed to happen. Gary Chapman writes:

> *When we look at Job and other biblical examples of people who were angry with God, it is clear that God did not condemn such anger. Rather, He entered into conversation with these people and helped them work through their anger. However, this does not mean He always gave a full explanation of why bad things happen to good people.* [4]

As Jacob wrestled with God, though I doubt our children will wrestle to such a profound degree, it is noted that God honored it.

> *So Jacob was left alone, and a man wrestled with him till daybreak. When the man saw that he could not overpower him, he touched the socket of Jacob's hip so that his hip was wrenched as he wrestled with the man.*
> *Then the man said, "Let me go, for it is daybreak."*
> *But Jacob replied, "I will not let you go unless you bless me."*
> *The man asked him, "What is your name?"*
> *"Jacob," he answered.*
> *Then the man said, "Your name will no longer be Jacob, but Israel, because you have struggled with God and with humans and have overcome."*
> *Jacob said, "Please tell me your name."*
> *But he replied, "Why do you ask my name?" Then he blessed him there. So Jacob called the place Peniel, saying, "It is because I saw God face to face, and yet my life was spared.* (Genesis 32:24-30)

Jacob walked with a limp all his life because his hip was struck while wrestling with God (God Himself or God's angel … we don't know for sure). The analogy of wrestling with God through the hard things of life is profound, yet how much are we actually comfortable with it? I don't like the idea of my child questioning God. I don't like the idea of him feeling unsure of himself in this world. Yet, as we allow our children to question

God—even bring our anger to Him—they might experience God in a new way. R.C. Sproul writes: "Even though God gave no answers, Job's questions were put to rest. He received a higher answer than any direct reply could have provided. God answered Job's questions not with words but with Himself."[5]

In the previous three chapters, fear, sadness, and anger were described as normal and likely responses in our children (and ourselves) as we teach and learn about global realities. If handled well, I believe these feelings will result in good and godly outcomes. I believe they are the responses God desires to the topics that He truly feels the same way about (in sadness and anger … God is not fearful). I don't know your child. I don't know what extra fears, angers, or sadness play into their lives that may be a good reason for you to shelter them from certain truths about the world … only you do. God will give us all wisdom on how to parent our own kids. My overall suggestion is that we not be afraid to allow our children to engage the world.

Tangible Acts in Response to L.E.S.S.:

1. **Find verses about God's justice … both to see His heart and to know that He will judge the world!**
2. **Find something you (or your kids) are angry about. Act on it! Pray! Punch a punching bag! Put it to further use by standing up for something!**

Chapter 18

Exposure—A Cure for the Disease of Apathy

Apathy and evil. The two work hand in hand.
They are the same, really…Evil wills it; apathy allows it.
Evil hates the innocent and the defenseless most of all.
Apathy doesn't care as long as it's not personally inconvenienced.
–Jake Thoene

In the previous three chapters, we described possible responses our kids may have to global issues. Between my own kids, I observed quite different responses during an interesting back seat car conversation: Adelaine was five and Lukas was seven. Lukas can be very introspective at times, so I wasn't that surprised to overhear his profound reflection: "If I had one wish in the whole world, I would take away sin … from myself and from all the evil people in the world who hurt people." My heart was full. I felt good about how deep, spiritual concepts were getting through. Then I heard Adelaine reply, "I totally know what you mean. If I had one wish, I would be a pony."

That's right, a pony!

While my kids had quite divergent responses (though my daughter is actually usually the first in our family to help anyone), I do want to acknowledge the *one* response that a parent does want to be most aware of when they introduce global issues—that is *apathy*. We want to pray most of all that our children *care*. I don't mean to freak anyone out who has a child who doesn't weep at every topic of global concern (or I'd be freaked out myself), but I do believe apathy can creep in and we should be aware of this.

The best antidote I have found for apathy is relationship. When the African Children's Choir came to stay with us for a week, our kids had a great time playing with kids from Uganda and seeing them perform. They had some new pals who were some really amazing kids. However, at one time, just after the kids left for a day of concert performances, my son asked:

"Mom, so t*hose* are orphans?"

"Yeah, buddy, for whatever reason their parents died or just can't take care of them. Those kids are orphans."

"Oh," he said as he quietly walked away.

The term "orphan" fleshed out more when he had a few friends who were orphans. My son and daughter shined that week in selflessness and caring … and in prayers. It was what God naturally does in relationship. I am so grateful for the connection that was made.

If we do encounter apathy in our children, we can be comforted by the reality that more is going on under the surface than we realize. I have been very surprised at times when I thought my kids didn't hear anything I shared about an issue close to my heart, but then later they reflect on it.

Though it is hard, the reality is that in the end it will be their choice. It will be our children's choices whether or not they choose to follow God, let alone love others fully through the gifts God has given them. However, it is our job to model and teach it until we let go of that responsibility.

Again with Sponsorship

I know I have mentioned child sponsorship more than once, but I will talk about it one more time because it is not just important for our children to have compassion. It is also *unbelievably* important in the lives of the children who are sponsored, helping them to have clean water, education, and more … an actual future, basically. Preacher, professor, and author Tony Compolo tells his story about such an experience in a village in Senegal years ago. "In this village, it was World Vision's loving help that had created this openness to the gospel message. But I have to add that even when we sense that such wonderful opportunities to preach the gospel might never be available, Christians are still to feed the hungry, clothe the naked, minister to the sick, and stand up for the oppressed. We do that because God loves us unconditionally, and He calls us to extend that love to others unconditionally. This is why World Vision is helping children in Muslim countries."[1]

I am blessed with many families in my life who model this engagement in many ways. Along with many other things, the Clarks have adopted a little girl from China, with their kids fully involved. They also have toured parts of San Francisco with them intentionally to find and talk about homelessness when their kids were very young. My friend, Celeste, recently organized a Valentine's party for women and children at a homeless shelter. My family was blessed to go and serve with her, though we received far more than we gave. Celeste's children range from 2-6…yet she is starting these activities/conversations/empowerment NOW!

I end this chapter with some words written in an email from a good friend of mine when I asked her how she got so involved in fighting apathy and caring for others with her family. Summer Bergantino writes:

> *Once our first child was born we deepened our faith through the Bible and church involvement. Our eyes opened up so much to the world around us now that we were responsible for raising other human beings. As our eyes opened and our faith deepened, the needs of others in the world became more apparent than they had ever been. Now we want to be sure our children are raised to see the needs of the world and to take action. We want them to know that faith without works is dead. We want them to know we can be the hands and feet of Christ on this earth. We want them to focus on the needs of others and not their own.*

Personally my childhood was a tough one and we felt the call to adopt because of our love of children, of God and the thought of preventing a child from going through the same struggles I faced growing up. Our third child was adopted and I believe all three of our children have learned and will continue to learn so much about God through the experience. They know there are children in this world who need parents and that all three of them were placed in this family by God even if they came in different ways. There is a great need in this world for all of us to see and it's one that's near and dear to God's own heart, to care for orphans.

In 2012 we hosted three children and two adults from Destiny Africa's Children's Choir for one week. We may have felt that we were blessing them with a place to stay, meals, and activities but we were blessed beyond measure by their visit. Our children knew that the children staying with us were orphans but what they didn't know was they were just children like them that loved God, wanted to run and play and have fun. But these children also performed daily, had wonderful attitudes and manners. We took them to Wal-Mart to buy toiletries and as we walked through the store I had to keep asking them if they wanted this or that; they wouldn't ask for anything. Our children did ask for things and we were able to use that as a teaching tool for them. We learned so much about their life in Africa and the children's center they lived at, it was such a wonderful experience for our children and sure was a tearful goodbye. We hope to have them back again and have them on our prayer list.

For the past few years we have been involved with an organization called Hartford City Mission. For a long time we searched for serving opportunities we could do with our children. The only one we found was the family missions trip at our church, but we wanted something we could focus on locally. HCM is a Christ-centered organization that provides summer and after-school care for inner city youth. They also have "field trips" to suburban homes on Fridays. So we became a volunteer field trip home. Once a month a group of 3-6 children come over for crafts, games, cooking, etc. It's a chance for the children to get out of the city and into another fun, safe environment. This is a serving opportunity where my children can get involved in the planning and execution of the activities. They know that these children come from broken homes, either they live with one parent or don't live with all of their siblings. They come from apartments without a yard, low income, little or no access to church. I love seeing how our older children want to be generous with them. Last year our children loved throwing Valentine and Easter parties at HCM in Hartford. They wanted to pick up extra gifts and be in charge of handing them out. Our children also attend a magnet school and they are just starting to make connections that many children come from Hartford and from similar situations as they do from HCM.

For the past four years our family has been going on a family missions trip through our church. We take our family up to Canada, camp in a tent for a week, and volunteer at local churches to run a vacation Bible school for community children. It's not an easy task, but it's the only week of the year I feel that we fully give our family to God. We are so thankful for the opportunity to expose our children to a missions trip at such a young age. Our youngest was seven months old when we first went. They know they are "missionaries" for the week. Before they could really help we told them they are modeling behavior for the other children and being lights. Now they are able to have assignments and take responsibility on the trip. They are able to have the opportunity to go to another country to serve God. Even though we drive there I feel it's a big deal for them and hope they will remember and want to do more as they grow.

I can honestly say in all instances we get way more back in many ways than we give. Our hope is that if we expose our children to serving, giving, and loving others we don't know, they will be inspired by God to take initiative themselves when they get older. We pray they will find their God-given gifts to do great things for His Kingdom.

I'd say this is an incredible model to launch from … from L (Living) and E (Exposure) to now S (Serving) and S (Sending), as I have seen so evidently in this family.

Tangible Acts in Response to L.E.S.S.:

1. **Sponsor a child: let your child pick him or her out online at World Vision or Compassion International.**

2. **Make a photo book of people to pray for that you know working internationally or living in hard situations—visuals and interactions are key to fighting apathy.**

Chapter 19
Serve With Them—Introduction

Christianity is not about building an absolutely secure little niche in the world where you can live with your perfect little wife and your perfect little children in your beautiful little house where you have no gays or minority groups anywhere near you. Christianity is about learning to love like Jesus loved and Jesus loved the poor ... and Jesus loved the broken.

–Rich Mullins

Intentionality

As we consider what it is like for us to serve *with* our children, it is these components of Intentionality, Availability, and Participation that make service most effective and genuine.

> *For by grace you have been saved through faith and that not of yourselves; it is the gift of God, not of works, lest anyone should boast. For we are His workmanship, created in Christ Jesus for good works, which God prepared beforehand that we should walk in them.* (Ephesians 2:8–10)

We have been saved for a purpose. For the glory of God, we are not to sit on our butts and wait for the rapture. "According to Ephesians 2:8–10, the purpose for which the Lord has saved us is to do good works. After explaining that our salvation is by grace through faith, Paul goes on to state its purpose: 'For we are God's workmanship, created in Christ Jesus to do good works, which God prepared in advance for us to do' (Eph. 2:10). Of course, our good works are not a necessary condition of our salvation but rather a natural fruit of our redemption."[1]

After hearing a sermon from my favorite Northern Ireland pastor, James Hyndman, I was also reminded of the Jeremiah 29 verse we all love so much:

> *"For I know the plans I have for you," declares the* LORD, *"plans to prosper you and not to harm you, plans to give you hope and a future."* (Jeremiah 29:11)

I had known from seminary that this verse has been taken somewhat out of context by many (sorry for all of you that have it plastered on your Christian paraphernalia). However, it is so much richer than a personal claim that God is working things out in our lives for some great future. Though I do believe God "works for the good of those who love him, who have been called according to his purpose" (Romans 8:28), this verse has a deeper context. God was speaking to the people in exile in Babylon. He was telling them that their exile will be a LONG time—for some of them their whole lives—70 YEARS! He told them to get comfortable, to thrive as much as they can there. He also says,

"Seek the peace and prosperity of the city to which I have carried you into exile. Pray to the LORD for it, because if it prospers, you too will prosper" (Jeremiah 29:7).

We are all in exile, right? We are not in our real home, where God has redeemed us all and the earth yet. We are stuck in illnesses, sorrows and struggles. This verse is rich for us … not as a sweet little inspiration, but deep acknowledgement our fallen situation. If we apply this Scripture, we are told to thrive as much as we can and to "seek the peace and prosperity of the city." That is so deep and amazing.

God is so good to include us in the redemption of His people both spiritually and holistically. The key here is not that we have to do *huge* works, but that they are intentional and led by God as he prepared them in advance for us. Shane Claiborne, trying to understand his faith and the desire to see God real, writes:

> *One night my friend Chris said to me, 'I've been reading Mother Teresa.' I knew we were in trouble then. He continued, 'She says that we can't understand the poor until we begin to understand what poverty is like. So tonight we are going to sleep out on the street.' My jaw dropped. I asked him not to mention this to my mom, and we headed out for the streets. Night after night, we would head down. The Bible came to life for us there.*[2]

Before you put your Pillow Pets and Pack N' Play in your car all ready for an exciting overnight family event on the streets, remember that Shane Claiborne was in college, single, with another guy, and God was moving in his life, calling him into this.

God may call some of us into some crazy experiences like this, and if He does, I pray I don't say "No." But without that specific call, wisdom may lead my family to go down to the homeless shelter during the day instead (in lieu of an all-out pajama party).

Our faith comes to life for our children as we serve with our children. It doesn't *have* to be sleeping on the streets of Philly. I have many friends who are incredibly intentional about the kids that they allow in their house … intentionally bringing struggling kids into their home whom they can love on, knowing their kids will hear words, see actions, and have to deal with relationships that are uncomfortable. That isn't easy stuff.

The next key to this intentionality is our availability.

Availability

Why am I relieved when a snow day happens or a meeting is canceled, or even sometimes if one of my kids has a cold and I have to cancel a playdate? Am I that overbooked that I am relieved to cancel good things? Soccer, piano, violin, acting, martial arts, drawing, Lego class, dancing, church youth group, etc? All of it? Do we really *have* to have two sports, one instrument, one dance, two church activities, and an art class going at the same time? No wonder we have panic attacks if someone calls and needs help. We have no room in our lives for our own planned schedules, let alone an interruption. How sad that is. I want *LESS*, not *more*!

We must have margin in our lives. We have to have room for others—for conversations with those we interact with—lest we have to rush to our next activity. In *Transformational Discipleship*, Geiger, Kelley and Nation write:

> *The way you integrate this command into your real life today is that in all these areas, you don't plow to the edge. You don't book meetings back to back in case there is a conversation God will bring your way. You don't spend all the way to the end of your paycheck in case there is an unforeseen chance to be generous. You don't overschedule your family with activity after activity to that there isn't a single second to spend with your neighbors in the yard.*[3]

In Leviticus (19:9–10), God calls us to not reap our whole harvest: "And you shall not glean your vineyard, nor shall you gather every grape of your vineyard; you shall leave them for the poor and the stranger; I am the Lord your God."

Our harvest is our finances, our time, our energy, and our resources. Let us not glean it to the very end, but leave some available for others—for the poor, stranger, and friend as an act of obedience and worship to God. We want to be intentional about our service, but we don't want to overschedule it, either.

Participation

For a year, I took my kids once a week to an urban ministry, Hartford City Mission's after-school program, to help out. On the first day, it was a disaster. The kids at Hartford City Mission were great, but my kids were not. Lukas, in particular, was whiny and complaining. I felt so embarrassed that my privileged son was the rudest kid there that first day.

When we got in the car, he could tell how angry I was. I expressed how disappointed I was about his behavior, especially in light of the fact that these kids have little support at home with family, finances, or anything that my kids have in abundance.

Lukas began crying and said, "But Mama, I didn't know. You never told me."

My heart sank and I apologized to Lukas. Though he should never whine and be rude in *any* situation, he thought we were just at a random place at the end of his tiring day spending our time with kids he didn't know. I hadn't told him what we were doing. How foolish of me! Similarly, a couple of years ago, when it was time to do Operation Christmas Child boxes, I was overly efficient shopping and was able to get the boxes filled without the kids knowing it. So on the day that they brought their boxes in, they were *totally* disconnected from the boxes they were bringing for children through Samaritan's Purse's wonderful ministry.

> *Train up a child in the way he should go, And when he is old he will not depart from it.* (Proverbs 22:6)

It is important to include our children in every aspect of what we hope to disciple in their hearts. Angie Quantrell writes:

> *The best way to teach your child how to give is to involve him in your giving. Let him carry a bag of groceries to the food collection box. Let him put money in the special bank or look to see who doesn't have a toy. Let him help you*

> *give time picking up trash for a neighbor. Your preschooler will learn from your examples and love being involved in your lifestyle of giving of yourself, your time, your money, and your energy.*[4]

There are *so* many opportunities for us to serve right in our backyards. We can choose a few and begin to serve with our kids. Kimmel writes:

> *A servant attitude assumes humility, gratefulness, and generosity. Bottom line: people who don't live with an attitude of constantly being available to serve the needs of others can never have the words 'truly great' describe them—'successful,' 'nice,' 'interesting,' maybe—but 'truly great'—never! The one thing that unhappy families have in common is how little effort they expend investing their time in others. My friends, if you want to be happy and influence your children to greatness, serving other people needs to be an attitude that summarizes your life.*[5]

In this chapter, I offer an idea of *days* as a possible tool to engage kids on different topics. Days on the calendar can create a rhythm in your home and a natural way to gather other families to serve with you. The keys are to:

1. Only pick one day a month or you will get overwhelmed.
2. Choose varying topics to cover different issues.
3. See if there are local events on the day and serve together.
4. Come up with an event or research, learn, and pray about it!
5. Choose other days outside this list if an issue suits you better.

January:

Martin Luther King, Jr. Day—Civil Rights
Human Trafficking Awareness Day—January 11th
Genocide Remembrance Day—January 27th
World Leprosy Day—January 30th
Child Labor Day—January 31st

February:

Freedom Day—February 1st
World Cancer Day—February 4th
World Day of the Sick—February 11th
St. Valentine's Day—Love—February 14th

March:

World Day of Prayer (1st Friday in March)
International Women's Day—March 8th
St. Patrick's Day—Missions—March 17th
World Water Day—March 22nd
Lent/Good Friday/Easter

April:

Autism Awareness Day—April 2nd
International Orphans Day—April 11th
International Day of Street Children—April 22nd
Earth Day—April 22nd
World Malaria Day—April 25th

May:

National Day of Prayer and Fasting—May 6th
World AIDS Orphan Day—May 7th
World Fair Trade Day—2nd Saturday in May
World Hunger Day—May 28th
Memorial Day—Last Monday in May

June:

International Childrens' Day—June 1st
International Day Against Child Abuse—June 4th
World Day Against Child Labor—June 12th
World Refugee Day—June 20th

July:

Independence Day—July 4th
International Justice Day—July 17th

August:

International Day of Indigenous People—August 9th
International Youth Day—August 12th
International Mourning Day—August 15th
International Day to Remember Abolition—August 23rd

September:

International Literacy Day—September 8th
International Day of Peace—September 21st
International Day Against Human Trafficking—Sept. 23rd
World Clean Up Day—September 24th

October:

International Day of the Elderly—October 1st
World Homelessness Day—October 10th
International Day of Mental Health—October 10th
International Day of the Girl—October 11th
Day of the Eradication of Poverty—October 17th

November:

Day of Prayer for the Persecuted Church—November 11th
Veteran's Day—November 11th
Make a Difference Day—November 15th
National Adoption Day—November 17th

December:

World AIDS Day—December 1st
International Day of the Disabled Person—December 3rd
St. Nicholas Day—Giving to Poor—December 6th
International Migrants Day—December 18th
Christmas—December 25th

Tangible Acts in Response to L.E.S.S.:

1. **Include your children in your family's giving**

2. **Consider marking special days on your calendar as a way to serve certain people.**

Chapter 20
Serve With Them—Build Them Up

It's one thing to tell my kids to reach out and love other people, but it's a much more real thing to take their hand and walk them into a place of desperate need and say, 'Let's love here. Now. Together.

–Lysa Terkeurst

Like most parents, from our children's early age, we have been firm believers in teaching them skills that they will need for life. Though I cannot perhaps yet teach my eight-year-old how to apply for a job or my six-year-old to change a tire on her own, we can start somewhere and work our way up to what we want to see in them when they leave our home. Therefore, when my son was five and my daughter was three, we began to have them try to sort some of their arguments out by themselves.

After a ridiculous dispute, Adam and I sent our kids upstairs with the instructions that they needed to talk to each other and could come down when they had worked it out. It didn't go as well as we hoped. We overheard:

Lukas: Adelaine, let's just do this.. Why are you mad?

Adelaine: MEOW.

Lukas: Cut it out, Adelaine. Mama and Daddy won't let us back downstairs until we have talked. Soooo … Let's talk.

Adelaine: MEEEEOOOOWWWWW.

Lukas: I'm trying here, Adelaine. Just tell me what I did wrong so we can talk about this.

Adelaine: MEEEEEEEEOOOOOOOOWWWWWWWW.

Had Adam and I not overheard this conversation (trying to muffle our laughter), we would have never believed our son when he came down saying, "Mama and Daddy, I am trying to work it out, but Adelaine keeps meowing."

So while that one didn't pan out, there are *so* many life skills we hope for our children to have, first just to survive in this world, but then to keep a strong faith, and finally we hope for them to be effective movers in the world.

The Kid's Got Skills

When I think about the most effective people involved in missions cross-culturally and most engaged in the world's global issues, there are many skills that come to mind:

<u>Ministry Skills</u>

- Comfortable speaking to or teaching small groups and big groups
- Know the Bible, basics of discipleship, evangelism, apologetics, spiritual disciplines, and classic spiritual books

- Scripture memorization—for own life and for sharing with others
- Prayer life—public prayer and personal prayer

Skills When Traveling Internationally

- Flexible eater and sleeper (Hudson Taylor even trained his body in rugged conditions for hardship)
- Self-defense or martial arts
- Know another language (Spanish, Chinese, and Arabic are the most widely used languages in missions right now)
- Navigation (public transportation in urban and rural situations, planning travel)

Skills When Living Internationally

- Handyman skills and cleaning
- Cooking skills (low-cost, healthy)
- Mechanical skills
- Outdoor survival skills (check out YWAM's Niko program)

Life Skills

- Good steward with finances
- Relationship health (peacemaking, friendship building, conversation skills, etc.)
- Physical health (exercise without fancy equipment or classes)
- Time management

When you look at this list (and you could add much more to it), let me ask: is this just a list of what we want for a child who might become a missionary or pastor? When I made this list prayerfully a while back, I realized that this is what I want for my children no matter what vocation they take. Discipleship is not just imprinting our faith in our children—it is about healthy habit formation and how to live life.

Though I love different activities like soccer (which can create teamwork and sportsmanship), dance (health and confidence) and so many more kid activities, I know the other skills are non-negotiable. If the wonderful extracurricular things don't make it into our schedule (without making our lives too busy), then so be it. *LESS* is more! Though we may not always have to choose between these things—at some point we choose what we have time and energy to teach. Believe me, this convicts me, too! I still want everything for them, but there isn't time and money for everything! Maybe you can relate?

Gifts and Passions

Each of our children has different gifts and talents. They have both abilities (drawing, athletics, mathematic skills, etc.) as well as spiritual gifts, once they know Jesus (teaching, intercession, hospitality, etc.). How wonderful to help our children figure out how God made them. Even at a young age, but definitely as children grow, we can look for our children's spiritual and physical gifting and affirm them.

> *As mission-minded families, we can seek God's direction and then begin to serve as God's facilitators and motivators. If we can encourage our children to discover God's plans and to want to develop specific God-given abilities, it will totally change everything. Instead of dealing with surface issues, we begin to train our children's hearts and to focus on staying aimed toward God's purpose. A change at this root level alters everything, from grades in school and success in activities to confidence in leadership and a spiritual desire to develop God-glorifying friendships.*[1]

As we expose our children to global topics and cross-cultural relationships, we may find that they grab onto certain issues (or perhaps it is just the story and person they care about regardless of the issue). As they get passionate and you see their desire to act or know more—*don't lose your chance!* It is that combination of gifting and passions (and where they meet the needs of the world) that they will find their most fulfilling activities and purpose in life as they worship God.

When discussing gifting with my son, I told him that I thought God had given him a gift for building (he creates and builds inventions all the time). He just smiled, flexed his muscles, and said, "Yeah, I know I have a gift of building…BODY-building!" Well, that's not quite what I meant …we are working on it.

Use Your Muscles

Helen Lee writes, "When children have the chance to use their skills and talents to serve, they remember those tangible moments, which help to build a spirit of generosity and tenderness toward those in need. Giving becomes a powerful antidote to combat the attitudes and behaviors of self-entitlement and self-indulgence that come when children are not encouraged to think beyond their own needs and desires."[2]

I love seeing how my children's gifts come out. My daughter's gifts are like mine: she likes to jump in deep, organize, and see things change. She wants to teach others about what she learns and is willing to sacrifice for the sake of it. As we did a Walk for Water with my women's group, Adelaine had so many ideas about how to make it better. She wanted to help with every step of the way and she endured a lot that seven-year-olds usually would whine through in order to see it be a success. I *loved* getting to share with her about the things I see in her.

My son is different. He is quieter about such things, but I see evidence of how he is moved under the surface and how he intercedes for others on his own, treats others with compassion and how he keeps asking to hear more stories of missionaries and Christians in other countries. He is willing to serve and help, but has no desire to be in charge at this time. Those are also gifts, and we can praise God for them and him. We must. "If we leave our child's cheering section, if our seat is vacant, the child will look for someone else to fill it. That someone is usually a peer. So dust off those pom-poms! Ready that megaphone! Be about the business of becoming your child's greatest fan!"[3]

My daughter's hero is Amy Carmichael—a missionary and abolitionist hero to India that could inspire anyone. I love that my daughter looks up to her. One might wonder how she became so incredible.

Amy Carmichael's mother Catherine was her biggest fan (and example) even *before* Amy began rescuing a thousand children from the abuse of Hindu temple worship and then raising them up in Christ. We learn:

When Amy's mother made soup for the sick and poor in the community, often she sent her children to deliver it. This was Amy's introduction to reaching out to the poor. She also loved to hear stories of India that her pastor's brother, Mr. Beatty, would tell. She couldn't learn enough about how the Lord worked in the hearts of the Indian people who had never heard about Jesus before ... When she gathered children from the slums to teach them about God, her mother opened her home and even provided tea for refreshments. When Catherine's friends whispered behind her back, saying it was improper for Amy to travel into the slums and invite the Shawlies to her church, Catherine turned a deaf ear and praised her daughter's giving heart. And when on January 13, 1892, Amy heard God's call to go to India, where she would spend the rest of her life, her mother gave Amy her blessing. Catherine Carmichael wasn't one to discourage her daughter from heeding God's call but instead encouraged her in both word and deed to do as God directed. She was a mother who trained up her child in the way she should go—and then let her go. She was an encourager who poured courage and confidence into her child by pointing to the One who gives us strength. When Amy wrote to her mother about going away to India, Catherine responded with the following letter. "Yes, dearest Amy, He has lent you to me all these years. He only knows what a strength, comfort and joy you have been to me. In sorrow He made you my staff and solace, in loneliness more than my child companion and now in my gladness my bright and merry-heart sympathizer. So, darling, when He asks you now to go away from within my reach, can I say nay? No, no, Amy, He is yours—you are His—to take you where He pleases and to use you as He pleases. I can trust you to Him and I do ... All day He has helped me, and my heart unfailingly says, Go ye." How did Amy rise up and call her mother blessed? She wrote, "There never was such a mother so good, so loving, so unselfish, so perfect in every way.[4]

Catherine Carmichael was an amazing mother who trained and then released her child to her amazing gifting, passions, and God's will to save Indian children from slavery and lead them into God's kingdom. Let us, too, bravely cheer them on!

Serve With Them

As we discover their gifting and passions, we need to serve *with* them—the first S of L.E.S.S. They can smell us out if we push things too much, so we want to (as much as possible) encourage them prayerfully and by example—with their specific desires in mind. To make the service stick, we should ideally reflect with them before and after the event.

For example, if you are serving the homeless, take the chance to talk about homelessness and how your children would feel if they were homeless. What would it be like to live like them? How did they perhaps get in the situation they are in? After the activity, see if they will share and reflect on their experience, and give them an opportunity to ask questions. Where did they see God at work? What would they like to do in the future?

So, What Can They Do?

Find a group of friends to serve with. Royal Ambassadors and Girls in Action are organized ministries of WMU that you can be a part of or start. (They have amazing magazines regardless).

Fundraise: make things to sell, start a lemonade stand (more for awareness than for actual funds), try "fun-run" raising, or do work for neighbors to raise money for a cause. They will feel accomplished after a deed is done and they are able to send money to a mission project or buy a cow from a relief organization. Kids of all ages can organize a food pantry. My kids enjoy organizing a clothes closet at our church, making them also quicker to give away their own things for the sake of it.

Research and plan: What interests them? What group is doing things to help others in a way that they care about? How do they advertise? Plan it with costs and schedule and delegating tasks. Execute! (This is skill building for any future job!)

There are endless ways to serve locally. Make lists about projects. Our family did a "Summer of Service" where each week we focused on a different topic, learning and serving in that area. It had to be intentional or it never would have happened. Just do something, and it will be part of finding their passions and gifting, too. My friend, Heidi, lives in a multicultural suburb, full of all different kinds of faiths. She is very intentional in her relationships with her neighbors and their kids. They are often in her home (she has the gift of hospitality and loving on kids) and her children are a part of that service. They have probably had more multicultural, missional interaction than most people I know—in their own neighborhood.

Do it over and over. Discipleship is just layer upon layer of life. It just keeps getting deeper as children and youth get older. Heck, hold onto the info for college applications (you type-A moms … or teach your kids how to do that for their future resumes).

If they want ideas, give them ideas through what other families have done (of kids who have done everything from small backpack drive at school to big service projects). Here is one of my favorite youths (who has written a couple books aimed at youth and teens, by the way):

> *In the spring of 2004, nine-year-old Austin Gutwein watched a video that showed children who had lost their parents to AIDS. Afterward, he realized these kids weren't any different from him, except that they were suffering. Austin felt God calling him to do something to help them. He decided to shoot free throws, and on World AIDS Day 2004, he shot 2,057 free throws to represent the estimated number of children who would be orphaned by AIDS during his day at school ... From that year forward, thousands of people around the world have joined Austin in a basketball shoot-a-thon called Hoops of Hope. By doing something as simple as shooting free throws, Hoops of Hope participants have raised well over $1 million. Children impacted by AIDS and poverty now have access to food, clothing, shelter, school, and healthcare, including a medical testing facility which could help save an entire generation.*[5]

I have a good friend who uses random acts of kindness as a guide to serve with her kids. She longed for it not to be just a feel-good list of things to do or brag about, but a way of life and a heart that is truly humble. Shawn George writes:

> *What I love about living Acts of God is it is a way of life. I want to not just know God's Word but to put what he says into practice.*

> *Therefore everyone who hears these words of mine and puts them into practice is like a wise man who built his house on the rock. (Matthew 7:24)*

> *I want to teach my children by my actions and be a witness to my husband that God's Word lived out is a gift that we can bring to others and make a difference in their lives. And it isn't the big stuff. I am a wife and a mom of three kiddos. I can't save the world ... and anyway that isn't my job, that is God's. It is offering to make my husband his breakfast, it is spending time reading or playing a game with my kids, it is smiling at a stranger, acknowledging the presence of and saying hello to the cashier at the grocery store or the bus driver that drives my kids every day to school. It is seeing someone holding too much and running ahead to hold the door. Asking someone "How are you?', and then stopping to listen for the answer. It is picking up the phone when your friend who is going through stuff calls and spend time listening to her even though there are other things I 'should' be doing. It is going without an extra box of snacks to give a few dollars to a cause at the table outside the store. It is paying for the person's coffee in line behind me. It is volunteering for an event at school, or at church. It is sponsoring that child in another country. It is living in the direction where my actions are lovingly purposeful, with nothing expected in return, and all point to the character of God.*

> How awesome!

Serve on a mission trip with your kids:

There are more and more opportunities out there for local and international mission trips with kids. In *Don't Forget to Pack the Kids: Short-Term Missions for Your Whole Family*, Jill Richardson reflects on mission trips with her kids:

> *It's not magic. Life lessons take, well, a lifetime. But we saw right away that they noticed more. They understood gratefulness on a new level. They flew to the TV to find out how "their" kids were after the earthquake in China. Things all the way around the world mattered.*[6]

My friend Jenny has allowed her son (starting at age seven) to go with her husband to Mexico to build homes for a couple of years now. They recently went as a family, bringing her young daughter as well. It has been profound in their lives and her kids are more and more invested in missions because of the friendships they have built there. This challenged me to bring my own daughter to Guatemala to serve in an orphanage (since she loves toddlers and helping out).

My trip to Guatemala with Adelaine on a on a Mother-Daughter mission was AMAZING…better than I could have ever hoped for. We went to serve at an orphanage run by the Block family under Lifesong. Adelaine had already had the oldest Block daughter, Addisyn, as a role model through her amazing blog, *Life as a Missionary Kid.* Addisyn could not have been more encouraging to my daughter. It was a real highlight for her to meet this great role model. However, the trip turned out to be full of role models. Though Adelaine was the youngest at age 7, the older girls on the trip (age 11-21), included her completely. She was surrounded by girls passionate about God and missions, praying powerfully and serving sacrificially. She found a Guatemalan girl at the orphanage, who was her age, that she really cared for and enjoyed playing with. She loved all the little munchkins there, some who had HIV. She heard incredible testimonies and got to serve the local poor and homeless. The ministry there was incredible and it was an honor to be a part of anything they are doing. It is a memory that I will never forget, as not only does my daughter reflect on it constantly, but I gained many friends on the trips of the other amazing moms.

In conclusion, activities like these give our kids life skills, identify gifts, and build up our kids. In all of these things, and in the daunting task of just raising our children at all, I am reminded of my desperate need for the Spirit of God in my life for such a task. I am so grateful He is up for the challenge!

Tangible Acts in Response to L.E.S.S.:

1. **Teach them about spiritual gifts. Go through one of the gift surveys.**

2. **Teach them the main current global issues in missions, community development, and justice. See what sparks their interest the most and dive in further.**

Chapter 21
Serve With Them—The Power of the Narrator

Have the courage to live under strain and pain to be a part of a better story. A larger story. Don't wimp out.
–Beth Moore

My son used to struggle with fear. It isn't uncommon for a young child, but it felt paralyzing for him, especially socially. Between the ages of three and five, Lukas had great anxiety about trying new things, going new places, and meeting new people. I'm sure some of it had to do with the frustrations of a severe speech delay—being unable to express himself.

Lukas was five the summer we moved cross-country from Oregon to Connecticut. Before we moved, we decided to better understand the gifts and weaknesses of a very anxious boy before he entered a new school system by having him go through a couple of ability tests (like IQ tests). We hoped to give a report to his teachers and speech therapists about his abilities, so he wouldn't just be seen for his language struggles. We were on our long drive out to Connecticut when we got the results of the tests, which confirmed different things we had already suspected about our son.

We had stopped for the night in Ohio when Lukas asked what the test had shown (having overheard our conversation in the front seat). As we walked to the hotel pool for a swim after a long day's drive, we weren't sure what to tell him. We didn't want him to be discouraged by his weaknesses or be overconfident about the abilities God gave him, but we wanted to tell him encouraging, true things. So for whatever it was worth, we chose to say this (though it branched outside of what the test could have shown): the test showed us things we already knew about you. You are smart. God made you smart. You are kind. God made you kind. You are *brave*. God made you brave."

Lukas was quiet, then softly asked, "Am I really brave?" Though I knew he was asking if the test showed he was brave, I answered knowing the truth of him, "Yes, Lukas, you are brave."

It was as if a switch had been flipped. We were at the hotel pool and my five-year-old son (who normally won't even jump off the side into my arms), started doing flips off the side of the pool. He was doing the most insane things that evening to the point that I was starting to picture us rushing to the hospital sometime that evening. We were awestruck and didn't know who this kid was. He was so different and so ambitious and risk-taking. It was such an incredible night and he was filled with such joy. We just delighted in what seemed to be fear draining out of him … in just one night.

As we walked back to the hotel room, we asked him, "Lukas, what got into you? Why were you doing so many crazy flips and dives? We don't even know who you are!"

He replied, "You said I was brave. I just didn't know."

Until that day, I had never seen so profoundly how quickly and how easily someone can influence our identity. Tim Kimmel, author of *The Danger of Raising Nice Kids*, writes:

> *Our kids are desperate for a vision. They are craving purpose. Millennials, as postmoderns, yearn to be part of a grand story. Their hearts long to be characters in a story that matters—one with a creative design, passionate characters and a noble mission ... A child with vision doesn't get trapped in the mundane. There is something he is shooting for. He has ideals and goals that inspire him. With an internal sense of purpose and a clear vision of what he wants to become, he is motivated to pursue his aims.*[1]

Though others will come into our children's lives, parents will have the biggest role in ultimately giving our children their vision of themselves, the world, and God. We have the role of naming them and narrating our children's lives (or leaving a void that they will fill themselves). We model to them with how we live our own lives, to whom we look up to, and who we verbally esteem in front of them. We can name our children—beyond their birth name—in who they will become, telling them what character qualities they have and can have. The most active everyday role we can have is as our children's narrator: helping them interpret and respond in the context of the grand narrative of what God is doing. We can give them heroes, name them, and actively narrate their lives with God's purposes.

Looking for Heroes

The Bible is obviously chock full of great heroes. From Noah's faith in a world of disbelief to Moses standing up for the oppressed in Egypt, there are many heroes to look up to. We have the incredible hero of Mary, who is pure, obedient, and faithful. We have some struggling heroes that we can relate to a little more like a lustful David that conquers a giant as a child and calls out to God in humility all his life. Peter has just as much foolishness as passion—which I can relate to personally, as well. Rahab, in spite of her shady past, risks her life to offer shelter to Joshua's men, and God redeems her.

However, even these hero stories are seen best in light of the grand narrative of the Bible. From Genesis to Revelation, we see where we were and where God planned to take us. We can see all these heroes through this narrative and eventually ourselves and our children. We see that God has blessed us to be a blessing—to call the nations to Himself:

Abraham: "*all peoples on earth will be blessed through you.*"
–Genesis 12:3

Moses: "*But I have raised you up for this very purpose, that I might show you my power and that my name might be proclaimed in all the earth.*"
–Exodus 9:16

Joshua: *"He did this so that all the peoples of the earth might know that the hand of the* LORD *is powerful and so that you might always fear the* LORD *your God."*
–Joshua 4:24

David: *"Sing the praises of the* LORD*, enthroned in Zion; proclaim among the nations what he has done."*
–Psalm 9:11

Isaiah: *"I will also make you a light for the Gentiles, that my salvation may reach to the ends of the earth."*
–Isaiah 49:6b

Jesus: *"He said to them, 'Go into all the world and preach the gospel to all creation. Whoever believes and is baptized will be saved, but whoever does not believe will be condemned.'"*
–Mark 16:15–16

Paul: *"Scripture foresaw that God would justify the Gentiles by faith, and announced the gospel in advance to Abraham: "All nations will be blessed through you."*
–Galatians 3:8

John: *"After this I looked, and there before me was a great multitude that no one could count, from every nation, tribe, people and language, standing before the throne and before the Lamb. They were wearing white robes and were holding palm branches in their hands."*
–Revelation 7:9

There are so many more verses than this, but just taking our children and ourselves through this red thread of God's redemption in the Bible strings all the hero stories together. It is God's common voice and heart in all of Scripture.

Amazingly, we can also see world history through God's plan for redemption. Ann Dunagan's books, *Mission Minded Child* and *Mission Minded Family*, have great ideas for all of this, especially with resources about missionary heroes—past and present.

I confess that it wasn't until these past two years that I knew maybe two famous past missionaries. I would even roll my eyes at the mention of them, thinking it was outdated or too old-school. Now that I am diving into the stories of those missionaries myself, being so completely inspired by their faith and God's work in the world through their lives; I am loving old-school missionaries! I am also making it part of my everyday curriculum for both my own children and Children's Missions at church. It is worthy of our time and energy to praise Him and learn from it.

YWAM (Youth With a Mission) has some awesome books for children on a vast array of missionaries. Voice of the Martyrs has an animated video series that my kids have asked to watch over and over again. If your church or library doesn't have them, and you don't want to purchase these things, then just Google the stories of these people— people like: Amy Carmichael, Hudson Taylor, David Livingstone, Eric Liddell, William Carey, Nate Saint, George Muller, Gladys Aylward, and so many more. Our children need to know who they are and their impact on missions today. I went to Thailand in college with OMF (originally China Inland Mission) and I didn't know much about Hudson Taylor (who started it) until recently. Having now been to Thailand and seen the lasting effects of his efforts, I am amazed. My kids love these missionaries now.

We don't need to stop at past heroes, lest our children think hero making has died. God is still doing amazing things in this world, through international icons and through ordinary people, many of whom are children and teens. *The Brickman Adventures* are amazing audio dramas about a family interacting with lots of different missionaries today and mission experiences in their family. Our whole family loves them!!! God has also moved the hearts of those who are famous, like Bono, Switchfoot, Jars of Clay (Blood/Water Missions), and Sara Groves to start big movements to help the poor—living out their faith in what they sing about, how they live, give, and what they stand for. Bethany Hamilton has used her fame and even personal tragedy to bring attention to international relief issues. My daughter loves Katie Davis, who I have mentioned before. After reading her book, *Kisses from Katie,* she gave her saved allowance money to Amazima ministry.

Zach Hunter is another young hero. Zach was 12 when he learned about modern day slavery. So Zach started Loose Change to Loosen Chains. The idea was that everyone has loose change around, and putting it together we can make a difference. He got his school involved and together they raised $8,500. Ten years later, millions of dollars have been raised and thousand of youth have come alongside him in education, advocacy, and activism. He has written three books, and now International Justice Mission is using LC2LC (Loose Change To Loosen Chains) as a way for students to get involved in abolitionism. He writes: "Most kids dream of being superheroes, fighting villains, winning battles. Well, I still have those big dreams. And I believe God likes it when kids dream big. I'd just turned fourteen when I started writing this book and I'm a modern-day abolitionist."[2]

So why can't my child be like this? Why can't yours? There is no reason they can't. We can't necessarily bank on this big of an external outcome (though God can do great things and loves to surprise us).

Our children can be heroes. They *must* be heroes—27 million slaves need heroes to help set them free. 150 million children are orphans in need of families. Over 200 million children work instead of going to school (of which half are in the worst forms of child labor). 2.7 *billion* people have never heard that Jesus came to free them from their sins and to offer them redemption in Him. There is a need for heroes: servant heroes, with humility knowing who the true Hero is.

> *I became a servant of this gospel by the gift of God's grace given me through the working of his power. Although I am less than the least of all the Lord's people, this grace was given me: to preach to the Gentiles the boundless riches of Christ, and to make plain to everyone the administration of this mystery, which for ages past was kept hidden in God, who created all things.* (Ephesians 3: 6–9)

> *For we are God's handiwork, created in Christ Jesus to do good works, which God prepared in advance for us to do*. (Ephesians 2:10)

We know clearly that this is indeed God's story and it is all about Him. He is in fact the main character. He is the writer. He is the *true* hero. However, as his sons and daughters, as his ambassadors, we are called to be like Him—to find our story in His and to point to His glory and redemption.

When Lukas was four, we let him watch *The Lion, the Witch, and the Wardrobe*. My husband has a deep love for the books of C. S. Lewis, and because we hadn't seen Lukas exhibit much fear over movies, we watched it around Easter time because it had such incredible symbolism.

Lukas *loved* the movie. He loved the characters, the talking animals, the adventure, the fight between good and evil, and he *loved* Aslan. Prior to the movie, we had explained to him about how Aslan was supposed to be a character like Jesus: all powerful, but sacrificial. We weren't sure how much he got it.

I knew that the scene of Aslan offering himself as a replacement for Edward's death to the White Witch would be hard. It is a hard scene to watch as an adult. I almost skipped it, but I kept feeling like it was so important for him to see and understand. Lukas didn't cry as he watched it and he didn't appear afraid, but he definitely wanted me to explain everything that was happening to Aslan. We watched as Aslan voluntarily walked up to the altar, was mocked, and then beaten by the evil creatures. Lukas squirmed as Aslan tragically got his mane cut off in big chunks, and then we were powerless but to watch as Aslan was killed. The White Witch loved her victory and we were left empty. Lukas was left confused until I whispered to him, "It isn't over … just wait."

His eyes were glued to the movie and it was as if nothing else in the story mattered until he saw another scene about Aslan. With his speech delay, he asked me "Ere's A'an? Ere's A'an?" (Where's Aslan? Where's Aslan?)

After the battle began, Lucy and Susan went to find Aslan and he wasn't there, Lukas' little body stiffened up and he held his breath. But then in the glory of the sun, the stone cracked and you knew He was not dead. Indeed, the story hadn't been over. Lukas fell back on me, relaxed, and breathed again.

Unsure whether we had let Lukas watch the movie too young (hold your judgey judgment, Mr. Judgerson!), we put Lukas to bed, checking to make sure he understood the movie and that he wasn't scared, etc. He didn't say much.

The next afternoon, I came downstairs after putting Adelaine down for an afternoon nap (she was two then) and found Lukas in the bathroom. I couldn't believe my eyes, and at first I didn't understand. He had been very, very busy in the short time I was upstairs. He had drawn marks all over his arms and legs with a marker. He also had scissors in one hand and a big handful of his hair in the other. I was about to yell in frustration at him (which of course I *never* do), but something flashed in front of my eyes, like a memory or scene I knew deep inside. It was a picture of Aslan: beaten and mocked, his body marked, mane cut. So I asked him in disbelief, "Lukas, are you trying to be like Aslan, the Lion?"

He just nodded.

I fell down to hug him and started to cry. My four-year-old boy loved and wanted to be like Aslan so much that he drew on himself and cut his hair. He knew that his hero was good and that he saw something worth copying. Christ, merely allegorized in Aslan, suffered and sacrificed himself to save others, to then conquer death and darkness. If our children can know the *true* hero of the world's story, I don't believe they will have a problem taking a servant, sacrificial position. They will know it is good. They will merely copy what they have seen modeled to them by Christ and Christ in us. For Aslan says, "If the Witch knew the true meaning of sacrifice, she might have interpreted the deep magic differently. That when a willing victim who has committed no treachery, is killed in a traitor's stead, the stone table will crack, and even death itself would turn backwards."[3]

Name them with a Mission in Mind

I hadn't gotten around to doing family haircuts for a while, and Adam was having a particularly "large" hair day. Adelaine was in the back seat and having a morning (not unlike many mornings) of talking a little too sassy to him. I was turning around, about to intervene, but Lukas did it for me by saying, "Adelaine, stop bossing around Fluffy."

After total silence in the car (including Lukas because he thought he'd finally gone too far), we all busted up laughing and Adam left the car to go into his university where he teaches, with the kids yelling "bye-bye Fluffy" and "have a good day, Fluffy."

I hadn't thought much of it until Adam got home and instantly asked me to give him a haircut.

Who knew that two little kids joking around could make a grown man actually insecure enough to get a haircut?

If I'm honest, I know that words can level me quickly, too. Even the words of my own children can deeply wound me. There are a few things they have said to me that have reached deep places in my heart. Words of kindness have given me incredible value of being a mom and I cherish them deeply. Words of unkindness (or just unthoughtfulness about how I look or what I do wrong as a mom) have hurt me deeply, still bearing the scars.

Well, if just the words of kids can affect us, what about adults? What about adults that spoke into our lives when we were kids? Lawyer and author, Bob Goff, reflects on his own life: "I used to think the words spoken about us describe who we are, but now I know they shape who we are."[4] That is so true, isn't it?

I know that the kind words—things that people have said about gifts they see in me, have given me confidence. The words of past and current mentors still ring in my ears, shaping how I view myself and even how I view my potential future. Rough critique from adults ring sometimes louder, and somehow the crippling effects take effect faster than kind words.

However, beyond just encouraging words and telling children what gifting we see in them, we have the power to name them.

A wonderful woman I know was named after Amy Carmichael. My friend, Amy (obviously), grew up knowing that she was named after this brave, beautiful, kind missionary. Amy took her faith seriously and even traveled to India, seeing the country Amy Carmichael served in. With such a legacy for a namesake, it isn't much of a surprise that my friend, Amy, now works in an incredible urban afterschool program in Hartford and intentionally lives in inner-city Hartford to help rebuild it holistically. My daughter, Adelaine, loves Amy Carmichael, too—she loves that she saved slaves. What is also neat is that my daughter loves my friend Amy, too. She loves how she cares for the struggling kids in inner-city Hartford. Adelaine asked that we also call her "Amy" for a season because she wants so much to be like those two Amys. With role models like that, we do it!

Seasons may carry different names, but we ought to let them carry a name at least for a while and really live it out. If they lose their identity or are never given it to begin with, they will search for it elsewhere: in relationships, success, or pleasures. Our children will possibly have times in teenage years when they try to separate from us, appropriately trying to verify their own thoughts as opposed to their parents'. This is where the importance of mentors comes in. Our children will need words to hold them up and shape them, even if they won't listen to us.

Words of encouragement are like that. They have their own power. And when they are said by the right people, they can change everything. What I've found in following Jesus is that most of the time, when it comes to who says it, we each are the right people. And I've concluded something else, that the words people say to us not only have shelf life but have the ability to shape life.[5]

Carri, a friend of mine, sets apart mentors for her children once they hit age eleven (just when they hit middle school)—adults whose role is to speak truth and identity into her children's hearts. (I have some of Carri's story in an upcoming chapter). I know my mentors have meant so much to me, telling me who I was and what my mission was. For every "follower of Jesus (including every *Christian child)* should have a 'life mission' aimed at finding God's purpose and fulfilling His potential."[6]

Be an Active Narrator

Bryant Myers, author of *Working With the Poor*, writes:

Everyone must have some kind of transcendent narrative that gives answers to questions of meaning and provides moral direction and social purpose. We need to know who we are (identity and purpose), where we are (location in the world and the universe), what went wrong (making sense of the poverty, pain and injustice we see), what we must do (what must change and how it can be changed), and what time it is (how our past, present and future fit into this picture).[7]

It is easy to forget to give children this narrative, or to procrastinate. In the day in and day out of life, we are making lunches for school, dealing with discipline issues, trying to juggle our own life, and honestly, just trying to make it to church on time, let alone outline for our children their place in God's great story. But if we don't give them a story, they will find their own lesser story.. Julie Ferwerda writes:

> *As I've begun learning about many kids out there who are doing so many inspiring things, nothing has become clearer to me than this: I have aimed far too low for my kids, and I have not adequately encouraged or readied them to reach their God-given potential. I have lived as if the world is God's gift to my children, instead of living like my children are God's gift to the world.*[8]

A big part of giving our children a story is to give them a life verse or a calling. Scripture gives us many, but there are several verses that paraphrase much of God's heart that we can offer to our kids:

> *Learn to do right; seek justice. Defend the oppressed. Take up the cause of the fatherless; plead the case of the widow.* (Isaiah 1:7)

> *Before I formed you in the womb I knew you, before you were born I set you apart; I appointed you as a prophet to the nations.* (Jeremiah 1:5)

> *And if you spend yourselves in behalf of the hungry and satisfy the needs of the oppressed, then your light will rise in the darkness, and your night will become like the noonday.* (Isaiah 58:10)

> *The Spirit of the Sovereign LORD is on me, because the LORD has anointed me to preach good news to the poor. He has sent me to bind up the brokenhearted, to proclaim freedom for the captives and release from darkness for the prisoners.* (Isaiah 61:1)

At the end of this book, I have a list of resources of books, movies, and even songs that are *awesome*. Just listening to one of these songs makes me want to live my life differently. Telling my kids that this is their song, explaining the lyrics, and having us dance and sing in the car has been awesome. Every time the song comes on, they yell "Turn it up!"

As we are active narrators, when necessary, we change their story.

Donald Miller describes a time when he was listening to a friend, Jason, talk about his thirteen-year-old daughter. He was saddened by her life and felt powerless to help her. She was smoking pot, apathetic about life, and dating a jerk. Donald writes, "Then I said something that caught his attention. I said his daughter was living a terrible story."[9]

That night, the idea kept rolling around in Jason's mind as he tossed in bed. He was thinking about his daughter's story and the role she was playing in her story. Donald explains:

> *He hadn't mapped out a story for his family. And so his daughter had chosen another story, a story in which she was wanted, even if she was only being used. In the absence of a family story, she'd chosen a story in which there was risk and adventure, rebellion and independence. 'She's not a bad girl,' my friend said, 'She was just choosing the best story available to her.'*[10]

So Jason decided to find a better story for his daughter and his family. He found an organization that built orphanages and found out that they needed $25,000 to build an orphanage in a village in Mexico or terrible things would happen to the children.

He didn't have the money, but he also knew that a good story involved risk-taking, so he went for it. He boldly brought the plan before his family.

At first, the family wasn't into his drastic idea and was angry for the intrusion. But slowly, they started taking steps toward it, warming up to the idea and warming up to each other. The daughter approached her father and asked if she could go meet the children. She then featured the children on a website she started as an active way to fundraise.

Amazing things happened in that family, and the daughter broke up with the jerk boyfriend. Her life turned around. Why? Because "no girl who plays the role of a hero dates a guy who uses her. She knows who she is. She just forgot for a little while."[11]

What story are we writing for our children? What story are we living already? Are we explaining that story to them, responding, reflecting with them, asking them where they see themselves in God's great narrative? Do we have the guts to totally change the story if it isn't working?

We can shape our kids in faith as we ask the question, "I wonder what God has for you?" and "I wonder how God is going to use your gifts for His purposes?"

Claude Hickman writes in *Live Life on Purpose*:

> *The Christian life is the story of a journey. We are travelers on a road that has a beginning and more importantly a destination. The journey wasn't created for you; you were created for the journey. That is where you*

> *fit. God formed you and blessed you so that you could live to use your talents, skills, abilities, and resources on the tracks of where He is heading. Only when we see all that God is doing, and place our lives obediently into submission to the cause, do we begin to find the most delight in who we are created to be. We can be ourselves—a unique, colorful, and specially designed piece. We fit.*[12]

What story is God writing with the children in your life, in your family, in your own life? We will all have a story of our own and a part in God's greater narrative. Will it be epic and eternal, or just fluff? Will we give our children a good story through naming them, giving them heroes to model after (including ourselves), and actively narrating for them so they might be sent out for a redemptive life?

Tangible Acts in Response to L.E.S.S.:

1. **Name three heroes you will research and tell your kids about—missionaries past and present, music groups using fame to spread mission, or young heroes.**

2. **Tell your story to the children in your life. Remember to ask the stories of others for them to hear—including possible mentors!**

Chapter 22
Send Them Out—Introduction

When I stand before God at the end of my life, I would hope that I would not have a single bit of talent left, and could say, 'I used everything you gave me.'

–Erma Bombeck

Classic car ride to Christmas Eve church service:

Adelaine and Lukas fighting over something in the back seat. Literally wrestling over it.

Me: Okay, give it to me, whatever it is, I want it.

Lukas (*giggles*): I can't.

Me: Lukas, it better be in my hand right now.

Lukas: Mom, it's imaginary.

Me: You all are fighting over something imaginary? Are you kidding me?

My husband: Lukas, I don't care if it's imaginary … give it to me.

Lukas hands "it" (aka … a handful of air) to Adam, who rolls down the window and throws "it" (nothing) out the window.

Adelaine begins to pout … you know, because she lost her…nothing.

Lukas: Adelaine, just reach in your bag and pull out another one … I mean (*giggles*), come on—it's imaginary.

My husband: Adelaine, don't you dare pull another out. I will throw imaginary things out the window all night if I have to.

At that we pull into church.

Isn't the ride to church just always the most delightful ride of the week? Even if you have more devotional, worshipful transportation experiences to your Sabbath communities, if we are parents or teachers, we can often find ourselves in this strange, beautiful mess of discipling, disciplining, and just plain chaos and survival. But, beyond that, I have found that in this life change toward being a missional family, I am not that different from my ridiculous daughter, pouting that her imaginary possessions were thrown out the window. Let me explain.

I like to pretend I have control, but in the end that control is, in fact, imaginary. My kids have always been God's and I am called to release them – first slowly and for small distances, but eventually as far as God wants to take them. As I have too many control issues with them, God will "throw them out the window all night if He has to."

> *Like arrows in the hands of a warrior are children born in one's youth. Blessed is the man whose quiver is full of*

> *them. They will not be put to shame when they contend with their opponents in court.* (Psalm 127:4–5

Ann Dunagan describes a friend who had the common mixed feelings about letting go of her child into the world to try out his skills. She writes, "I leaned over and whispered in my friend's ear, 'You know, Karen, it's not enough to just aim our arrows; to hit the target we've got to release the string … If we are going to raise a generation of world changers, it is likely that we will need to surrender our children into areas that may make us uncomfortable.'"[1]

Sending them to Capitol Hill

We had an amazing experience this last homeschool year with something that turned a lot bigger than a history lesson, mostly because we dared to step out and send our kids out into the world, even if ever so slightly.

I gave my kids the necessary pep talk about not doing anything horrifically rude or vulgar before we went inside the enormous government buildings. It was strange that it was the letters of these two little rascals (who were now making silly faces at each other) that had brought us to the Senate Building and the House of Representatives for meetings with our state's elected officials. I confess that I could barely remember what I had learned in elementary school about the different parts to our government systems, and yet here I, too, in all my ignorance, was walking up the steps.

It had started with a school project on the Civil War in December. As my five-year-old daughter and seven-year-old son learned about amazing abolitionists like Harriet Tubman, Frederick Douglass, Harriet Beecher Stowe, and Sojourner Truth, they proclaimed confidently that if there was still slavery, they would be as brave as them. My son paused, however, recalling that I had mentioned before that there was still slavery in the world, though I had not gone into too much depth about its horrors. So he asked about slavery today.

Since I primarily knew facts about sex trafficking (and didn't care to share that with a five- and seven-year-old), I looked for more materials on other types of slavery. I knew a little about families stuck in bondage at rock quarries, but as I read, it wasn't long before my eyes were opened further to the horrors of slavery in carpet factories, industries like clothing, rice, and sugar, and, of course, slavery in the cocoa and coffee world. At first, I was shocked by some of the stats. I mean, I thought I knew about this stuff. Surely cocoa wasn't *that* bad or the places I shop wouldn't sell it, would they? I mean seriously—would they? So as my children asked more and more about slavery today, we learned. We learned together. We learned more than I wanted to know.

Initially, my son wanted to "Do a Boston Tea Party." Now that just sounds a little like a super hip dance move or a retro party theme, but he actually referred to the idea of taking all of our coffee, cocoa, and other products that are made by slaves and throwing it in the river. He figured that if it got the attention of political leaders long ago and was in history books, surely it would work again. After a long discussion on pollution (and my desire not to get heavily fined or go to jail), we settled on the kids writing our elected officials—as well as the President—about slavery. We might as well make it a school lesson about the government too, right?

My daughter's letter was sweet, with her sadness about slavery, her hope in the President's care for kids in particular, and her ideas about how to make it stop. My son just got straight to the point. He just didn't like slavery. He wanted it to stop. He wanted people in power to stop it (and by the way, does the President like Sonic the Hedgehog as much as he does?). The End (with a comic drawn of Sonic the Hedgehog for President Obama to enjoy). So with all that, we thought we had our history lesson, went the extra mile with the letters, and assumed it was mostly over. We made our list of products we would try to buy differently, but we hadn't made any plans to change any laws.

However, at the beginning of the year, when the Trafficking Victims Protection Reauthorization Act (TVPRA)—a bill that protects victims of trafficking—didn't pass, this little Civil War slavery talk changed. My kids really cared about this issue and let their friends, relatives, and representatives know. They were invested. I was more invested in politics than I'd ever been in my life and wanted to hope in the process.

In March, when the TVPRA did finally pass—a spark lit in me. It was unexpected. Can my voice matter as a citizen? As I told my children that the bill passed, they began to run around the house with shouts of joy and spontaneous happy dances. My son then wrote up a "Newspaper" (complete with comic, maze, and Wii tips for light reading on the back) about how our country is going to help to fight against slavery. He wrote that he had been a part of it. Uh oh … that little spark in me just got fanned and it is a little brighter now. My kids are in on this now. We might just have a voice. This might just matter.

So, there we were a month later, going to meet with the staff of our Representative and our Senator to thank them for supporting the TVPRA against trafficking and ask that they keep the full funding for the bill. I was in D.C.—a place that I had once thought had no place for me. I was now here with my kids as they carted up enormous Thank You cards they had made. Though they decided that the Senator's office was a great place to start a round of potty talk, we made it through our meetings.

However, the story didn't stop there. A few months ago (over a year since our first letters), we got a message from our Representative's office. She wanted to do a press release about our family. Apparently our simple stop at her office made a difference to her. She had been at the beginning of her term in office. She was still learning what her constituents cared about. When a family (and kids to represent kids internationally without a voice) wrote, called, and stopped in…she decided to co-sponsor the TVPRA bill. This was unbelievable to us!

In the famous words of William Wilberforce: "We are too young to realize that certain things are impossible…so we will do them anyway."

As I reflect, I recall that the boy with the fish had *no idea* that Jesus was going to multiply his lunch into a feast for thousands. He just wanted to offer what he had. That is all anyone could have asked. So often we look at that boy and think, "Don't even try…there are too many people, the system is too messed up". But he offered it up all the same. We don't know when our offering will remain small or be multiplied. All we are asked to do is offer whatever we have. Jesus will do the rest.

The boy with the fish didn't teach me this. My kids did. Since then, they have wanted to write to our representatives about different issues. Now I'm afraid that they think I have the President on speed dial or something. Pretty soon, they will ask, "Call the President—tell him to get me a pizza here ASAP!" But it is amazing to see kids who believe that they can be part of something big. Adelaine makes bracelets that she plans on selling to send money to orphans. She truly believes that she can start a business and fund the lives of other kids.

Big and Small Sending

Sending our children out into the world starts small and then gets bigger … and harder. Small is letting them lead their own campaign or project, while you're acting more as an advisor than the director. That takes a while of training them and building them up. It can include (as mentioned before) mission trips locally and globally with or without you.

My husband points back to a mission trip to the Ukraine as being a turning point in his life at the age of 15. After delivering Christmas gifts to orphans there, Adam came back to his high school social worries as well as athletic successes with a different set of lenses on. He didn't care so much about who thought he was cool and who didn't. He also didn't think so highly of himself when he excelled in sports. Adam was changed.

Regardless of the process of sending them out, it is always painful for us, scary for them, and extraordinary in our worship of how we offer them back to God. If we dedicated our infants once, let us continually dedicate our children to God's call. In this last section of L.E.S.S., the S of Sending them is perhaps the hardest to grasp—the least tangible, but something that we can prepare for now in prayer, conversation, and small acts in preparation for their final release!

Tangible Acts in Response to L.E.S.S.:

1. **Write to missionaries, invite them over, and visit them abroad.**
2. **Pray for a community of other kids that you can send your children off with in small and big ways.**

Chapter 23

Send Them Out—Little Birds

If you can't feed 100 people, then just feed one.

–Mother Teresa

Carri's son was turning eleven. While most of us plan big parties of mass expense to celebrate these occassions, Carri worked hard and long on a different agenda for his birthday … but not just for a birthday party, for an entire *year*! Carri created a year-long Rite of Passage plan for him, including mentors and a service project that he had to choose, plan out, and implement. Carri explained for me:

> *It has always been my greatest desire that my children would grow to become confident, godly adults. I have three sons and one daughter. That is a great responsibility and an even greater honor. In our pursuit to guide our children, my husband and I created a Rite of Passage for our first born last year. We wanted to instill in him the knowledge of what is, and how to be, a real man. My husband met with our son each month and taught him nine virtues that we felt were most important. Loyalty, Servant-*

Leadership, Kindness, Humility, Purity, Honor, Self-discipline, Excellence, and Perseverance. Knowing the true definitions of these virtues at such a vulnerable age is important to combat the many other messages and worldly pulls. We also selected three mentors to be role models and examples to our son. We wanted him to know that he is a part of a group of men that live with integrity and faith. That no matter what he goes through, these men will stand by him, guide him, pray for him, and be examples to him of what a good man, brother, friend, son, boyfriend, husband, and follower of Christ look like.

The Rite of Passage included a service project of his choice. We wanted him to learn to see outside himself and see the hearts and needs of others. Often, American kids are raised to think they deserve anything and everything they want. Sadly, that excludes the knowledge that helping others brings a greater fulfillment than any 'thing' they could ever acquire. Americans also tend to assume others are already taking care of the people in need, and that they don't have what it takes to do something. As followers of Christ we wanted to show our son how anything and anyone can make a difference and that all of it matters. Our son chose to build a home for a family in Juarez, Mexico. We teamed up with Raise the Walls and he helped raise funds and brought together his friends and family to help put together the walls of the house for a single mother of two kids. It was one small way that he could see the power every person has to make a difference for others. If an eleven year old, can build a home and change a life for a family in Juarez, nothing is impossible with God.

This Rite of Passage has planted seeds in a deep way. We have been encouraged to see our son starting to make choices that reflect his becoming a godly man. We recognize that our role has not ended with this experience, and we look forward to partnering with Christ to helping those seeds grow more and more every year. We in no way have expectations for a perfect kid, or one that won't go

> *through growing pains and suffer consequences. We hope, though, that through this process he will continue to grow more sensitive to the Holy Spirit, and that he will have the tools and support to guide him through all that he encounters in life.*

Believe me, this is on my To Do list for my kids for so many levels of their identity and skill building. I had never met Carri's son until this last summer, and though he may have always been a confident, cool kid, I was just amazed by what a kind, personable ten-year-old he was. What ten-year-old boy talks to a group of moms and helps out with little kids? One who has been trained and raised up for this. One who has also been sent out to do good things. I praise God for the work He is doing in that family as Carri and her husband Brent have worked hard to Live, Expose, Serve with, and now Send out their children.

I have so many friends who have empowered their children to choose service projects as their birthday parties. They raise money for a mission organization in lieu of getting gifts or collect items for a shelter instead of collecting more plastic toys. My friend Laurie has five kids. This last year, her kids' birthdays were each a different theme that matched a mission organization (like the movie *Planes* as a theme, but kids were asked to bring donations to Missionary Aviation fellowship instead of gifts). Even just after one year—that is a LOT of money that went to missions and not to plastic toys. My friend Megan asked her daughter, Madeline, what she wanted to raise money for and it ended up being our adoption that benefitted from their generosity.

This not only blessed us, but completely impacted my own children to see Madeline's family care for us. In fact, it in turn, inspired my children in their birthday parties to do similar cool things. The ball keeps rolling. My friend Angie organized an international food-packaging party for a birthday party: rather than doing crafts that end up in the recycling bin, they instead fed thousands of hungry kids through the local church in different starving countries. They will remember this type of birthday party, more than what plastic gifts they got.

Their Own Ideas

So, what *are* their ideas? What things *would* they like to do? Before we groan and realize that it may be a lot of work, let us remember two things I have mentioned before:

1. These are life skills that they need: decision making, planning, finding their gifting and purpose, teamwork, etc. As I mentioned before, we might as well teach them now.

2. We really can empower them to do a *lot* of the actual work. Though we may not want them surfing the internet for lots of information, *they can* make the posters and clean the house for the organizational meeting coming up. They need to know all that goes into these efforts and feel proud that they did it as much as possible. YWAM encourages us to: "not limit the areas in which young people can express their desires for service. Find out what interests them and seek opportunities for them to be mentored, and express themselves in those areas. "[1]

If kids are running low on ideas, look up Isabel at SHOES for KIDS where she collects shoes for kids in countries where they have no shoes. Kids could add an element of going a week barefoot as a conversation piece to raise money or shoes. Kids can also be part of SOLE HOPE, which is the making of show parts to send to Uganda for a microenterprise ministry.

Check out the sisters at *Africans by Amerikids*—a project that both benefits the environment and fights oppression. They take old crayons and melt them into new crayons, selling them to raise money to fight against slavery.

Compassion International has a kids' section (and a kids' magazine) with stories of kids that are doing great things, as does GA (Girls in Action) and RA (Royal Ambassador) magazines. These ideas become reachable in our kids when they are continually exposed to generous ideas of other kids.

Random ideas are great, too! The youth group at First Christian Church in Yuma, Arizona, raised over $5,000 through wrapping presents during the Christmas season (in addition to bake sales). They were so successful that they planned more projects to raise more for Blood: Water Mission[2].

A boy named Jack Chlebanowski raised his own money to go on mission trip as a nine-year-old to Ethiopia and Uganda with his parents. He came back so moved by what he saw that he wanted to raise more money for a well for his new friends there. So what did he do? He walked half a mile every day for a week to get his water rations for the week from another location in honor of those who have to walk much farther for dirty water every day. He also did a lemonade stand where he sold things from Africa. Everywhere he went, he told people about his desire.[3] His parents could have told him that he had done enough or that his desires were too grand. They didn't. They launched him out and he won!

I am blessed to be part of great churches that have empowered kids to serve on their own or with their friends – through food packing events, writing cards to people in nursing homes, and making packs for the homeless with cards and warm hats/gloves.

Conferences can be a great way to send kids out when they are old enough. Urbana, The Justice Conference, Passion (fighting slavery), and IJM's youth conference are all designed to empower youth to engage the world as a generation for change. These are amazing opportunities!

Staycation Mission Trip

If we are working up to the actual sending, there is much that we can do where we are.

> *The Great Commission says to 'go,' but we don't always need a passport. Because we are part of a global society, our missions work has become much easier to accomplish. The world literally has come to us. A Christian family can 'go' in one sense without leaving their own country. How? By sharing the gospel with the diverse people of 'all the world' (Mark 16:15) who live all around us. It is up to us to meet and get to know these people, to share the gospel with them.*[4]

Though it may be a bit of a stretch in our normal experiences, we can find refugee and immigrant families in our communities pretty easily if we look. They often need help in a variety of ways and also need friendships. We need them in our lives, too. These people groups (as well as international exchange students) could be key in changing not only the communities they reside in here in America, but in whatever countries they visit or return to abroad. They also graciously open our eyes to experiences and cultures that we normally don't see.

Since Muslim/Christian conflicts seem to always be in the media, specifically having friends who are Muslim takes the fear out of other religions and makes it about people we care for. They are lovely people and we are blessed when we care for and build friendships with these families, who too need Jesus.

Teach It

If there is a science fair coming up—why not do something on dirty water internationally and purification systems? If there is an international fair, why not have the kids focus on your sponsored child? Of course, this is part of **S** of **Sending** your kids out, so they need to be your youth's ideas, but there are a *lot* out there: irrigation in the developing world, effects of famine on the brain, effects of trauma on the brain, prosthetics for the developing world, etc. Cool stuff actually for someone to learn and then teach—not only to know better themselves, but as a platform to educate others. They can feel proud to educate others *and* people receive difficult information (like dirty water) more readily from children. I taught global issue games at Soulfest, a week of Christian concerts. My kids assisted me (and at other times have lead teaching). Their knowledge, excitement and engagement was profoundly different than if they had just sat in the crowd again.

Serve

As my kids are learning Tae-kwon-do, they are not just learning a few moves in order to fight—it has to become a natural reflex and response for it to be useful to them. They have to practice over and over and over: serving at nursing homes, food kitchens, homeless shelters, teaching ESL, tutoring, picking up trash, intercession for missionaries, writing our senators about a bill, etc. Serving in these capacities must be drilled over and over until it becomes part of life and faith. I know it has been a learning process for me not to feel awkward. As our children learn to sense God's leading and feel His heart for others, great things can happen. Send them out in their own service!

There is a story I can close this chapter with of a *young* kid who did great things. Ryan Hreljac of Kemptville, Ontario, was six years old when he heard in school about a fundraiser to dig a well in Uganda for clean water. He learned about how long kids had to walk in Uganda and diseases they got from the water. He learned that kids died from the dirty water.

> *Ryan came home and told his parents that he had to raise the $70 that his class had mentioned. His parents didn't take him seriously. But, after he persisted again and again, they gave him jobs around the house. After three months, he had earned $35—not the $70 he needed to and by now the fundraiser was over, but Ryan wasn't done. He kept working. He finally gathered $75 (said the extra $5 was for lunches for the well-diggers) and went to the well organization. Unfortunately, the organization explained to Ryan that it wasn't $70 needed to dig a well, but $2000. Though disappointed, Ryan was determined to get this well for the people he had envisioned in Uganda. The newspaper heard his story and people started making checks made out to "Ryan's Well"... and it wasn't too long that Ryan's well was dug. One would think Ryan was tired of chores and done, but he wasn't. He found out that a Power Drill in Africa could dig more wells in Africa, but it cost $25,000—an inconceivable amount to a six-year-old. Perhaps it was good that it was inconceivable because it didn't stop him. Ryan appeared on The Oprah Winfrey Show and he started a foundation. His organization has raised millions of dollars to drill wells in South Asia, Central America and Africa for more than 800,000 people. When Ryan was 8, he got to see a well. The children were shouting his name. When they got to the village, an old man stood up and said, 'Look around at our children. You can see they are healthy. This is because of Ryan.'*[5]

If this is just a little bird, I can't wait to see him when he is grown up soaring.

Tangible Acts in Response to L.E.S.S.:

1. **Find an issue or people group your kids care about and have them create a plan to be involved and help make it better. Empower them to do it on their own as much as possible. Just be their consultant.**

2. **Give them a topic that they have to learn about and then teach others.**

Chapter 24

Send Them Out—Releasing the Arrow

I had known about Jesus dying for me, but I had never understood that, if He had died for me, then I didn't belong to myself. Redemption means buying back, so that if I belong to Him, either I had to be a thief, and keep what wasn't mine, or else I had to give up everything to God. When I came to see that Jesus had died for me, it didn't seem hard to give up all for Him.

–C.T. Studd

The Trust of Hannah

I think it is easy to wonder how Hannah, though barren, could make such a promise to God to give away her two-year-old, after having prayed so hard for him. But, if we are honest, we try to make that kind of deal with God all the time, offering anything to God when our child is in danger or in desperation of ourselves. Hannah is no different in her desire to be pregnant:

> *And she made a vow, saying, "LORD Almighty, if you will only look on your servant's misery and remember me, and not forget your servant but give her a son, then I will give him to the LORD for all the days of his life, and no razor will ever be used on his head.* (1 Samuel 1:11)

The most amazing part, however, is that she actually holds true to her word and gives Samuel back to God—to serve at the temple. How do you have a child for just two years and then give him up? How could she do it?

Hannah must have looked at her child differently than most mothers. She must have viewed him all along as set apart for God. We also must remember that Hannah had experienced God intervening in her life and seeing her in her despair. He had done a miracle in her and she felt loved by Him. This proved to her that God was trustworthy—capable of taking care of her child.

Ann Dunagan writes, "Like Hannah, we must realize that our child is actually God's child—entrusted to us for only a short time. We need to release our child to God and then follow His guidance to raise His child for His divine purposes!"[1]

They are to be Christ's ambassadors … that means that they leave and go. They don't stay, and *that is hard*!

> *Therefore, if anyone is in Christ, the new creation has come: The old has gone, the new is here! All this is from God, who reconciled us to himself through Christ and gave us the ministry of reconciliation: that God was reconciling the world to himself in Christ, not counting people's sins against them. And he has committed to us the message of reconciliation. We are therefore Christ's ambassadors, as though God were making his appeal*

through us. We implore you on Christ's behalf: Be reconciled to God. (2 Corinthians 5:17–20)

SEND Them on a Plane

It is true that sometimes mission trips are more about the travelers than the recipients. I totally agree that these trips can sometimes be overdone, when we could simply send the money to locals to make three churches for the price it costs to send a whole team down to make just one. However, the relationships between churches, cultures, and especially youth are invaluable seeds planted for future missions and life perspectives. "Over three-quarters of trip-goers report that the short-term experience altered their life in some way. Those who have been on a short-term trip understand the life-changing event that it can be."[2]

You are the light of the world. A town built on a hill cannot be hidden. Neither do people light a lamp and put it under a bowl. Instead they put it on its stand, and it gives light to everyone in the house. In the same way, let your light shine before others, that they may see your good deeds and glorify your Father in heaven. (Matthew 5:14-16)

As I referenced before, in *The Zambia Project* you can read reports of more youth that were affected by their mission experiences, particularly through Wheaton Academy's relationship with Zambia. It makes you want to start a savings account just for mission trips (which I think is actually a decent idea if it is a priority for this kind of travel, as opposed to vacation travel). Read the results of Ryan Souders's heart transformation:

> *For years I sat around and was completely satisfied with fake food. I ate it up, all of it. I got up and went about things like everyone else. I had quiet time devotions, attended small groups, went to church, and did everything I was supposed to do. And these have had significant value, irreplaceable value in my life. Yet once I got ahold of that real food, I have never been the same. It fills me up like nothing I have ever had before. Its taste is like nothing I have ever tried. And most incredibly, there is always more than enough.*[3]

Wow, I'd love for my kids as teenagers to be talking about their faith like real food. Furthermore, Chip Huber reflects on all the kids who went to Zambia:

> *I hear in my head voices of a generation of students who regularly scream at me that they want to do something. They want to bring change to people's lives in this very day and time. And when the Holy Spirit has clearly led them to step out in faith to do something magnificent on God's behalf, I will continue to try to clear the way of all that would distract and keep them from moving forward as they lead from a place of unbridled trust that God will show up in their lives.*[4]

In that book, you read about where the students are now today. It is amazing to see how most of the students are still extremely involved in missions on their college campuses and some are heading up ministries … all because they got involved in Zambia. They are ministry leaders, and changing justice and charity even now (while most of the pews are full of older adults who aren't). There must be something about actually *going* and *being* with the people! But it isn't cheap, and we do need to check our hearts, knowing that mission trips are usually about the one going and not the ones receiving. Nonprofit Christian organizations are doing amazing work these days and are able to do incredibly efficient things with time and relationships for God's kingdom. Obviously, I'm all for mission trips, but this honest conversation needs to be in our hearts before God as we decide how to use our resources.

SEND Them in a Car

If you don't have the chance or finances to send your child so far away, hearts can change deeply in most inner-city mission trips. You can serve in places like Appalachia—a "developing world" in our own country or go on a inner city project through World Vision US, Urban Plunge, Serve Seattle, The Hartford Project or serve refugees through Experience Mission. There are so many more!

When I was in college, I helped chaperone a high school trip that went up to Vancouver, Canada, to serve the urban poor. Not only were *so many* of the youth transformed (some still serve in a variety of missions opportunities today), but the high school trip to Vancouver proved to be more impactful to me as a leader than I ever imagined.

Our tasks varied throughout the week. One day, we gave flowers to prostitutes to remind them of God's love and to continue to build relationships with them and a ministry there in town. It is powerful to see the youth come face to face with prostitution—no longer giggling at it like it is part of a Julia

Roberts love story film, but horrified by a 17-year-old leaving in the car with a 50-year-old. They realized that each girl had a story and didn't want to be there. They saw the disgusting men that preyed on them. Unfortunately, they also saw the young boy prostitutes. Even the older "cool" high school boys were affected. Because there were faces and stories behind this issue, a "hooker" or "pimp" was no longer the punch line of a joke.

We did worship services for homeless shelters, brought food to the homeless in parks, did cleanup projects, and served in drug-rehab centers. The kids heard real stories of people struggling in life and real stories of redemption. These were people who looked like them—some of them kids, too. These were people they began to care about, which, like I mentioned before, is the first part of getting kids to want to be involved.

One of the most meaningful days was when we were supposed to be "homeless for a day," just to feel what it was like (just barely). We were told to dress grungy, go on one of the wealthy shopping streets, and ask for money. Pretty easy directions, but I dreaded it. I easily could have opted out of it, claiming I was "management," but I knew it was intended just as much for me. So I grubbed myself out and sat next to a trashcan.

I held up a sign that asked for spare change. That was a no go. No one even looked at me and certainly no one gave money. I then tried shyly asking people who passed by if they had any change to spare. Again, no one responded. I got a little louder, because I thought that maybe they didn't hear me, but it became clear that I was heard, but just intentionally ignored. It felt horrible. I personally felt like trash. I couldn't believe how much someone ignoring me completely hurt … even just for a short time of doing it.

And then I saw her. It was me. Well, not "me," but a version of me. It was someone who looked like me and dressed like me. So, I asked her, "Do you have any spare change?" She just started fiddling around with her purse, like she didn't hear me and was trying to find something in there. She heard me. I knew she heard me. She knew she felt awkward, embarrassed and unsure what to do for me, but in the end—she heard me and didn't even look at me. What completely killed me was that I knew I would have done the exact same thing to someone. Who am I kidding? I *had* done the same thing—countless times. Since I *knew* I didn't want to give change to a homeless person and I didn't want to have to say "No," I would just try to act like I didn't see them. But now I knew that they didn't buy the act. They knew I heard them and it hurt. It hit the core of their humanity and it took them farther away from who God says they are. I took them farther away by not acknowledging them as a person, made in His image and of value, in front of me. I was so ashamed and it changed me. The real kicker was that the only person who stopped to acknowledge me that day was an actual homeless person. He apologized for not having any food or money to offer me. Well, isn't that a kick in the pants? He did offer me a cigarette, though. I passed. I mean, come on! I was on a church mission trip. ☺

To clarify: I do not think we have to give every time a homeless person asks us for money. In fact, I think it is generally unwise to do so most of the time for many reasons. However, we must, must, must, *must* acknowledge people in front of us—people who are talking to us. We can always say "Hi" or smile. We can introduce ourselves and ask their name. If they ask us if we have anything to give them, we can come up with a way to express care, but still say "No."

Kay Warren asks, "How many times have you passed a homeless man or woman holding a 'Will work for food' or 'homeless veteran' sign with your eyes averted? As long as you don't make eye contact, it's fairly easy to drive past him with no twinges of guilt. But if you make eye contact, suddenly you are confronted with the truth that this is a *fellow human being* with a name, a face, and a story."[5] We can take them to a sandwich shop if we want to get them food or make a quick drive to McDonalds to bring them back something if we feel led to. We can have things in our cars or purses ready to go—food (granola bars are easy) or gift certificates. Regardless, we can always say Hello and give dignity. We must. It changes them…and us…and our kids.

No matter where the trip is—to live with family or friends who serve as missionaries in South America, to build a house in Mexico, to serve at an orphanage in Eastern Europe with a church group, to serve the inner-city homeless, to teach English in Asia, or to help bring supplies and teach in Africa—whatever it is, find out what interests your kids and send them. I looked more into TeenMissions—a summer mission program where teens go to a two-week bootcamp for missions and then spend four weeks in a mission project of their choosing. They have some preteen ones in the states and other camps for younger kids too. I am so excited about this (though it won't be easy).

Send them! We just want to hold them close and pour our love all over them…and we can. But it must be in preparation for sending them out to share that love with others or our system is broken. My husband's church in Scottsdale had a motto, "Grow and Go," which is pretty brave. A lot of churches remind me of a group of flowers that are planted too close together: some seeds are good, but too many planted all together over time choke each other out fighting for space and sunlight. They are best if the seed is spread around—for themselves and for the gospel.

God's Will

While we receive God's will all along as we grow up (His ultimate Will is that we know Him and make Him known—plainly put), the specifics of what that looks like usually come slowly as youth become adults. It is important that we send them out with the ability to know how to hear God's will for their life. Claude Hickman writes, "God gives people direction more than directions. He will not rob you of the faith building experience of obeying Him for what He says, not what you see. We cannot expect to get all the detailed instructions before we are willing to begin walking the path. The Bible doesn't lay out a 'map.' It gives us a 'compass.'"[6]

So, what is the compass and how can we help our kids get it? Well, as I see it, the True North is as I mentioned before: Loving God and Loving others. Or put another way: Loving God and making Him known (in word and deed). They are the greatest commandments in the New Testament.

Theologian Frederick Buechner wrote that, "Vocation is where our greatest passion meets the world's greatest need."

This definition of our calling has made sense since the day I heard it and has shaped how both my husband and I have made our big life and career decisions.

"Calling" and "God's Will" are both ways of knowing God's heart and sensing His leading in who He has made our kids to be. He reveals little pictures of it, and we chase after it and He reveals more, all along changing us and making us into more obedient, refined servants. We are called to share in God's heart and be obedient. "What is a call is as practical as reading a missions book, having a map up on the wall that you can't get out of your mind or having your heart broken by a statistic."[7] We can send them out in their careers and future lifestyles, always considering God's mission on earth and how he created them uniquely.

Counsel

Our kids will undoubtedly be broken by the suffering they see in the world at some point. We need to be ready to enter into that pain and the hard questions with our children. Kay Warren remembers one of her hard moments: "But nothing, absolutely nothing, in my experience or my faith had prepared me to speak to a homeless woman dying of AIDS and living under a tree. I smiled on the outside, but on the inside I was in total panic—angry at God, angry at the brokenness of the world, searching the dim recesses of my mind for something halfway spiritual to say."[8]

We may just see that this Living, Educating, Serving, and Sending pans out. In a letter to her parents, who always told her to "Just do what God tells you to do," the daughter of Ganila Baumnan (author of *Releasing Your Children to the Lord*) writes: "Your desire to follow Jesus was modeled in your life and was one that I wanted to follow….Now I get to bless other people with the same desire to follow Jesus. You blessed me with boldness to go anywhere Jesus would lead. "[9]

Tangible Acts in Response to L.E.S.S.:

1. **Pray—entrust the Lord with your children! Give them back continually.**

2. **Send them off somewhere!**

Chapter 25
Do Something Big!

All we have to decide is what to do with the time that is given us.
–J. R. R. Tolkein

We have friends who lived and worked for a year and a half in the slums of Thika, Kenya, starting up a center for pregnant mothers, young children, and babies. They had two young kids, a four-year-old boy and two-year-old girl when they arrived. They lived in a part of the country that had "rape gates" (wooden and metal locked doors on the house and even bedrooms), bars on the window, and a security guard at all times.

The underlying motive for this "unsafe" move was to follow God's call on their life. They relied deeply on God's insistent call on their life and the prayers of many. They believed that spiritually, the "safest" place for their family to be was in God's will. That is a different kind of safe living. It doesn't feel the same. It feels risky. But it builds faith, it trusts God, and it views eternity correctly.

During this time they were away, it was amazing to hear their stories, to see their kids embrace Africa and new friends. They even got pregnant there and had their youngest daughter in Kenya. It wasn't easy—by any stretch. It cost them a great deal—of heartbreak, sorrow, effort, and finances. But they also gained so much as they were part of an amazing ministry (I'm pretty sure at least 20 babies were named Ian or Anne). They, indeed, in this time, saw God protect them and provide for them.

After a year and a half, the commitment didn't stop as they started a nonprofit (Ameena, named after their daughter who was born there) that feeds and educates the children in the slums of Thika, using the contacts they had met when they were there.

This has not only changed them, but all the friends and family who are now involved as well. Our other friends are donating huge amounts of services, finances, and time into this awesome ministry. Our friends' kids have started their own little ministries to raise money for it. Once a pebble is thrown, the ripple effect continues.

Why not go for a month or a year? *Sticky Faith* reads:

> *When Rob was a ninth grader, his whole family spent ten weeks serving at a missionary-run school for two hundred boys in Honduras ... This trip deeply impacted Rob's faith and that of his brothers, two of whom had been adopted by the family from another Latin American country ... Now Rob is thinking about how to replicate those kinds of experiences with his own kids. He notes, 'That's definitely*

an outflow of the priorities of the home I grew up in. Those seeds were planted a long time ago.'[1]

I want to suggest that we have the power to do radical things … to do crazy *big* things. Living missionally with L.E.S.S. can look very habitual, and that is wonderful. It takes time to start things slowly, to wash off lies and bad habits, and put on new living. However, there may be times when God calls us to do something *big*—whether it looks big in your eyes or in the world's eyes.

Some big act (like moving to another country) can become the identity of a family, or make children more fully invested in those God has called them to serve. Our friends, the Ambroses, moved to inner-city Hartford to care for and reach the people of Hartford holistically. Their kids go to Hartford inner-city schools—revealing that they are totally committed because they *live* there. They followed God's call and have been blessed for it, becoming leaders in the city and in their community.

Our friends, Craig and Natalie, have felt like God may be calling them to work somewhere else to serve God. A wise friend told them, "You don't have to jump in all at once. Just be in a place where you can go if you are called." So they have. They have been cleaning, organizing their lives, and getting rid of excess junk. They are preparing their life in such a way that if they are called, they are already ready. Even if they don't go anywhere, they are feeling the lightness of LESS is MORE so that they can give more fully to organizations that they care about. I am very motivated by their modeling of this.

Our friends, the Bergers, lived as missionaries in Turkey for the majority of their four childrens' growing up years. Though that life call placed some very hard realities on them and their children, God has done some amazing things in and through them. They have been back in the States for many years, very intentional with cross-cultural ministry here, and my children have had the pleasure to see their intentional life and have their grown up children as role models who love Christ.

One thing to mention here…we don't all need to go and be international missionaries. However, if we are making the decision not to go, then we are making the decision to stay. Though it may not feel like an intentional decision – it is a decision by default. My husband begged a challenge on us as a family. He said, "What if we considered ourselves as missionaries HERE? How would our lives look differently if we actually felt called here, in a foreign land, hoping to have relationships where we could share the gospel?" I know some families that do that very well. We are still figuring it out.

Giving

Besides relocating or founding a nonprofit, there are countless other big things we can do. What about big, *sacrificial* giving that we include our kids in? As we know that most of the things we spend our money on day to day doesn't last, we could sacrifice some extras and save it to give to some ministry or people that *will* last.

Lysa Terkerust, writes:

> *Sacrificial giving is one of the few times God asks us to test Him. Yet for many years I found myself unwilling to accept the challenge. I was willing to tithe but not willing to go beyond what I felt comfortable giving. Leaving our comfort zone, however, is the very place God calls us to. He wants us to venture into truly abundant giving. He wants us to get out from under our own selfishness with our possessions and accept His invitation to become radically obedient with what we own. Then, not only will He bless us, but He will lavish blessing upon blessing on us.*[2]

Our faith could change, our kids' lives could be impacted, and surely the lives of others could be impacted by what we give. With all of these things, we, of course, must pray and not be guilted into things. However, we must renew our minds by God's call to live a holy, sacrificial life of honoring service and worship.

> *And be not conformed to this world: but be ye transformed by the renewing of your mind, that ye may prove what [is] that good, and acceptable, and perfect, will of God.* (Romans 12:2)

Traditions

One area that we can change—though not necessarily easy—is in our holidays. It can be easy in the sense that you don't have to leave the country or sell your house. Most likely, it won't cost you anything However, changing the ways that we have always done things (and how everyone else is still doing things) does feel very costly (and very big) in other ways.

I will highlight one holiday in particular: Christmas!

To Santa or Not to Santa?

There have been lots of debates about whether or not to include the jolly red man in our holidays, and people fall across a huge spectrum about this question, even in Christian circles. I had originally asked myself the question that many ask themselves about lying to my kids about Santa versus letting them have a childlike magical spirit, and did some debate. However, it was when I found out *who Saint Nicholas actually was* that my mind was made up.

Santa Claus (Santa comes from Saint, and Claus comes from a Dutch form of the name Nicholas) has many possible stories of who he was in actual history, but one thing is for sure: he was generous to the poor and oppressed (as a story goes, he helped three girls not have to be given as prostitutes by putting money in their socks) and he defended the Christian faith. As you learn more about who this bishop was, it is tragic to consider what he would think about how he has been remembered. He was a man who gave up his own comfort to care for others and wanted the glory of God, yet the modern day Santa image supports materialism and selfishness and deters from worship of Christ at the time of His birth. Makes my stomach hurt. J. Rosenthal and C. Myers wrote a poem comparing the two:

Santa Claus belongs to childhood;
St. Nicholas models for all of life.
Santa Claus, as we know him, developed to boost Christmas sales—the commercial Christmas message;
St. Nicholas told the story of Christ and peace, goodwill toward all—the hope-filled Christmas message.
Santa Claus encourages consumption;
St. Nicholas encourages compassion.
Santa Claus appears each year to be seen and heard for a short time;
St. Nicholas is part of the communion of saints, surrounding us always with prayer and example.
Santa Claus flies through the air—from the North Pole;
St. Nicholas walked the earth—caring for those in need.
Santa Claus, for some, replaces the Babe of Bethlehem;
St. Nicholas, for all, points to the Babe of Bethlehem.
Santa Claus isn't bad;
St. Nicholas is just better.[3]

So, what do we do then with Santa Claus? Well, that is for each family to decide. In Holland, they celebrate St. Nicholas Day on December 6th, which we did this last year—deciding to give to the poor in honor of St. Nicholas. What about the stocking? I don't know. We are a family still in the process of figuring it out, but I want to *choose* what we do on this sacred holiday to honor Christ and even remember a great hero who was a man named Nicholas, not someone that Coca Cola framed into a fat man with busting presents on his shoulder (seriously, check out how "Santa" came to be).

> *Therefore the Lord himself will give you a sign: The virgin will conceive and give birth to a son, and will call him Immanuel.* (Isaiah 7:14)

What *is* Christmas all about? How the heck does it correlate to the poor and suffering? Mike Slaughter writes:

> *The traditional Christmas that we have grown up with is about a feel-good, insulated, holly-jolly Santa Claus Jesus who leaves us isolated from the needs of the world. We are detached from the servant Son of God who would not be exempt or insulated from pain, suffering, or death. Jesus experienced the injustice and unfairness of life in its extremes when, beginning at age two, he lived with his family as refugees in Africa to escape the Judean genocide. He was executed as a criminal of the state around the age of thirty-three. So will someone please tell me: Where is the disconnect between Jesus's birthday, refugees, genocide, and Africa?*[4]

In some ways slowly and in some ways drastically, my family is changing—we are changing how we do Christmas and Easter. We are reclaiming them.

Adoption

At the outset of this section, let me note that adoption is not for everyone. However, I believe that everyone should be caring for orphans in some way.

Ryan Hooker and his wife Jess met Daniel when he was 18 months old in their adoption process through Guatemala. It was then that stories of a corrupt system and stories of trafficked babies came out. UNICEF blew the whistle, and they shut down adoption in Guatemala. The Guatemalan government froze adoptions for five years while 4,000 children were stuck in the middle. 4,000 kids that had already met their new families were suddenly unable to be adopted, with no prospect of safe families in Guatemala to pick up the call. The Hooker family remained committed to Daniel, spending unheard of amounts of money on 36 trips to Guatemala to visit their son and advocate for him—passing up a job, moving, and all the other things they could have spent their money on—as well as other adoptions. The Hooker family was the first to have their adoption pass after a five-year wait. Their son was six when he finally came home to them under a new law.[5]

That is love. That is faithful, Christ-like love that fights through boundaries, naming someone as their own and bringing them home. That is adoption.

Adoption is a hot topic right now. It is probably a pretty hot topic most the time. However, media likes to make adoption either into saint-like behavior or something that greedy people do in the context of corrupt countries. Besides a few sickos out there, it is truly neither.

First, I will say that there is indeed corruption in adoption, as there is corruption in anything that makes money, particularly in developing countries where people are in poverty and easier to be taken advantage of. However, I also need to say that adoption as a whole has gotten a bad rap. UNICEF as an organization—though they do many great things—has failed millions of children by shutting down adoption. In their effort to keep kids in their own countries (to support community development, which I'm totally behind), they haven't dealt with the reality of the current problem—which is about 160 million orphans globally. The result? Trafficking has increased. Now that in-country institutions are busting at the seams because kids aren't adopted, or the process takes so long to adopt, there are more kids than ever on the street. This allows traffickers to take their pick of the litter. At least when adoption is happening, there can be some sense of control (see *STUCK*, the documentary).

I am not saying I have the answers, but I am saying that children need homes, and it is *always* God's will that kids have families. We can't just wipe our hands clean of the system and say that we don't want to be a part of it because we've heard rumors about it being corrupt. Things need to be changed. Community development needs to lead the way. Bad people need to be prevented from adopting, but adoption needs to continue so long as there are kids without homes that are not being cared for.

> *God sets the lonely in families, he leads out the prisoners with singing; but the rebellious live in a sun-scorched land.* (Psalm 68:6)

I've always felt a call to adopt. Ever since I held little orphans in Haiti, I remember promising in my heart to the kids (in general without families) "I'll come back for you." When my husband and I met, we actually talked about adoption on our first date. My husband grew up in a family that did foster care, so caring for kids that were not biologically related to him was natural. Also, my brother and his wife had a very successful (though not easy) first adoption through foster care and are in the thick of a second adoption, painfully helping their son deal with his past. They have done an incredible job with these kids, and if I think about the redemption of these kids, I could be stuck in tears for hours. So after much praying and seeking (and what seemed to be at the time a very direct call from God), we too started the international adoption process. We emptied our savings account, praying our car would miraculously putt along, and moved forward with the process. We applied for some grants and did a little bit of fundraising and prayed!

I can't even explain how awesome this process has been in terms of finances so far. Somehow, our car made it a year with about four warning lights, and then we were gifted a car by my generous parents. We received grants and some fundraising, and even extra money from my husband's job. Since Ethiopia's adoption process has slowed down greatly as they correct some problems (having some of the same media attention as Guatemala), we have been waiting quite a bit longer than initially expected. Adoption is not for the faint of heart. It is a humbling process, yet God has been so good to sustain us, confirm His call, and even bless the time as we wait in different ways. I have felt more deeply for orphan issues than ever in my life. I have laid in bed and cried for the mother that gave her child up due to extreme poverty or illness or death. I have felt like orphans, as a whole, was my issue because I could imagine parenting and loving so many different kids.

> *The Spirit you received does not make you slaves, so that you live in fear again; rather, the Spirit you received brought about your adoption to sonship. And by him we cry, "Abba, Father." The Spirit himself testifies with our spirit that we are God's children. Now if we are children, then we are heirs—heirs of God and co-heirs with Christ, if indeed we share in his sufferings in order that we may also share in his glory.* (Romans 8:15–17)

I have different friends that have adopted infants domestically, foster kids of different ages, kids from South Korea, China, Rwanda, Guatemala, Ethiopia, Ghana, Russia, Ukraine, and more. All of these stories have some level of "REALLY HARD" in them, but they are also all BEAUTIFUL. I am proud of all of them.

A different friend, Lisa, lived in Grenada when her husband was in medical school there. She visited an orphanage and met a couple with an amazing story. The couple had come to Grenada and visited the orphanage and fallen in love with a little boy. They knew that little boy was *their* little boy, but Grenada doesn't allow adoption out of their island country … so what did they do? Did they give up? Did they find another kid at another orphanage? Did they try to fight with lawyers? All would be fair responses for most people, but they did not do any of them. They moved to Grenada, and they spend as much time as possible volunteering at the orphanage to be with the boy they consider their son. Though they hope that eventually the country will see their intentions and make an exception to their adoption rule, they have no guarantee of that—no real hope of it, really. They moved from their home to be in a poor country to be with a child that may never be theirs. That is crazy. But that is the gospel. Do we get that?

Christ came for us. He left His home and glory to be in a dirty, poor place knowing not all the children would be His. That is why adoption is so powerful. It isn't only that we change lives. It isn't only that it brings the reality of compassion, grace, and restoration into our homes. It is that we are re-enacting the gospel. Even if we don't adopt, adoption will forever have changed me. This seeking after the lost and fatherless is part of the gospel, and I applaud all those who have—not because they are awesome people, but because they have listened to the call of Christ. I am so grateful for those who have supported them, too—perhaps not adopted, but made it possible for them to adopt. It wouldn't have been possible otherwise. Most countries aren't adopting out—and they have millions of orphans. Someone needs to take care of them physically, prayerfully, and financially. We can all have our role. We are not all called to adopt, but we are all called to care for orphans.

Steven Curtis and Mary Beth Chapman adopted three girls—one of which died in a tragic car accident at their home. Their family is dedicated to adoption, making it possible for thousands of others to adopt (we got a grant from their agency, actually). Steven writes: "It's scary for me to think we might have missed all of this….Mary Beth and I could have missed the joy of adoption by not seeking it out. Now, we look at our family, and we can't imagine missing something so key in what it means to walk close with God."[6]

Do something big! No matter what you do, remember the God that will provide, protect, and sustain you in it. He is the God who came for you when you were an orphan.

What a promise to remember:

I will not leave you as orphans; I will come to you. (John 14:18)

Tangible Acts in Response to L.E.S.S.:

1. **Dream up a list of big acts with your family—pick one to work toward!**

2. **Take a look at the waiting children with several adoption agencies that also have good reputations for their community development work. If adoption isn't on your heart, pray for those children to find families.**

Chapter 26

The Joy of Isaiah 58 and living with L.E.S.S.

I want to live a life that demands an explanation.

–Shiela Walsh

Adelaine (at age three) is having a profound spiritual moment in her room yelling prayers to God like, "God, where are you? Jesus, I want to see you. You are beafiful [beautiful] … Jesus, won't you talk to me? God? Are you there?" There is a long pause, and then I hear a low, booming voice responding to the call saying, "Yes?" Wondering if God is truly responding to my little girl, I go quickly into the room and see that five-year-old Lukas, hiding behind a pillow, has taken it upon himself to use a long cardboard tube to change and echo his voice to impersonate God's. Poor girl just wanted to hear from God and all she got was a rascally brother pranking her.

We all long to hear God's voice. We all want to hear and know His will for us. Though there is much that we can gain from seeking God's specific wisdom and direction, the truth is that He has already given us so much of the map, yet we don't live like we understand. The end point is God's redemption of the lost in this world. The end point is to bring glory to God through a life of humble, sacrificial service and worship to God. Isaiah 58 is one of my most favorite passages in the Bible—not only because it reveals God's amazing heart for the hurting, but because it tells me who I can be when I join God in that effort.

Jen Hatmaker writes: "We must run, not walk, the way of Isaiah 58, embracing authentic faith manifested through mercy and community. Living on mission requires nothing less. It is a grand adventure, a true voyage into the kingdom of God."[1]

"Is not this the kind of fasting I have chosen:
to loose the chains of injustice
and untie the cords of the yoke,
to set the oppressed free
and break every yoke?
Is it not to share your food with the hungry
and to provide the poor wanderer with shelter—
when you see the naked, to clothe them,
and not to turn away from your own flesh and blood?
Then your light will break forth like the dawn,
and your healing will quickly appear;
then your righteousness[a] will go before you,
and the glory of the LORD will be your rear guard.
Then you will call, and the LORD will answer;
you will cry for help, and he will say: Here am I.
"If you do away with the yoke of oppression,
with the pointing finger and malicious talk,
and if you spend yourselves in behalf of the hungry
and satisfy the needs of the oppressed,
then your light will rise in the darkness,
and your night will become like the noonday.
The LORD will guide you always;

he will satisfy your needs in a sun-scorched land
and will strengthen your frame.
You will be like a well-watered garden,
like a spring whose waters never fail.
Your people will rebuild the ancient ruins
and will raise up the age-old foundations;
you will be called Repairer of Broken Walls,
Restorer of Streets with Dwellings. (Isaiah 58:6-12)

What sweet words we (the restored) might hear as we work with God in His redemption that we find in Isaiah 58 and this incredible work He invites us into: "Repairer of Broken Walls, Restorer of Streets with Dwellings."

I am not my own. Repeat: **I AM NOT MY OWN.** My money, my time, my gifts are not my own to do with a please. LESS is MORE. This isn't confining. It is glorious, for I cannot imagine other purposes more amazing than restoring the lives of others. For in the restoration of others is where I continue to be refined and redeemed. This too is true then for the children and youth in our lives.

> *If you want God's attention, if you want to please Him, and if you want your prayers to be heard, then you need to live the 'True Fast'—to seek justice for the oppressed, share your resources with those in need, break the structures of oppression, honor the Sabbath, and pour yourself out for the hungry .... The promises of Isaiah 58, the third part of the message, offer assurance that if you live the True Fast then God will heal you, guard you, guide you, strengthen you, and listen to you. God will show up.*[2]

What can I whisper to my children at night about their future?

- You will be successful (no one can guarantee that even if someone works hard)
- You will be happy (can't guarantee that either)

  What can I offer then in light of scripture if they follow this call?
- You will be called a "Repairer" and a "Restorer."
- When you call for God, He will say "Here I am."

I can pray for nothing more.

Joy!

I watch horribly sad documentaries about child soldiers, sex trafficking, street children, etc. I cry at night because I know about some current world issue that is oppressing and killing thousands … or because I am reminded about tragedies like trafficking or the reality that our adopted kids have biological parents who have to go through their worst nightmare before our children will end up in our families. My children know more about missionaries, global issues, and people around them struggling than they do about Disney characters or Superheroes. Yet in the midst of what sounds like an emotional hole, I have never had more joy in my life.

I wake up every day with purpose.

I have futures to offer my children that will give them identity and value regardless of how successful they are in the world.

Though there are horrifically hard stories I know because of this life change, there are so many miraculous stories of redemption that I wouldn't otherwise know.

I go to bed every night amazed that my children are healthy and safe.

I don't take my days for granted.

I often weep in bed out of gratitude for my life, the gifts I've been given, and that God has included me in His great plan.

I have experienced God so much on this journey, more than I could have ever dreamed.

I have joy. When I see my kids serve others, I see joy in them as well—not the fleeting happiness of a toy or experience, but a satisfaction and peace and fulfillment of loving others and serving God.

Mark Lutz summarizes: "Poverty is frequently the bedfellow of inexplicable gratitude. With all my richness, I had not truly experienced it. On that dark night, God showed me my inner poverty. He replaced the emptiness of my pride with the gift of joy and gratitude."[3]

Upside-Down Kingdom

We shouldn't be surprised by this joy and gratitude. We see the promise in Isaiah 58. We see it over and over in scripture. The gospel changes everything. It flips everything on its head. LESS is More and if we lose ourselves, we will find ourselves. It is the amazing thing about God's upside-down Kingdom and the mystery of His redemption.

Suffering, death, and hardship take on different forms in light of Christ and purpose. We run as fast as we can from any form of pain. We do it because we can, especially with our money and our medicines within short reach. But there is a deeper joy that we have missed in life when we hide too much from pain and don't live in the reality of death.

Whenever God unsettles me and I am again broken by an issue or by a new awareness that I painfully must change my life or heart, I am overwhelmed with gratitude. It means that He is working in me. It means that He isn't finished with me. It means that He saw me and cared enough to not let me sit stagnant. Our transformation comes primarily through struggle. We can choose much of what this struggle takes…in our homes, with our support and with our narrative.

It is easy in our culture to deny this kind of transformation. Nothing else in our society suggests that this is how we find fulfillment. No commercial has ever been made that sells joy through hard work and sacrifice for the sake of others. We are told that happiness is in receiving. That is what we are fighting in our children as they are fed this more than we ever were. Yet if our faith and our lives aren't thick in the midst of the brokenness of this world and ourselves where God truly resides and wishes to redeem—we will come up empty. We will have not only missed our chance to do great things in this world purposed by God, but we will have given our children a shallow faith that may not stand against temptation or suffering.

> *But at the end of the day we thought our Christian life would be more than this—somehow larger, more significant, more vivid, and more glorious. But it's not. Driving to church on Sunday feels a bit like Groundhog Day, the movie where Bill Murray's character is forced to pathetically relive exactly the same day over and over again ... Indeed there comes a time in the life of every believer and over every church where a voice inside us simply asks, Now what? . . .This is, I believe, a voice of divine restlessness. This is a voice of sacred discontent. This is the voice of a holy yearning for more. This is the moment in which we can see that all the work that God has been doing in our lives and in the life of the church is not an end in itself; rather, the work he has been doing in us is a powerful means to a grander purpose beyond ourselves.*[4]

God is on the Move

"They say that Aslan is on the move" (a great quote from the Chronicles of Narnia).

And we say, "God is on the move!"

God is doing amazing, radical things in many churches—small ones, huge ones. Certainly not just in America (as we are actually behind on much of this). God is transforming the Church, globally. Though we have always had this call, there is a sense within those working in international development and justice organizations that God is doing something big. There has been a movement of hearts for these issues and a release of God's redemption (as His people have come to Him fasting, praying, and in obedience) that has not been seen in our generation before. But it is not easy. However, as Gary Haugen said at the Justice Conference, "Do-gooders show up late and leave early." This work of training our children in L.E.S.S., for a lifetime of service, perseverance, and loving Christ, is a long, slow, tedious race. The reward, however, will be great.

Joy in Big and Small Packages

When we were living in Oregon, we befriended a couple from Uganda that had come for a year to train at the seminary there. Moses and Christine quickly became our good friends. Being new to the United States, they needed a little assistance, especially with a three-year-old (who quickly became friends with my kids). When they became unexpectedly pregnant shortly after they arrived and didn't have insurance, they needed a lot more assistance. Many people helped and cared for them. They were delightful to be with, so it wasn't much of a stretch to care for them deeply throughout their year in Oregon. Though it was indeed effort, it didn't feel like anything miraculous.

However, then the real miracle was born—a little girl, healthy and beautiful like her mama. Her name? Anna Joy. I am still beyond humbled to have my name on the face of such a sweet little girl. We are blessed to have a relationship still with this family as my husband has gotten to visit them a couple times after they returned to Uganda. We now help their girls just a little in school as Moses and Christine faithfully serve God in missions in many capacities in Uganda.

Joy shows up in unexpected places. I have found it more on this journey into the darkest places of the world. I have found it in the softest places of God's heart for the least of these and in teaching compassion to my children through real relationships. I even got to see joy in the face of a beautiful little girl from Uganda.

Please join me in seeking Christ in the missions with our children, for in some of these hard places lie our greatest joy and their greatest future! Though some of this may be overwhelming—remember that we are on a long distance run. I, too, look at scripture and other parents, teachers, and pastors whom I admire and am trying to just change my response to God's call one day at a time. Be encouraged—you (and I) are in the race to live out Isaiah 58 with our children! I thank God that you joined me in this book! I am humbled to be any part of His great plan of redemption.

God is on the move … and so are His children!

Tangible Acts in Response to L.E.S.S.:

1. **Frame Isaiah 58, put it on your wall, and live by it.**
2. **Rejoice in the Joy that will be deeper than anything we could create on our own with L.E.S.S.**

Chapter 27

Resources For Further Enrichment

You may choose to look the other way but you can never say again that you did not know.

–William Wilberforce

I wrote what I did because as a woman, as a mother, I was oppressed and broken-hearted with the sorrows and injustice I saw.

–Harriet Beecher Stowe

There are more resources out there than those I list below, but these are my current favorites:

Adult Books

Hole in Our Gospel by Rich Stearns—Rich Stearns, President of World Vision USA, reveals his journey to become involved with relief and community development work and with God's work on his heart. He gives great detail and personal openness about his own story and the stories of those he has met in developing countries. His second book is called ***Unfinished***.

Terrify No More by Gary Haugen, President of the International Justice Mission, writes about one particular planned raid in Cambodia to free some girls who are slaves in a brothel. You read actual stories of girls and an intense, true account of lives risked to save others.

Interrupted by Jen Hatmaker—An incredibly witty, thoughtful, and honest account of a pastor's wife whose heart became broken for the least of these, leading her and her husband to start a church plant that meets the needs of urban and global poor. Easy to connect with and unintimidating, but still inspiring. Another amazing book of hers is ***Seven.***

Dangerous Surrender by Kay Warren—Awesome account of Kay Warren (wife of Rick Warren who authored *Purpose Driven Life* and is pastor of Saddleback Church in California) and her journey of getting her heart broken into action for HIV/AIDS. Well written and honest. She has a newer book titled ***Say Yes to God***, which is wonderful as well.

One Million Arrows by Julie Ferwerda—Wonderful perspective of seeing our children as our arrows into the world (Isaiah 49), and then goes on to inspire more youth ministry and adoption.

Christians in an Age of Wealth: A Biblical Theology of Stewardship by Craig L. Blomberg—Great scriptural engagement with God's view of stewardship in a Christian's life and tackling with some of the basics of how we are to live.

Serving with Eyes Wide Open by David A. Livermore—A wise introduction to short-term missions.

Just Courage by Gary Haugen—President of IJM writes extraordinarily about being brave to stop horrible things in this world. My favorite part is the amazing stories at the end of the book. His first book was ***Good News about Injustice.*** He has a new one out, ***The Locust Effect***.

Fields of the Fatherless by Tom Davis—Really wonderful explanation of God's heart for the downcast and least of these. Well written with true, personal stories throughout. God reveals His heart for the orphan through the scriptures that Tom doesn't allow us to escape from. Another great book by him is ***Red Letters***.

Son of God is Dancing by Adrian Plass—Best, easiest read to explain how the AIDS epidemic got so bad in Africa. Gives personal stories so it is less easy to judge mass groups of people and see how the disease crept up and took lives like a thief. Also has a great deal of hope!

Outlive Your Life by Max Lucado—In a way that only he can, Lucado inspires us to use our life in ways that really matter. He also wrote ***Live to Make a Difference.***

Awake by Noel Brewer Yeatts—Important and impactful stories from around the world about caring for one person at a time.

Overrated by Eugene Cho—An challenge to stop talking about justice/mercy and start doing it.

He Walks Among Us by Richard and Renee Stears—An extraordinary devotional that brings the reader into the lives of the poor/oppressed, while reflecting on God's work in our lives.

Everyday Justice: The Global Impact of Our Daily Choices by Julie Clawson—How do our everyday choices and purchases affect the world for God and love for God?

Half the Sky by Nicholas Kristof and Sheryl WuDunn—These authors highlight some of the issues that plague oppressed and poor women globally through real stories, as well as reveal ways that they can be alleviated and empowered.

Global Soccer Mom by Shayne Moore—An inspiring account of how God allowed an ordinary soccer mom to be part of the beginning of the ONE campaign. Encouraging for us all. She also coauthored ***Refuse to Do Nothing*** and is working on another book.

A Thousand Sisters by Lisa Shannon—So hard to read, but important to not look away and to weep with the children and women in Congo who are still being used right now as weapons of war (through killings, rape, and mutilation).

A Long Way Gone by Ishmael Beah—A boy recounts his real-life experience as a boy soldier in Sierra Leone. Gives real, personal insight into its horror. Well written.

Mission Minded Family by Ann Dunagan—Extraordinary ideas to include not just missions, but actual missionaries as heroes throughout. Encourages intentional parenting toward missions. ***Mission Minded Child*** is similar in style but full of loads of different resources and thoughts.

The Middle of Everywhere by Mary Pipher—A great book explaining refugees in our country.

Not for Sale by David Batstone—Overview of human trafficking and what we can do to help.

Faith in Action BIBLE—Put out by World Vision, it has pictures, stats, and amazing study notes throughout so we can read our Bible and not miss God's heart on every page!

Poverty and Justice BIBLE—Highlights God's heart for justice and includes extra study. Supported by many major relief and justice organizations.

I am Najood, Age 10 and Divorced by Najood Ali—Given in marriage at age 10 (not uncommon in her area), Najood decides to break the norm and fight her way out of it. Heartbreaking and amazing.

Kisses From Katie by Katie Davis and Beth Clark—Katie Davis was 18 and fell in love with Uganda. She gave up college and all of the "comforts" and family of America to become the mom of 13 adopted girls and lead hundreds of kids to Christ and education through her ministry, Amazima. Insightful, educational, inspiring.

Toxic Charity by Robert D. Lupton—An important read for anyone doing justice, relief, inner-city and missions work. It addresses how we help people without hurting them. You'll be surprised how necessary and convicting it is to read.

Left to Tell by Immaculee Ilibigaza—She tells of 91 days she spent in a cramped bathroom hiding with seven other starving women during the Rwandan genocide.

Deepening the Soul for Justice by Bethany Hoang—An extraordinary read and devotional regarding gaining a heart for justice as well as the essential time with God in any compassion and justice work.

Books that are also powerful in Audio form

The Heavenly Man by Brother Yun and Paul Hattaway—Amazing testimony of a pastor in the underground, persecuted church of China.

Running for My Life by Lopez Lomong and Mark Tabb—A lost boy from Sudan tells of his journey to a family and all the way to the Olympics. AMAZING!

The Cross and the Switchblade by David Wilkerson—The amazing beginning of Teen Challenge in the hardest parts of NYC.

Love Has a Face by Michele Perry and Heidi Baker—Missionary work in Sudan, full of miracles and God's heart.

In the Presence of My Enemies by Gracia Burnham and Dean Merrill—Held hostage in missionary work in the Philippines.

I Dared to Call Him Father by Bilquis Sheikh—A Muslim woman risks everything to know Jesus.

Peace Child and ***Lords of the Earth*** by Don Richardson—New Guinea and Iranian missions.

End of the Spear by Steve Saint—The story of Nate Saint, Jim Elliot, and others who were martyred by Auca Indians in missionary work.

Youth/Teen Novels (Not all Christian, but still culturally significant)

Shooting Kabul by N. H. Senzai—A girl is separated from her parents by the Taliban and has a plan to relocate her parents.

One Crazy Summer by Rita Williams-Garcia—three girls travel to look for their mother who abandoned them, set in the 60s.

Wonder by R. J. Palacio—A boy with a severe facial deformity is mainstreamed in school—deals with everything.

Inside Out and Back Again by Thanhha Lai—Escaping Vietnam, a girl with her family comes to live in America.

Out of My Mind by Sharon M. Draper—About a girl with cerebral palsy.

A Long Walk to Water: Based on a True Story by Linda Sue Park—A boy named Salva, during a long two-hour walk for water becomes one of the "Lost Boys of Sudan."

The Breadwinner by Deborah Ellis—Another insightful book about living in Afghanistan.

Iqbal by Francesco D'Adamo—Pakistan girl sold to carpet factory.

Real Kids Adventure Series by David Gustaveson—Mission adventure fiction books.

Airquest Adventure Series by Jerry Jenkins—Mission adventure fiction books.

Found in Translation by Roger and Kristi Bruner—Girl finds her faith and perspective on a mission trip.

YWAM's International Adventures Series

My Hands Came Away Red by Lisa McKay—Danger and adventure on a mission trip.

I Would Die for You by Brent and Dianna Higgins—Challenge by a 15-year-old to be willing to die for Christ.

If We Survive by Andrew Klaven—A group of kids stuck in danger during a mission trip.

Children's Books

The Good Garden by Katie Smith Milway—WONDERFUL! About a teacher that changes a village by coming in and teaching about plants and giving power to the people.

If You're Missing Baby Jesus by Jean Gietzen—Amazing book for Christmas time: true story about a family who encounters a family in need at Christmas. It changes them all.

Fly Away Home by Eve Bunting and Ronald Himler—A moving book about a homeless boy and his dad who live in the airport moving from terminal to terminal to not get caught. Reading Rainbow also has the book on DVD with additional real stories from kids and families who are homeless and people who help them.

A Shelter in Our Car by Monica Gunning—A little girl and her mom live in their car.

Material World by Peter Menzel—Photos and families from around the globe. Really good looks at some lives in other places.

The Carpet Boy's Gift by Pegi Deitz Shea and Leane Morin—Children stuck in a carpet factory learn of possible freedom

Mohammed's Journey (A Refugee Diary) by Anthony Robinson and Annemarie Young—True story of a boy fleeing Iraq.

Hamzat's Journey (A Refugee Diary) by Anthony Robinson—True story of a boy leaving Chechnya after a run in with a landmine (there are more Refugee Diaries than these).

Kids Against Hunger by Jon Mikkelsen—Some kids try to figure out why their friend is ditching them at soccer, only to find that he is helping at a food kitchen.

Little Critter—Just Critters Who Care by Mercer Mayer—1st Reader book: Kids learn about a neighbor and decide to help. Really cute.

Four Feet, Two Sandals by Karen Lynn Williams—A sweet and eye-opening book about a refugee camp in Pakistan. Two girls each find one sandal of a matching pair off of a refugee truck after not having any shoes of their own. They decide how to deal with it between each other.

A Day's Work by Eve Bunting—A Latino immigrant grandfather teaches his grandson integrity.

One Smile by Cindy McKinley—One girl decides to smile and it has an effect on person after person after person.

CUMBAYAH by Floyd Cooper—The famous song used as a prayer with beautiful accompanying photos from around the world.

The Lord's Prayer by Tim Ladwig—The Lord's Prayer with beautiful pictures of a girl walking with her father through the inner city.

Beatrice's Goat by Page McBrier—A girl's life changes because of the gift of a goat.

Window on the World by Daphne Spragget and Jill Johnstone—Praying for different kids in different countries.

Every Child Everywhere by Debby Anderson—Reminder about every kid everywhere being made by God.

For Every Child by UNICEF—The rights of the child in word and pictures.

Not Forgotten by Cal Ainley—A little African girl's journey to a needed surgery.

Papa, Do You Love Me? by Barbara M Joosse—An African father's everlasting love.

My Sister, Alicia May by Nancy Tupper Ling—A book about a little girl with Down syndrome.

In Jesse's Shoes by Beverly Lewis—A sister realizes God's perfection in her special needs brother.

Tight Times by Trina Schart Hyman—A boy's family is changing because money is really tight and things are hard with everyone.

Those Shoes by Maribeth Boelts—A boy struggles with not having the same shoes as everyone else.

One Hen by Katie Smith Milway—The change in a family when a small loan is given (true story).

Ordinary Mary's Extraordinary Deed by Emily Pearson—Random acts of kindness for a little girl have unending positive effects.

A Life Like Mine by Unicef—More visuals and facts about how children live around the world.

My Name is Yoon by Helen Recorvits—A girl from Korea moves to the USA and is scared to start school.

The Can Man by Laura E. Williams—A couple kids go from judgment and discomfort to helpfulness and relationship with a kind homeless man.

Mimi's Village by Katie Smith Milway—A picture book about how healthcare transforms a village.

The Small One—A Good Samaritan by Katherine Brown—A different story based on one we all know.

DVD Documentaries

Half the Sky—Long, but really great at showing issues. It focuses on bringing in celebrities (knowing they have a strong voice) to these horrible issues facing women. Interesting to see how it affects them all differently, but it is the stories of the suffering (and often so strong) women that are amazing and horrifying and empowering (all of it).

Isaiah 58—New DVD available through www.live58.org showing poverty and justice issues globally. Only mild things above young eye's understanding. I was comfortable allowing my young children to see it and explaining some of the hard stuff in explainable, less-scary ways.

Walk to Beautiful—Struggle of many women in Ethiopia.

Born into Brothels—Stories of children born to prostitutes in India.

Beyond the Gates of Splendor—Documentary after "End of the Spear" movie of Jim Elliot and his fellow missionaries that lost their lives in order to give the gospel as well as the people who continued to minister to these tribal people of Ecuador. Powerful.

Mary and Martha—Two women meet up who have lost their sons to Maleria while in Africa. It sparks a transformational journey for them and those they want to help.

China's Lost Girls—Stories of orphan girls in China.

We Are Together—Story of South Africa's Agape Choir, beautiful film, pretty accessible to youth.

Beyond Belief—About two women who gave birth to two children after losing spouses to 9/11. They turned their grief into a way to actually minister to Afghanistan widows. It isn't necessarily a Christian documentary, but convicting and inspiring nonetheless.

Angels in the Dust—An orphanage started in South Africa for 500+ kids in response to AIDS crisis—gives lots of individual stories of kids—what they have been through.

Girl Rising—Inspiring and educational documentary on the challenges facing girls internationally.

Stuck—Documentary about International Adoption

Stolen Childhoods—Many different types of child slavery portrayed.

War Dance—Kids who suffered at the hands of the LRA in Uganda use dance as a source of healing and expression.

Emmanuel's Gift—Inspiring true story of disabled orphan in Ghana, not giving up and changing lives around him.

Small Voices—Documenting struggles of garbage dump children in Cambodia.

Lost Boys of Sudan and ***God Grew Tired of Us***—Stories of boys who were in refugee camps most their lives and then brought to America.

Call and Response—Slavery today.

Flesh and Blood—Women who take in medically complex foster kids.

Invisible Children—Boy soldiers.

DVD Movies
Trade of Innocents—The most approachable (for the widest audience) movie on sex trafficking I've ever seen. Still hard to watch, but redemptive and shows both international and domestic issues.

Blood Diamonds—Revealing the very real, disgusting cost of most commercialized diamonds: child soldiers, exploitation, and war.

Holly—Story of one girl in Cambodia stuck in sex trafficking.

Children of Heaven—Appropriate for younger viewers, though if I recall it has subtitles. Two poor children trying to get a new pair of shoes in the Middle East. Really sweet film.

The Trade—Sex trafficking: though hard to see, doesn't show too much and is somewhat redemptive.

Kite Runner—Based off a best-seller. Really important to see life in the Middle East, but some difficult scenes.

End of the Spear—Based on the famous story of Jim Elliott and his fellow missionaries, passion, and death while serving a tribe in Ecuador.

Pursuit of Happyness—Beautiful movie of man who is trying to make a better life for himself and his son. They are briefly homeless while he is trying to get a job as a stockbroker. True story.

Searching for Antwone Fisher—Man dealing with his past abuse and loss as a foster child. There is a level of beautiful redemption in this movie.

Tears of the Sun—Rescue operation of some missionaries and the effect of seeing the struggles of people in a war-torn country. Really an excellent film of people moving from seeing Africans as *others* to people they care about.

Crash—Hard to watch, but shows that there are prejudices everywhere. Also shows a lot of different poverty, race, and trafficking issues in America.

Temple Grandin—About a woman with autism. Very insightful and beautiful.

Radio—Caring and standing up for a mentally disabled boy who wants to help on a football team. Some powerful scenes.

The Killing Fields—About the genocide in Cambodia. Horrifically hard to watch, but true and so important to know the background of Cambodia.

Slumdog Millionaire—A boy's winning streak on a TV show is tracked through his hard life's events in India.

Constant Gardener—A mystery/action movie that uncovers a dirty secret of a company in Kenya.

Faith Like Potatoes—True story of a South African farmer. Beautiful.

Maria Full of Grace—Woman caught in Colombia drug war. Not easy viewing.

Reign Over Me—Aftermath of a man's life after losing his kids and wife to the 9/11 tragedy.

Amistad—Shows some of the horrors of the American slave trade during a mutiny on a slave ship in 1800s. Graphic.

Amazing Grace—Amazing story of William Wilberforce, among other abolitionists, working to end the slave trade in 1800s.

The Visitor—One man is changed by his interactions with some illegal immigrants.

Beyond the Gates—Catholic school is used as a place of refuge for Rwandan Tutsis during the genocide. Some faith questions. It shows the genocide and death while showing minimal actual killings. Well done movie, but tragic.

Under the Same Moon—Little boy tries to sneak to America to get to his mother, only barely shows all the horrors that could have happened. Beautiful movie.

Bella—Amazing movie of redemption. Gentle approach against abortion.

Beyond Borders—Some pretty incredible landscape, eye-opening scenes of poverty and war in this film.

The Good Lie—Reece Witherspoon in an incredible movie about war refugees

Journey to Jamaa—Short film on poverty and sponsorship. Free online through World Vision.

Not Without My Daughter—Sally Fields stars in a movie that reveals darker part of some Muslim womens' lives

Soul Surfer—Great faith, true story, but key is how her perspective changed when she visited the poor after the tsunami. Good for young eyes.

The Blind Side—A rich white family is changed when they meet a kind boy who was lost in the cracks of society. True story of football player.

Ultimate Gift—Rich, selfish man gets a chance at a new life through a series of tests to get an inheritance.

Tsunami: The Aftermath—Helps a person understand what the tsunami in Thailand of 2004 was like.

Grace Card—A cop, whose child was killed by a black drug dealer, is teamed with a black partner and deals with his racism and bad family life. Faith and redemption.

Music (Soundtrack)

Kingdom Come, With Every Act of Love—Jason Gray
Banner of Love—Luminate
Live Like That—Sidewalk Prophets
God of This City—Chris Tomlin
We Are—Kari Jobe
Compassion—Rough Draft
I Will Go - Starfield
Tanzania—Alli Rogers
God of Justice—Tim Hughes
My Own Little World—Matthew West
Give Me Your Eyes—Brandon Heath
Micah 6:8, Chainbreaker—Charlie Hall
Daylight—Ten Shekel Shirt
I Saw What I Saw, Eyes on the Prize—Sara Groves
Gloria—Brenton Brown
Rise—Robbie Seay Band
Beautiful Things—Gungor
I Refuse—Josh Wilson
Instead of a Show—Jon Foreman
All the Poor and Powerless—All Sons and Daughters
God is Justice, God is Mercy—Dan Bursch
Missions Flame, Fill Us Up and Send Us Out—Matt Redman
If We are the Body, Until the Whole World Hears—Casting Crowns

Children's Resources

Voice of the Martyrs Torchlighters DVDs
YWAM Missionary Biography Books, International Adventure Series and downloads
Lightkeepers Series Books
Trailblazer Series Books
Reel Kid Adventures books
Brickman Adventures Audio Stories
10/40 VBS Materials
WMU—Missions Magazines for Kids, Family Mission Trips

VBS
Voice of the Martyrs
Regulard Baptist Press
10/40 Window
WMU

Websites with extra resources
World Vision
Compassion
IJM
Justice Kids
Stand Up For Kids/Pioneers
Harvest Ministry
Kids of Courage—Bold Believer Series
Wycliff
YWAM—Mission opportunities/Training
Perspectives Journey
One Mission Kids
My Passport to India
WeaveFamily
SIM Kids
OM New Zealand
WindowKids

Works Cited

Chapter 1

1. Kay Warren, Dangerous Surrender (Grand Rapids: Zondervan, 2007), 20.
2. http://positivelyorphaned.org/hiv-adoption/
3. http://www.fromhivtohome.org/faqs/
4. http://www.bbc.co.uk/news/mobile/health-13381292?SThisEM
5. Faith J. H. Mcdonnell and Grace Akallo, Girl Soldier: A Story of Hope for Northern Uganda's Children (Ada: Chosen Books, 2007), 118.
6. Beyond the Gates film
7. Kay Warren, Say Yes to God (Grand Rapids: Zondervan, 2010), 108.
8. David Batstone, Not For Sale (New York: Harper One, 2010), 1.
9. (Dangerous Surrender, 97–98)
10. Gary A Haugen, Terrify No More (Nashville, W. Publishing Group, 2005), 41.
11. (Terrify No More, 240)

Chapter 2

1. Dallas Willard, The Great Omission (San Francisco: Harper, 2006), 15–16.
2. Gary Haugen, Just Courage (Downers Grove: IVP, 2008), 41.
3. Mark Labberton, The Dangerous Act of Loving Your Neighbor (Downers Grove: IVP Books, 2010), 26.
4. Jen Hatmaker, Interrupted (Colorado Springs: NavPress, 2009), 27-28.
5. Tony Campolo, Let Me Tell You a Story (Nashville: W Publishing Group, 2000), 28.

Chapter 3

1. Katie Davis with Beth Clark, Kisses from Katie: A Story of Relentless Love and Redemption (New York: Howard Books, 2011), 30, 32.

2. Richard Stearns, Hole in the Gospel (Nashville: Thomas Nelson, 2010), 22.
3. Ronald J. Sider, Good News and Good Works (Grand Rapids: Baker Books, 1993), 10.
4. Jim Wallis, The Call to Conversion (New York: Harper, 1981), 8.
5. (The Call to Conversion, 8)
6. Scott C Todd, PhD, 58: Fast Living (Colorado Springs: Compassion International, 2011), 46.
7. Rick Warren, "Purpose Driven in Rwanda," Christianity Today http://rickwarrenquotes.blogspot.com/2010/04/rick-warren-and-compassion-of-god.html

Chapter 4

1. Beyond the Gates film
2. (Kisses from Katie, 22–23)
3. www.compassion.com stats accessed in March 2012
4. (Terrify No More, 240–241)
5. Max Lucado, Outlive Your Life (Nashville: Thomas Nelson, 2010), 6.
6. Cory Trenda, Reflections from Afar (Federal Way: World Vision Resources, 2011), 7–8.

Chapter 5

1. http://www.courierpress.com/news/2010/feb/09/entitlement-culture-gives-youth-unrealistic
2. Tim Kimmel, Raising Kids for True Greatness (Nashville: Thomas Nelson, 2006), 169.
3. Julie Ferwerda, One Million Arrows (Enumclaw: Winepress Publishing, 2009), 43
4. http://sadd.org/stats.htm
5. http://medicalmarijuana.procon.org/view.answers.php?questionID=000336
6. http://www.sciencedaily.com/releases/2008/03/080328112127.htm
7. Todd Ahrend, In This Generation (Colorado Springs: Dawson Media, 2010), 188.
8. (One Million Arrows, 22)

9. http://www.education.com/reference/article/why-so-many-students-bored-school/?page=2
10. http://ed.stanford.edu/news/driven-succeed-how-were-depriving-teens-sense-purpose
11. Jean M Twenge, Ph.D. Generation Me (New York: Free Press, 2006), 106.
12. http://www.teendepression.org/stats/teenage-depression-statistics
13. (Let me Tell you a Story, 91)
14. (NurtureShock, 141)
15. Claude Hickman, Live Life On Purpose (Enumclaw: WinePress Publishing, 2008), 22.
16. (58: Fast Living, 179)
17. (Kisses from Katie, 11)
18. (One Million Arrows, 98)

Chapter 6
1. Helen Lee, Missional Mom (Chicago: Moody, 2010)107.
2. Tim Kimmel, Danger of Raising Nice Kids (Downers Grove: IVP Books, 2006), 183.
3. (Just Courage, 125)
4. Michelle Anthony, Spiritual Parenting (Colorado Springs: David C Cook, 2012), 18.
5. Francis Chan, Crazy Love (Colorado Springs: David Cook, 2008), 68–80.
6. John Piper, Let the Nations be Glad (Grand Rapids: Baker, 1993), 46.
7. David Platt, Radical (Colorado Springs: Multinomah Books, 2010), 179.
8. Ann Dunagan, The Mission Minded Child (Colorado Springs: Authentic, 2007), 10.
9. (Just Courage, 34)
10. http://lysaterkeurst.com/2012/01/i-dont-want-to-raise-a-good-child/

Chapter 7
1. Barbara Campbell, I Don't Want to Wait until I'm Grown Up (Wheaton: ACMC, 1991), 3–4.

2. Po Bronson and Ashley Merryman,"See Baby Discriminate" in Newsweek, pg 3. http://www.thedailybeast.com/newsweek/2009/09/04/see-baby-discriminate.html
3. Po Bronson and Ashley Merryman, Nurtureshock (New York: Twelve, 2009), 62
4. Robert Coles, The Moral Intelligence of Children (New York: Plume, 1997), 213-214.
5. Jolene L. Roehlkepartian, Teaching Kids to Care & Share (Nashville: Abingdon Press, 2000), 11.
6. Angie Quantrell, Families on Mission (Birmingham: WMU, 2005), 10.
7. http://www.gcchildmin.org/certification/course3.pdf
8. http://leaningtowardjustice.wordpress.com/2006/05/29/fowlers-stages-of-faith-development/
9. http://leaningtowardjustice.wordpress.com/2006/05/29/fowlers-stages-of-faith-development/
10. http://prevetteresearch.net/wpcontent/uploads/image/all/14 percent20Faith percent20Development percent20Theories.pdf
11. (The Mission Minded Child, 13)
12. Wess Stafford, Too Small to Ignore (Colorado Springs: Water Brook Press, 2007), 212.

Chapter 8

1. Sally Clarkson, The Mission of Motherhood (Colorado Springs: Waterbrook, 2003), 85.

Chapter 9

1. http://www.relevantmagazine.com/culture/books/features/19094-qaa-with-donald-miller
2. (One Million Arrows, 9)
3. (One Million Arrows, 56)

Chapter 10

1. (The Dangerous Act of Loving Your Neighbor, 185)
2. Michelle Perry, Love Has a Face (Grand Rapids: Chosen, 2009), 12–13.
3. (Say Yes to God, 83)
4. (Just Courage, 32)

Chapter 11

1. Brenda Salter McNeil, The Justice Conference 2013 http://thejusticeconference.com/videos2013.html
2. Sally Clarkson, The Mission of Motherhood (Colorado Springs: Waterbrook, 2003), 293.
3. (Radical, 109)

Chapter 12

1. Bethany H. Hoang, Deepening the Soul for Justice (Downers Grove: IVP, 2012), 8.
2. http://www.micahchallenge.org.au/prayers
3. (Just Courage, 23)
4. Laurie Delgato, ed. Working for Change (Federal Way: World Vision Resources, 2008), 17.
5. Janet Morley, Harvest for the World (Norwich: Canterbury Press, 2004), 149.
6. http://thewaterproject.org/bottled_water.asp
7. http://thewaterproject.org/bottled_water.asp
8. http://www.healthkicker.com/764599612/the-truth-about-water-bottle-vs-tap/

Chapter 13

1. (The Spirituality of Fundraising, 31)
2. Dr. Craig Blomberg, "What would Jesus do with all your stuff? " www.revolutionarygenerosity.com
3. Russell Earl Kelly, Should the Church Teach Tithing (Bloomington: Writers Club Press, 2000)
4. C.S. Lewis, Mere Christianity (San Francisco: Harper, 1952), 67.
5. Jonathan Acuff, Stuff Christians Like (Grand Rapids: Zondervan, 2010), 129.
6. (Hole in Our Gospel, 207)
7. Matthew E. Narramore, Tithing http://tekoapublishing.com/books/tithing/chapter2.html
8. Ronald J. Sider, Rich Christians in an Age of Hunger (Nashville: W Publishing, 1999), 101–102.
9. (Seven, 158–159)

Chapter 14

1. (The Danger of Raising Nice Kids, 91)
2. Atticus Finch in To Kill a Mockingbird film (1962)
3. Henri Nouwen, Compassion: A Reflection on the Christian Life (New York: Doubleday & Company, 1983), 4.
4. Gregory Boyle, Tattoos on the Heart (New York: Free Press, 2010), 63.
5. Maiz Szalavitz and Bruce D Perry, M.D., Ph. D. Born for Love (New York: William Morrow, 2010), 9–10.
6. (Just Courage, 51)
7. (The Zambia Project, 65)
8. (Dangerous Surrender, 71–72)
9. Donna S Thomas , Becoming a World Changing Family (Seattle: YWAM Publishing, 1998), 30.

Chapter 15

1. http://www.aholyexperience.com/2012/12/the-truth-about-sandy-hook-where-is-god-when-bad-things-happen/
2. Cheryl Sacks and Arlyn Lawrence, Prayer Saturated Kids (Colorado Springs: Navpress, 2007), 116.
3. Os Guinness, Unspeakable Os Guinness (San Francisco: Harper, 2005), 15, 61.

Chapter 16

1. (The Mission Minded Child, 139)
2. (Reflections from Afar, 18)
3. Tom Davis, Fields of the Fatherless (Colorado Springs: David C Cook, 2008), 112–113.
4. (Let the Nations be Glad, 77)
5. (Let the Nations be Glad, 88)
6. Henri J. M. Nouwen, Here and Now (New York: Crossroads: 1994), 99.
7. http://www.janjohnson.org/articles-_spiritual_growth_-_weeping_prayer.html
8. http://www.passionatehomemaking.com/2011/10/teaching-our-girls-to-cry.html

Chapter 17
1. http://bible.org/seriespage/righteous-anger-ephesians-426-27
2. (Just Courage, 63–64)
3. (Radical Compassion, 57)
4. Gary Chapman, Anger (Chicago: Northfield, 2007), 156–157.
5. R.C. Sproul, The Holiness of God (Wheaton, Tyndale House Publishers, 1998), 142.

Chapter 18
1. Tony Campolo, Speaking My Mind (Nashville, W Publishing House, 2004), 181.

Chapter 19
1. Sung Wook Chung and Dieumeme E. Noelliste, "Toward a Theology of Political Engagement" Christians and Political Engagement, Denver: Denver Seminary's Vernon Grounds Institute, 2009), 35.
2. Shane Claiborne The Irresistible Resolution: Living as an Ordinary Radical
3. Eric Geiger, Michael Kelley, and Philip Nation, Transformational Discipleship (Nashville: B&H Publishing, 2012), 190.
4. (Families on Mission, 64)
5. (Raising Kids for True Greatness, 79–80)

Chapter 20
1. Ann Dunagan, The Mission Minded Family (Colorado Springs: Biblica, 2007), 30.
2. (The Missional Mom, 137)
3. Sharon Jaynes, Being a Great Mom, Raising Great Kids (Chicago: Moody, 2000), 79.
4. (Being a Great Mom, Raising Great Kids, 106–107)
5. Ed. Laurie Delgato, For the Least of These (Federal Way: World Vision Inc, 2011), 58.
6. www.amylsullivan1.com/2012/08/taking-kids-on-short-term-missions.html

Chapter 21
1. (The Danger of Raising Nice Kids, 51)
2. Zach Hunter, Be the Change (Grand Rapids: Zondervan, 2011), 12.
3. Lion, Witch, and the Wardrobe
4. Bob Goff, Love Does (Nashville, Thomas Nelson, 2012), 84.
5. (Love Does, 88)
6. (Mission Minded Child, 1)
7. Bryant Myers, Working with the Poor (Maryknoll: Orbis Books, 1999), 20–21.
8. (One Million Arrows, 145)
9. Donald Miller, A Million Miles in a Thousand Years (Nashville: Thomas Nelson, 2009).50,51,54.
10. (A Million Miles in a Thousand Years, 51)
11. (A Million Miles in a Thousand Years, 54)
12. (Live Life On Purpose, 23)

Chapter 22
1. (Mission Minded Family, 11, 14)

Chapter 23
1. (Understanding God's Heart for the Poor, 281)
2. www.yumasun.com/articles/well-66539-nations-africa.html
3. www.edmondsun.com/local/x277237863/Walking-for-Water-Edmond-9-year-old-will-walk-a-mile-each-day-to-raise-money-for-African-village
4. (Becoming a World Changing Family, 26)
5. (Real Kids, Real Stories, Real Change, 87–91)

Chapter 24
1. (A Mission Minded Child, 10)
2. (In This Generation,187)
3. Chip Huber, The Zambia Project (self published, 2012), 103.
4. (The Zambia Project, 59)
5. (Say Yes To God, 116)

6. (Live Life on Purpose, 36)
7. (Say Yes to God, 74)
8. Gunila Baumann, Releasing Your Children to the Lord (Seattle: YWAM Publishing, 2012), 154.

Chapter 25
1. Dr. Kara E. Powell & Dr. Chap Clark, Sticky Faith (Grand Rapids: Zondervan, 2011), 136.
2. Lysa Terkerust, What Happens When Women Say Yes to God (Eugene: Harvest House, 2007), 129.
3. http://www.stnicholascenter.org/pages/compare-santa-st-nicholas/
4. Mike Slaughter, Change the World (Nashville: Abingdon Press, 2010), 116-117.
5. http://www.denverpost.com/nationworld/ci_21504636/american-couple-caught-middle-guatemala-adoption-reform
6. (Fields of the Fatherless, 18)

Chapter 26
1. (Interrupted, 134)
2. (58:Fast Living, 52)
3. (Unpoverty, 84)
4. (Just Courage, 28-29)

Made in the USA
Lexington, KY
24 March 2015